MW01036719

LOVE
AND
FRIENDSHIP

Jules Toner

LOVE AND FRIENDSHIP

BOOK 1
THE EXPERIENCE OF LOVE

BOOK 2
PERSONAL FRIENDSHIP:
THE EXPERIENCE AND THE IDEAL

MARQUETTE
UNIVERSITY

PRESS

Marquette Studies in Philosophy
No. 26
Andrew Tallon, Series Editor

Library of Congress Cataloguing-in-Publication Data
Toner, Jules J.
[Experience of love]
Love and friendship / by Jules Toner.
p. cm. — (Marquette studies in philosophy ; no. 26)
Includes bibliographical references (p.   ) and index.
ISBN 0-87462-650-1
1. Love. 2. Friendship. 3. Love—Religious aspects—Christianity.
4. Friendship—Religious aspects—Christianity. I. Toner, Jules J.
Personal friendship. II. Title. III. Marquette studies in philosophy ;
#26.
BD436.T6 2003
177'.7—dc21
                                    2002156089

© 2003 Marquette University Press
Reprinted with corrections, 2005
Reprinted 2016
All rights reserved

Association of American
University Presses

MARQUETTE UNIVERSITY PRESS
MILWAUKEE

The Association of Jesuit University Presses

BOOK I
THE EXPERIENCE OF LOVE

CONTENTS

BOOK 2
PERSONAL FRIENDSHIP:
THE EXPERIENCE AND THE IDEAL

CONTENTS

[For convenience the Table of Contents for Book 2 is repeated on page 179.]

EDITOR'S FOREWORD

Jules Toner and I made contact on the occasion of my asking him, in my capacity as director of Marquette University Press, to read a manuscript as a referee for the Press. I had only known him by reputation, chiefly as a result of reading his great book *The Experience of Love*. That book had impressed me very early as the best thing I had ever read on the subject.

I found him at Colombiere Center in Clarkson, Michigan, a place described in its letterhead as Conference Center, Health Care, Jesuit Community. It was the first I knew of his failing health and weakening condition. We struck up a correspondence, in the course of which I mentioned my continuing admiration of his 1968 book, lamenting its having gone out of print (along with all the wonderful books brought out by that enlightened house, Corpus Books, before it ceased publishing). I asked him whether he would consider allowing Marquette University Press to reprint his book on love, and he said he would do so. He then mentioned that he had been working on a new book, on friendship, and asked whether I would be interested in having a look at it. Would I?! I read it and found it a marvelous work. He set to work completing it and having it typed to disk by a friend. Before we could get it into print, he died.

I have truly found it a labor of love (and friendship) to edit these two volumes—combined in one for this special edition—and to dedicate them to the memory of Jules Toner.

My modest duties in preparing Toner's work for this edition have been to review and edit the digital versions word by word, to construct a single bibliography and index for the combined books (*The Experience of Love* had an index but no bibliography; *Personal Friendship* had neither), and to reformat the notes in accordance with our house style, which is that of the *Chicago Manual of Style*, 14th edition. Mainly the latter consisted in converting reference notes to embedded form and in bringing content notes into the text, either in parentheses, or, where the ideas flowed well, without parentheses. The result is a book without notes. It is part of my "philosophy," grown into as director and editor, that authors usually overdo the use of notes, and I have been a major offender myself. When asked about style now I tell authors to use the author+date method (favored Chicago Manual style) for contentless references; and I tell them that when they are tempted to write a note with content to ask themselves whether it is important enough to be in the text, perhaps in parentheses, and, if so, to put it there, and, if not, to *drop it*. The result should be a text that flows without the convention we have all endured of interrupted reading as we drop to the bottom of the page for footnotes or, worse, turn to notes at the end of the chapter or back of the book; the effect is the same: one is distracted from the flow of the text and then forced to try to regain the original flow, either by ignoring or by integrating (sometimes successfully, sometimes not) the material from the notes.

Toner used gender neutral language in the Friendship book, so I thought it would be his wish to have the book on love read the same way, and I have made it so. My preferred method has been to use plurals rather than to say "he and/or she" (or "s/he"), which require subsequent "him and/or her," etc., or to alternate between masculine and feminine pronouns, which was Toner's method. For "man" I have used several substitutions, such as "humanity," some plural pronoun (as above), or the second person (following Toner's lead in the Friendship book). I have not forced the Friendship book into my inclusive method for the love book, but respected Toner's way. I trust this will be less distracting than other methods of achieving inclusive language. He was not always consistent in alternating between "he" and "she," often using both, which I presumed he intended for whatever reason, and so those remain as he wrote them.

Fairly frequently Toner referred in the Friendship book to his book on love; because these are bound in one volume, I have deleted those references; let the common index suffice for cross referencing.

Toner often speaks of a "loved object" where "loved one" is to be understood; he has in mind, no doubt, either the Latin of his training (where *res* did not distinguish persons from nonpersons), or the general notion of an *epistemological* object (which included subjects) in the sense, i.e., of the goal of a conscious intention (as intention is used in a phenomenology of intentionality). He most definitely does not exclude persons (thus his use is *sensu aiente*, not *sensu negante*).

Because of their frequency in both books, for Aristotle's *Nicomachean Ethics* I use NE, and for Aquinas's *Summa theologiae* I use ST.

In concluding this brief Foreword, I permit myself a few remarks about Toner's ideas. It was a rewarding experience to reread Toner's *Experience of Love*, and I discovered anew its clarity and insight. I still maintain that this is the best philosophical analysis I've ever read on the subject. Let me say why, first, and then offer a few remarks on the experience of friendship.

The first impression one has of Toner's work is that it is extremely well balanced and sane. All analyses have the ring of fair appraisal and inclusive, positive appreciation for what his sources are trying to do. What a tragedy that we do not have more by this wonderful thinker. But what a blessing that we do have his final work, fruit of the same careful, thorough review of sources and synthesis of the best of their conclusions. And yet this is so much more than a synthesis of things read: Toner's lasting contribution is his own penetrating grasp of the essence of love as affirmation, as YES to the other, a YES charged with *affection*, a YES that is both *more than affection* and *more than volition*, by being an *act of the person* constituted by affection, cognition, and volition. His key concept is the act of affectivity as an *affective response of the total concrete person* (p. 65). No truer pages than those on "The Unifying Center of the Total Experience" (67-69) were ever written about love.

Toner has done exceptionally careful and meticulous analyses where others have passed over the really difficult work by resorting to evocative language, anecdote, or poetry. The result is a work much accurate than it is easy of access. Some readers may have found the thoroughness an obstacle, but everyone who stayed with him, I would wager, found the reward well worth the work. For those who may have still found some difficulty in comprehending the central concept in the midst of the detail, his first three chapters to *Personal Friendship* may be just what is needed, a summary of his main idea. When we first talked about this book it was not clear how Marquette University Press would present it, whether separately or in combination with the reprinted *Experience of Love*. Toner might have chosen to exclude those first chapters had he lived to know that the latter way of presenting these books was chosen. As editor I could have made that decision myself, but I think we all would have missed a lot, since the value of his own summary is like a fresh look offered after years of mature experience. In 1999 I asked him what it would mean to revise *The Experience of Love*. He said: "Revision of *The Experience of Love* is changing my expression of thought to make it clearer or more precise. I find no need to revise my thought. Fuller development of it will be found in *The Experience of Personal Friendship*, but no change."

When we realize that the communing that is friendship is our ultimate goal as human pesons, we understand that everything beneath human communion (as the *act* of communing) and human community (as the *habit* of communing), and, I submit, everything above human communion and community (including communing with God, even with a transpersonal God far more mysterious than any earthbound epiphany), are somehow for interpersonal communion, then Toner's final chapters appear to point to an emergent property of the species as a whole. (On the model of every angel as a spiritual form which is a species unto itself, we humans all together share a spiritual form and are thus "conspecific," so that ultimately communion is connatural to us). Speaking philosophically one might extend Toner's reference to Christianity for transcendence of the tragic end of his dream of universal friendship by invoking one of his favorite sources, science fiction. David Brin's uplift saga (in two trilogies) imagines our evolution from lower intelligences to our present levels of life—and future levels as well, which is the point here—to have been aided by a more advanced species, one that by a kind of noblesse oblige has done for us what was done for them, i.e., raise us to our next higher potential. One can imagine this assistance coming from them without recourse to a god, Christian or otherwise, or imagine these loving helpers as angels, incarnate or not, or integrate all such god-talk or angel-talk into a human history of gods (or demigods) and angels, from Greek mythology (or earlier) up to today. In other words, we may have no clue beyond our endlessly searching imaginations and faiths and hopes to account for this dream of human communion, but that the dynamism is there does not depend on how we explain it. So we find Toner's *Love and Friendship* the work of a single vision, all the more credible for uniting in our emergent consciousness all three intentionalities, with the affective as the deepest dynamism of love, the cognitive as the questioning, understanding, and critically testing and judging intentionality, and finally as the volition that turns the affection and cognition into an ACT, into the affirmation in love that is commitment of one person to another and, in hope, to all. To add editorially to the author's own conclusion is not to deny it but to open it ecumenically in a way he shows he would welcome, i.e., interpretatively, by which I mean he would agree that the *experience* of our affective dynamism toward universal human community is primary, and the way we *understand* its possibility secondary, including the Christian way he espouses at the end of the second book.

Acknowledgments

Marquette University Press
is pleased to give special mention and thanks to

Maureen and Ken Rosenston,

who scanned the original manuscripts
left by Jules Toner, and to

Marguerite G. McCarthy,

who facilitated the project all along the way.

BOOK 1

THE
EXPERIENCE
OF
LOVE

by

Jules Toner

MARQUETTE
UNIVERSITY
PRESS

Previous Library of Congress Catalog Card Number: 68-15784
for *The Experience of Love*

Published in 1968 by
Corpus Instrumentorum, Inc.
1330 Massachusetts Ave., N.W.
Washington DC 20005

PRINTED IN THE UNITED STATES OF AMERICA

I
THE QUESTION AND PROCEDURE

The content of this book was at one time conceived of as the central part of a projected book on the foundations of ethics. The longer I worked at the ethics, the clearer it became that the understanding of love should shape ethical theory rather than that ethical theory already formed on some other basis should determine what we consider in the experience of love. But it also became progressively clearer that the results could be deplorable without a detailed, precise, deep, consistent, accurate, understanding of love, which could be achieved only by a demanding philosophically serious study of love in its own right, free from concern for moral or clinical implications, free even (insofar as this is possible) from the screening and molding influence of an already accepted philosophical anthropology. For the latter also should be shaped by rather than shape our understanding of love.

This book is the account of a prolonged effort to produce an intelligible description of the human experience of love, that is, conscious human love with no further qualification. On the one hand, I have not attempted to achieve an ontology or a metaphysics of love, built on an analogous notion of love embracing all levels or dimensions of being, including impersonal or even non-conscious being, as is done by Plato, St. Thomas, Paul Tillich, or Teilhard de Chardin. My concern is with the human and in the human with what is conscious. On the other hand, I am not directly concerned with any of the qualified forms of conscious human love as such, for example, mature and immature, morally good and morally evil, romantic, parental, religious and so on. My aim is to uncover within these differently qualified forms of human love that by reason of which every one of them can without equivocation be called love if, indeed there is any such thing to uncover. Other topics or questions frequently discussed at length in writing on love (its power, its growth, its importance in human life) are relevant only insofar as they are helpful toward that limited goal. In the measure that we know precisely and deeply what human love is, we can with confidence of proceeding accurately take up in any depth the kinds of love, the growth of love, morally good and evil love, etc. And only when we know what conscious human love is can we hope to speak intelligently about love as a metaphysical category without danger of hidden equivocations.

The reaction of those who discovered I was writing a book on love has convinced me that it is imperative to justify "another book on love." And this is especially necessary for a book that intends a philosophical answer to the question, what is human love? For I am sure there will be two principal reactions: isn't this a hopeless task? Or, hasn't this question been answered a hundred times?

The latter question reminds one of Hilaire Belloc's remark to the effect that many people live and die under the illusion that they have read *Das Kapital*. Similarly, most of those who ask this question live under the illusion that they have read some author who takes this question in all philosophical seriousness and answers it satisfactorily. Surely, to say the question has been answered a hundred times is supreme understatement; but to say it has been answered in all philosophical seriousness a half dozen times would probably be an overstatement. Let me explain what I mean.

It is a strange and striking fact that even those who write best about love devote very little space to considering what love is. The important problems are evidently thought to lie elsewhere. After a brief unquestioned and undeveloped declaration of or a few paragraphs on the nature of love, there are long discussions about the kinds of love, the power and effects of love, the stages of growth in love, the moral and psychological norms for love, the relation of love with knowledge, sex, justice, and so on. It is assumed that readers and writer know what love is and agree on what it is.

When, however, we examine carefully the explicit or implicit notions of love in the literature on the subject, we find a bewildering mass of different and often conflicting notions swarming before us. (For a detailed and discriminating account of the diverse opinions on love, see Hazo 1967. Unfortunately, I could not make use of this book which appeared after mine was already in press.) The disagreement is on the nature of the act itself and on the object of the act. Those who agree in some general way on the nature of the act of love may still differ on what the object can and ought to be. And conversely, those who agree on what the object is or ought to be may differ on what the nature of love is. Some will differ from each other on both counts. We even find one and the same author delivering several different definitions which are never integrated for us and sometimes do not seem reconcilable. The reader gets the impression that there is little general agreement among those who write on the subject except on one point: all agree that there are many current unsound notions of love. But there is notable disagreement on what notions are sound and what are unsound.

Further, among these many notions of love, a good proportion are really not statements about human love in its basic reality at all but rather about what characterizes one sort of human love as against another. We are told the difference between *agape* and *eros,* mature and immature love, *amor amicitiae* and *amor concupiscentiae,* gift-love and need-love; we are told what is peculiar to romantic love or motherly love or married love or Christian love or some other *sort* of love. But what is love which can take these diverse forms we are not told. The adjectival is discussed, the substantival is passed over or confused with the former. And when authors do intend a substantival statement about love, the almost universal practice is to begin with a definition. Sometimes this definition is explained but hardly ever is there a serious effort to justify it in the face of other opposing definitions. The psychic realities pointed to by other definitions are brushed aside as "not really love," or "not worthy of the name love," without a criterion established for what really is love or worthy to he called love and what is really a simulacrum of it.

It would be a misunderstanding of my meaning in the preceding remarks, if the reader thought I intended to deny value to the work of those to whom we all owe so much. On the contrary, I wish to show a great deal more respect to them than they frequently do to each other. For in almost every case I find that in their positive statements about what love is, they have given us at least some partially true insight into the total concrete experience, and that what they build on that positively in their treatment of other questions, does have value. The total concrete experience has many elements; and to have light thrown on this or that element, even when it gets out of perspective or is mistaken for the central element, is truly a gain. It is hardly to be thought that the many sensitive and intelligent writers who have given us their observations and thinking on love were all missing the reality of love altogether and merely spinning out non-sense. I am only pointing out that most of what they say does not pertain to the particular question taken up in this book and that what does pertain to it is for the most part asserted without serious effort to justify it in the face of many conflicting views—that, therefore, an important task remains to be done.

It would also be a misunderstanding if readers thought I expected them to take my word for the preceding large assertions about the history of writings on love. These assertions are made in order to explain what I *mean* when say it is difficult to find even a handful of authors who have taken up with philosophical seriousness the question of what human love is. Without a detailed, documented, historical study to back up my assertions, I could not expect to win anyone's assent. On the other hand, it is my hope that what I have said and what is to be said in the historical chapters of this book may give pause to any hasty assumption that the question being dealt with here has already been adequately answered by many others.

There are those who say that if in asking what love is, I am looking for a description or definition of what is essential to every love, then I am embarked on a hopeless quest. I must fail as everyone else must fail for the very good reason that there is no such thing as the essence of love. They see all the diversity of notions about love as unavoidable. Thus, Douglas Morgan, in his excellent historical study of love in Plato, the Bible, and Freud, will have no part in searching for the essence of love.

> It is finally in order here to disavow any intention of expounding the "real meaning" or "essence" of love. There is no such thing. *Love is,* as the currently fashionable phrase has it, an "open concept." If we are to be satisfied with only a unique, universally applicable, all-time definition of "love," we may as well not even enter upon our adventure (Morgan 1964, 3).

Carried to an extreme, to which I have no reason for thinking Mr. Morgan would want to carry it, this way of thinking ends in a nominalistic view. It is this way of thinking that Ortega y Gasset repudiates:

> Clearly, it would be much more simple and convenient to think that love has infinite forms, that it is different in each case, etc. I hope always to remain aloof from the intellectual abasement which elicits this way of thinking and flatters inert minds so greatly. The ultimate mission of the intellect will always be to search for the "essence," that is to say, the unique mode of being of each reality (Ortega y Gasset 1957, 196, n. 5).

Some who agree with Ortega's anti-nominalistic attitude and even disagree with Morgan, nevertheless speak of two or more irreducible "loves," each of them descriptively definable. The implication of this position is that there is no answer to the question, what is human love? The question has to be qualified: what is eros-love and agape-love (Nygren 1953)? What is gift-love and need-love and appreciative love? (Lewis 1960, ch. 1-2, esp. 11-14, 32-33; lest there be any misunderstanding, the "four loves" in the title of the book do not refer to four irreducible loves or elements in love but to three of these

Lewis found combined in various ways in the four loves to which the title refers.) What is benevolent love, appetitive love, adoring love? (Benoît 1955; esp. ch. 1 and 8; there is some indication that Benoît thinks of a common element in benevolent and appetitive lose which is not common to adoring love.)

In response to Morgan, it may fairly be required that before adopting such a position as he does we first examine experience to see whether in those experiences called love we do not find certain essential elements, structured in certain constant ways. I do not find that he or anyone else has done this and arrived at his conclusion. And in response to him and to those who hold several irreducible loves, we may fairly require that, before adopting such positions, an examination of experience be made to see whether there is not one radical element which is a necessary constant in all love and, if there is, whether there is not some common aspect in experiences generally called love which justifies a general concept of love. To my knowledge none of those who give us too or three irreducible forms of love have ever done this.

Assuming that the reader will grant tentatively the legitimacy of asking and trying to answer the question, what is human love, let me indicate how I intend to proceed. There are two main steps or parts. The first of these is a dialectical survey of opinions about what love is. The second is a reflection on the concrete experience of love.

It might be thought, on the basis of what has already been said, that the principal or even sole reason for the first part is to show the confused state of thought on the nature of love and so to exhibit the need for what is to be done in the second part. If that were so, the historical material would be treated in a different way than it is, with many more authors included and a much less thorough discussion of any one of them. It is true that the first part is calculated to serve what might be called a negative purpose, showing that the question has not yet been adequately answered; but it has also and more important a positive function. To go directly to experience without any help from others who have done so and to achieve any accurate and deep descriptive analysis is far more difficult than might be imagined by one who has not tried it. The successes and the failures of others are of greatest importance—even when what has been said is only an assertion which is not established by any careful description nor defended against opposing views. What the most intelligent, sensitive minds have seen in the experience of love can give us important leads. The consequences of their observations within their own thought and the conflicts between different views can enable us to take these leads critically. And, since the concrete experience of human love is a manifold of many elements, we may find hidden in an apparent jumble of opinions precious materials that can be clarified, made more precise, and related to one another in such a way as to help form an accurate description of what is in the full concrete experience.

The first part, the survey of opinions, is, therefore, undertaken primarily because of its positive value for the second part; and its scope is measured with that in mind. It does not pretend to be a thorough canvass of opinions nor a history of thought on love. The content is quite frankly and obviously selective, chosen and arranged with a view to the second part. Thus, there is a grouping of the many notions of love in such a way as to limit the confusion, to indicate the several main lines of thought along which opinions tend to converge, and to relate these dialectically rather than chronologically.

Attention should be called to certain consequences of the limited aim in the first part. Some famous contributors to the history of thought on love will not receive the attention the reader might expect if the aim of this study were broader in scope. For instance; those who have focused their study of love on some qualified form or forms enter our discussion only indirectly (e.g., Charles Williams on romantic love and Anders Nygren on *agape* and *eros).* Further, when an author is mentioned as presenting some notion of love in a certain book, I do not imply that this is the only definition of love. Authors may change their opinions over the years or may even within a single piece of writing at one time of life have worked with several notions of love, which notions may be compatible and complementary or may be incompatible and in tension within their thought. One and the same author, therefore, may appear under more than one heading. Thirdly, the notion of love chosen for our purposes when taken out of its full context will usually lose something of its complete and nuanced meaning Nevertheless, what remains will be accurate and sufficient for our purpose. That purpose is not to offer a fully balanced and adequate picture of any individual's thought on love. I am aware and want to insist that the reader be aware that the full meaning of any author's formula can only be fairly understood in its context. At the same time, I do not think I am distorting anyone's opinion: an inadequate presentation can be but need not be a misreading one unless it is presented as adequate. Finally, in this survey, no evaluation of the author's views is intended. The criticism which one author makes of another is sometimes necessary in order to bring out one's own thought and to highlight the conflicts which do exist. But, while drawing up a picture of the situation within which we will begin to rethink the whole question of love's nature, I wish myself to remain strictly expository. It may be necessary to criticize one author's understanding of the other in order to make the latter's view clear and accurate. But in presenting each author's own notion of love, I shall try to maintain myself in the position of expositor until I begin the second part of the book, the direct study of experience. Here disagreement with the opinions presented in the survey will inevitably arise.

The second part is, then, the principal part of this book. It is an attempt to answer the question, what is love, by a methodic reflection on the experience of love, bringing the main conscious constituents of the total experience into the focus of attention, noting their interrelations, discerning what is radical among them, and making a descriptive analysis of the various aspects of that radical element. In doing this, full account will be taken of the main ways of thinking about love as these have appeared in the survey of part one, offering a reasoned evaluation and criticism.

The two parts taken together should provide what I mean by a response which takes with full philosophical seriousness the question, what is human love? Should you, the reader, not find the content of my answer to that question acceptable, you may nevertheless agree that there is a task still to be done, a task that can be done; and you may find in this effort some indication of how it is to be done.

Part 1
Dialectical Survey

2
LOVE AS DESIRE AND JOY

Whatever love is in its proper meaning, most people think of it as that mysterious element in unanalyzed human experience which is the deepest moving force of human activity. The literature of all times and cultures testifies to this natural conviction. Now, desire (conscious drive or urge or tendency) is the most obvious claimant to that title and so to the name of love. To say that it is the most obvious claimant is not to confer legitimacy on its claim. As we shall see, there are many who will dub it a false pretender. Nevertheless its claim is so powerfully backed by evidence that there seem to be more, both learned and unlearned, who accept its claim than they would the claim of any other affection. As might be expected, therefore, it is also the one which is more often attacked than any other by those who hold a variety of other notions about love. For this reason alone love as desire would in any case be one good starting point for a dialectical survey of opinions on the nature of love, because most of the other important opinions are developed in relation to desire. That is to say, the notion of love is explained by opposing it to desire as a contrary, as a source, or as a goal of desire.

A preliminary comment on the meaning of the words used here may help to avoid misunderstanding. Such words as desire, drive, urge, and tendency, as referring to conscious affective acts, all have a basic common meaning: they all refer to some *affective movement toward, a psychic going-out-to* an object which is in some way distant, as yet unattained. Some of the writers who use these words are very clearly using them with this common meaning; for they use the words interchangeably. Paul Tillich usually employs the word "drive" when he is giving an explicit definition of love. However, he easily substitutes other words in the course of his discussion and even sometimes in explicit definitions. Thus we find him using such words as "desire" or "urge" or "movement" or "process" as well as "drive" (Tillich 1954, 26-34, 37, 48; 1962, 136). Others are not so clear about what is implied by speaking of love as tendency. They distinguish desire from love and yet speak of the latter as a tendency, a going-out-to and so on (Ortega 1957, 12, 15; Gilleman 1957, 101-02, 131- 32). Or some distinguish two kinds of love, one of which is desire, and then speak of the other as a tendency. Thus Johann (1955, 10) clearly opposes what he calls "direct love" to desire and is emphatic that in direct love the lover responds to the object absolutely as opposed to desire which always refers its object to another (6, 17, 45, 59); nevertheless, he continues to speak of this love as a tendency (12-13, 45). It is not made clear how one can have a tendency toward an object with which one is already in union insofar as one is in union (one can, of course, tend toward further union or even continued union) or how a conscious affective tendency to an object which is in some sense distant can be anything other than desire. However that may be, for the authors whom we will consider now under the heading of love as desire, there is no need to distinguish between the conscious experiences of desire, drive, urge, tendency. The terms can be used interchangeably.

If we now ask what evidence there is for asserting that desire or tendency is love in the basic meaning of the word, we must give a twofold answer. On the one hand, there is a vast mass of evidence gathered from observation of ordinary human experience and from clinical reports which points to desire as *a* root of some other affections and of action. In fact, the evidence is so impressive that one readily tends to think that desire is *the* root affection, which makes our human world go round, that is, love. On the other hand, there is evidence that desire itself derives from a less obvious because more radical affection. Let us first consider how it looks to those who make desire irreducible and identify it with what people usually mean by love.

The two classic statements of this position are those of Plato and Freud. Superficially alike but radically different, they yet concur in asserting that desire is the essence of those experiences commonly called love in human conscious life. An interesting and valuable contemporary position is that of Tillich who, in a carefully systematized development, controverts Freud and joins the Platonic with the Christian tradition, integrating *eros* and *agape* as he understands them. These three, Plato, Freud, and Tillich, will give us a well-rounded understanding of this way of thinking about love. Along with this notion of love as tendency, we will consider Spinoza's notion of love as joy. There are two reasons for doing so: first, it has much in common, as we shall see, with the notions of love as desire or tendency; and second, most of those who conceive of love as the source of desire conceive of it also as the source of joy.

Plato

Plato's statement of love as desire is found in his major dialogues on love: the *Lysis*, the *Symposium*, and the *Phaedrus*. The *Lysis*, an early and purely dialectical dialogue, prepares the way by raising and discussing the major questions about love. It clearly indicates the direction of Plato's thought; and, despite its apparently inconclusive ending, readers are not at all surprised when they take up the *Symposium* and read the premises which Socrates lays down as basic to any discourse on love (*Symposium* 199B–201C). Here Socrates not merely implies but insists that love springs from need; that whoever love, desire; and that whoever desire, lack and need what they desire. Therefore, love cannot be good nor beautiful; for we love what is good and beautiful; and if we do, then we must lack goodness and beauty. In other words, love cannot be an expression of nor constitutive of goodness and beauty in the lover. There is in Socrates' analysis no room for love that springs from fulness of being.

This does not mean that love is evil or ugly. Love, he says, is neither good nor evil, neither beautiful nor ugly; and, what is of primary importance in understanding love's function in life, it is neither mortal nor immortal. It is *of* the good, *of* the beautiful, *of* immortality ("of" in this context having an objective rather than possessive meaning). For it is a drive toward, a desire for, the immortal possession of the Good, the Absolute Beauty, in the possession of which human happiness consists. *Eros,* as it arises in human conscious life, is a drive toward immortal union with that which we need to make us happy (*Symposium* 201D–207A).

To speak in this way does not mean that for Plato as lovers we are neither good, nor beautiful, nor immortal. Clearly Plato thinks of us as "participating" in the Good, in the Beautiful. It is this participation by the human object of love which is the occasion for rousing the *eros* in human lovers (*Phaedrus* 250A–251B). We are good and lacking good, beautiful and lacking beauty. So also, we are immortal and mortal. Because we are souls, we are immortal; because we are in bodies we are mortal (*Phaedrus* 245C–246D). Love arises not because of what we already are or have but because of what we as yet lack. Whether lovers respond with heavenly or vulgar *eros* expresses something of what they already are—or, more precisely, what they know; but that they respond with love at all expresses lack and need. Now immortality belongs to the gods, and any mortal being who would participate in immortality and happiness can do so only through generation. Thus, when *eros* shows itself in beings less than human it does so as the force which drives bodily beings to repair their loss or injury and to generate offspring. In these ways they attain whatever immortality is possible to them. When this drive, which runs through all of temporal reality, arises in human consciousness, it does so as a conscious desire which makes us seek and strive in all the ways that we do. And in all our seeking and striving, Plato says, we are reaching for immortality whether we understand this or not. So, like the animals, we strive for immortality by physical generation. The desire for sexual pleasure is, more deeply, a desire for parenthood (*Symposium* 206C–207A). At a higher level, Plato says, we strive for immortality through spiritual generation by which we attain lasting fame as soldiers or poets or a public servants. It is the philosopher who strives for true immortality in wisdom. The philosophers are not wise but seekers of wisdom. The ultimate goal of philosophy is the vision of the Absolute Beauty. To this are directed all the steps in the philosophers' intellectual ascent through which the energy of *eros* drives them (*Symposium* 207D–212A).

In all these strivings, it is one and the same energy finding outlet at different levels of human life, an energy which is from the first directed to the ultimate good of true immortality in perfect wisdom. It is, however, misunderstood by most people, who are ready to let it come to rest in sensual desires or ambition for earthly things (*Symposium* 206C–209E). The experience of "falling in love" described in the *Phaedrus*, with all its high emotional flurry and sexual excitement, is understood by Plato entirely in terms of *eros* driving us on to the vision of the really real, the world of forms. It is a moment of crisis in human mortal life. It is a moment in which we must choose to follow the way of heavenly *eras* in the highest form of friendship and philosophy, or to succumb to the stunted way of the vulgar *eros* in sensual love (*Phaedrus* 250D, 253C–256D). If we follow the way of philosophy and friendship we will come to that which is from the beginning the goal of *eros*, that *is*, to the vision of Absolute Beauty (*Symposium* 210E–211C).

There seems no reason to think of love as significant once the ultimate goal is attained, if it can be attained with any permanence. It is obvious, of course, that if the vision may be had in a flash from time to time during life in this world, *eros* is always needed to keep one striving toward it again and again. But when and insofar as union is achieved, love ends. This seems to be a logical conclusion once love is understood in terms of desire (drive or movement), whether love is identified with desire or conceived of as essentially a principle of desire. (This logical conclusion is not usually seen and accepted by those who describe love as tendency to, going-out-to, movement toward, the loved one). This raises grave issues. If one thinks of human fulfilment as endless movement toward a goal, then one has to discount the end value of any contemplation of truth achieved or joy in a goal attained. On the other hand, if one thinks of contemplation and joy in truth achieved as goals, end values, then one is faced with the conclusion that love as one sees it is nothing but a means, that the greatest depths of love, even of mutual love in friendship, is of no value in itself and ceases with the goal attained. Plato shows no unwillingness to accept this position and makes fulness of life consist in intellectual vision. Love is only the driving energy towards immortal life where love has no importance. The gods do not love.

Freud

Influenced by Nachmonson and Pfister, Sigmund Freud was under the impression that his own views on the origin and function of love and its relation to sex largely coincided with those of Plato. There are obvious points of comparison; but there are equally obvious points of contrast flowing from contrary views of human nature. For Plato, a human is a soul that happens to be in a body; for Freud, we are bodily organisms whose psychic lives are totally rooted in matter. The consequent differences in their concepts of *eros* will appear as we see what love meant to Freud, that is, what it meant to him for most of his professional life, at any rate. For it does seem that some revision was in process near the end of his life. "It dawned upon him [Freud] late in his life, although he never clearly acknowledged it, that love is a psychical power in its own right" (Freud 1961, SE 18, 91; for a more comprehensive account of Freud on love together with a comparison and contrast of Freudian and Platonic *eros,* see Morgan 1964, 129-74.). This is the judgment of Theodor Reik, one of Freud's own pupils. Some other Freudians besides Reik frankly deplore Freud's views on love and develop other theories of love that sometimes bear little or no resemblance to his (Reik 1957, 16; see, e.g., Reik's criticisms [1957, 12-24] and Fromm's [1956, 34-36]).

To give any historical account of the vicissitudes of Freud's thought on love would be out of place here. My account will be grounded principally on a book written when he had achieved maturity and in which he expresses more fully and clearly and compactly than any-where else his views on love. I refer to *Civilization and Its Discontents.* This will serve the dialectical purposes of our discussion, even if any-one would want to say that this does not give an adequate view of Freud's thought.

Adopting nineteenth century materialism without question, Freud assumes that human psychic life is entirely rooted in the physical organism. The driving force of human life is our instincts. In the final form his theory of instincts took, there were two irreducible ones, namely *eros* and the death instinct (Freud 1961, SE 21, 118-225; for a summary account of his preceding theories, see Freud 1961, SE 21, 117-18). *Eros is* the one that is of interest to us. *Eros is,* as in Plato, a drive to happiness; but for Freud, happiness is pleasure, not the vision of Absolute Beauty (Freud 1961, SE 21, 76-77). Now the energy of *eros* is what he calls *libido,* and *libido* is love. *Libido* is di-rected to pleasure and is ruled by the pleasure principle. The pleasure at which it aims is directly and primarily sexual pleasure, sexual in Freud's meaning of the term.

It is true that Freud widened the meaning of sexual beyond the merely genital. However, it is also true that for him the prototype of all pleasure and of all happiness is the pleasure of genital sexuality (Freud 1961, SE 21, 81-82, 101; on this point, which is of central importance for understanding what love is essentially and radically for Freud, see the passage on love as *libido* in "Group Psychology and the Analysis of the Ego," SE 18, 90-91). And further, he makes it very clear that he thinks no one would seek any other form of happi-ness if one were not frustrated in seeking of happiness in sexual plea-sure. When we do seek objects other than sex objects and pleasures ordinarily thought of as higher than sexual pleasure, it is our *eros* still energized by *libido* which drives us to this. The energy is simply dis-placed, not replaced, and is sublimated to these other objects. In the unconscious it still remains essentially a purely sensuous drive. All the forms of tenderness, of brotherly love, of parental love, and so on, all arise by inhibition of the direct sexual aim, and at root, in the unconscious, are still sexual (Freud 1961, SE 21, 79-82, 97, 101-02). Even beauty is first of all in Freud's thought the sexual attractive-ness of the object, and any other notion of beauty arises as a result of the inhibition of sexuality (Freud 1961, SE 21, 80-83). Whatever else, then, may be said about the complex development of the in-stinct from primary narcissism to object-love and the manifold forms of object-love which arise from inhibition of the direct sexual aim with consequent sublimation, the essential notion of love in Freud is desire, primarily sexual desire, for an object which gives the lover pleasure. Those who, like the saints, achieve what appears to be an unselfish and universal love are really only using some psychological mechanism to escape the pain of being frustrated in the direct aim of love. The pleasure desired in love is blocked by so many obstacles that we must generally settle for a negative happiness, the avoidance of pain, as our main and realistic aim (Freud 1961, SE 21, 26-27). Someone like Saint Francis of Assisi, in Freud's estimation, was merely someone supremely successful in contriving a mode of response to reality that would be suffused with universal tenderness but would not really be a love for any individual being and so would avoid all the pains of frustrated sexual love. Francis was successfully exploiting universal love to escape pain and to gain an inner feeling of happiness (Freud 1961, SE 21,102).

(The reader who is at all familiar with the available evidence on Francis of Assisi cannot but think that Freud, whether he was aware of it or not, was really deducing what the case "had" to be with Francis, given Freud's hypothesis. Certainly no study of the evidence could have led Freud to find here confirmation of his hypothesis. What we find is someone who loved personally and intensely, who had very special loves, e.g., for his first Franciscan companions and above all for Clare, who willingly accepted the anguish that comes with concern for those he loves and bore all the pains of life with unflinching fortitude. The Francis Freud is talking of never existed by that name outside Freud's imagination.)

Freud's *eros,* then, is essentially Plato's vulgar *eros,* which rises above the sexual to seek other satisfaction only because frustrated of its own proper aim. It never arrives at what Plato calls heavenly *eros.* On the other hand, Plato's *eros* is essentially a heavenly *eros* which becomes vulgar by being frustrated of its proper ultimate direction to the vision of Absolute Beauty. This frustration, it would seem, is caused by bad education and/or bad heredity, which account for our not understanding what human *eros* is really driving toward. The contrast could be deepened by seeing how Plato and Freud view the relation of *eros* to human culture; but this would carry us far beyond the aims we have in mind here.

Tillich

Paul Tillich clearly develops his views of love in reference to Plato and Freud. Like both of them he looks for and finds one unqualified love in all the forms of love (Tillich 1954, 5); and, as in their thought, this unqualified love is drive, desire. Where Plato and Freud differ on the object of this drive, Tillich puts himself firmly in the Platonic tradition. In his analysis, Freud's description of *libido,* to which all Freudian love ultimately reduces, is merely a description of love as it can be distorted under the tyranny of the pleasure principle in our human state of estrangement (Tillich 1954, 28-29, 116-17). In Tillich's highly systematized thought, some important implications of a Platonic position are made explicit; and not only is the relation of *eros, epithymia,* and *philia* given a clear systematic statement, but also the relation of all these three to Christian *agape.* For these reasons, Tillich's treatment of love is well suited to rounding out a discussion of love as desire.

Tillich notes two main sources of confusion about love. The first is that of seeing the root meaning of love as an emotional one (Tillich 1954, 3-4, 24; Tillich 1963, III, 134). The other is thinking that there are types of love (Tillich 1954, 5). As anyone at all familiar with Tillich's thought would expect, he seeks the root meaning of love and the resolution of confusions in ontology (Tillich 1954, 17).

According to Tillich, the ontological question is: what does it mean *to be*? To ask this question is to ask: what are the structures common to everything that is, to everything that participates in being (Tillich 1954,19)? The attempt to answer this question, he says, precedes every other cognitive approach to reality, not always historically, but always in logical dignity and basic analysis. The best way, Tillich asserts, to discover the primacy of the ontological question is merely to make a careful analysis of the writings of the leading anti-ontological philosophers or of the anti-philosophical scientist and historian. For one will see on almost every page they write a number of surreptitious and often wrong basic ontological concepts. One simply cannot escape ontology if one wants to know (Tillich 1954, 20).

How does ontology go about its work of understanding being? Ontology attempts to describe the manifold texture of being. Being is one and the elements and qualities of being constitute a texture of connected and conflicting forces. This texture of connecting and conflicting forces is one insofar as it gives the power of being to each of its qualities and elements. Thus it is one without being a dead identity or a constant sameness. This does not mean that ontology attempts to describe the variety of beings in the world, whether in their universal qualities or in their individual ones; ontology is concerned with the texture of being itself, a texture effective in everything that is. Being is present to everyone in every encountered reality. Ontology analyzes the encountered reality in order to separate those elements which are constitutive of everything from whatever is generic or particular. Ontology, therefore, is analytical and descriptive. It is not metaphysics, but the foundation of metaphysics; the constructs of metaphysics are built upon an ontology (Tillich 1954, 19-20, 23). The way in which an ontological judgment is verified is not by experiment, therefore, but by experience, by intelligent recognition of the basic ontological structures within an encountered reality, including the encounter itself (Tillich 1954, 23).

What then does it mean to speak about an ontology of love? What does it mean to arrive at an ontological notion of love? Looking at what Tillich actually does, it would seem to mean two things: first of all, it means seeing that love is one of those elements of the real which are constitutive of everything that is (Tillich 1954, 21-23; this is the implication of all he says in these pages); and secondly, it means discovering what is common in every experience of love. Tillich himself puts it succinctly in a key passage:

> Life is being in actuality and love is the moving power of life. In these two sentences the ontological nature of love is expressed. They say that being is not actual without love which drives everything which is towards everything else that is. In human experience of love the nature of life becomes manifest. Love is the drive towards the unity of the separated (Tillich 1954, 25).

Because it is the drive, the urge, toward union not merely of the separate but of the separated, the estranged rather than the strange, Tillich more commonly speaks of love as the "reunion" of the estranged or of the separated. Reunion, and therefore love, presupposes the original unity and the separation of what belongs essentially together. Those elements which belong essentially together cannot be "strange" to one another, but only "estranged" (Tillich 1954, 25).

Love, then, shows its greatest power in overcoming the estrangement between individual selves, persons; for these are independent, self-related, centers, indivisible and impenetrable (Tillich 1954, 25-26). But this must not lead us to thinking that love is only something humans experience in our conscious personal lives. The drive toward reunion of the separated is universal, the moving power of all life. "It is effective in all three life processes; it unites in a center, it creates the new, and it drives beyond everything given to its ground and aim. It is the 'brood' of life and therefore has many forms in which the dispersed elements of life are reunited" (Tillich 1963, III, 134).

Although Tillich can on occasion slip into speaking of love as reunion or even just union instead of a drive or urge or movement
toward reunion, it is clear in the whole context of his thought that
when this happens, it is a slip in perfect accuracy of language, nothing more. Love for Tillich is *not* union. That this is so shows up in
two consequences he draws consistently from his basic notion of love
as a drive to union of the separated. The first is that it is hard to speak
meaningfully of self-love. Self-love cannot really be a concept, Tillich
says, but only an ambiguous metaphor, which we would do well to
remove from our vocabulary. "Is there any separation in the structure
of self-consciousness" to be overcome by love (Tillich 1954, 6; 33-
34)? The second and even more striking consequence of Tillich's basic notion of love is that love ceases in the measure that reunion is
achieved. Fulfilled love is the end of love, for without separation there
is no love and no life. Love necessarily remains unfulfilled, for its
complete fulfilment would mean the elimination of the lover and the
loved (Tillich 1954, 27; 1963, III, 253). (Tillich's understanding of
the emotion of love, as we shall immediately see, in terms of a response to an imagined union, a response of *anticipation,* fits with
and confirms the position that love ceases insofar as union is actualized.)

Love is forever driving to reunion, and this is a force in the very
texture of all being. Because it is ontological, it is not something
partial in any being. It is "the whole being's movement toward another being to overcome existential separation" (Tillich 1963, III,136).
On this basis, Tillich rejects as a confusion and a source of distorting
connotations any description of love as emotion (Tillich 1954, 3-5).
Emotion in Tillich's meaning is "feeling," merely subjective and only
in a "corner" of human life, as opposed to the whole being's movement (Tillich 1957, 38-40). Thus to think of love as emotion is to
falsify the former's ontological status and significance. Nevertheless,
Tillich does not want to mean that love is without emotion; on the
contrary he claims there is no love without emotion. Love without
emotion is only "good-will," and that is not love (Tillich 1963, III,
136; 1954, 26). How then is emotion related to love defined ontologically? The ontologically founded movement of the whole being,
which is love, finds expression in emotion. Love as emotion is "the
anticipation of the reunion which takes place in every love relation."
It is the feeling of happiness at this reunion experienced in imagination (Tillich 1954, 26-27). (Note that the emotion is said to be a
response to *imagined* union. As we have seen, when union is attained,
insofar as it is attained, love in its ontological meaning ceases; pre-

sumably love as emotion does also. In the following paragraph of the text, p. 27, Tillich speaks about the "ambiguity" of love fulfilled as being at the same time happiness and the end of happiness. What this means is not clarified. But consistency would forbid that the happiness of love fulfilled should involve love either as an ontological force or as an emotion. The former requires separation for its possibility, and the later is anticipation.).

Besides the confusion of love with emotion, the other main confusion which Tillich notes is that of confounding qualities of love with types of love. Love, his ontological analysis reveals to him, is one. There are no types but only different qualities of one love. These qualities are four: *epithymia, eros, philia,* and *agape.* The first is also called *libido.* Tillich rejects the hedonistic interpretation of it as based on bad psychology. *Libido* essentially is not governed by the pain-pleasure principle but strives for vital self-fulfilment in union. Pleasure is an accompaniment of this. *Eros* transcends *libido* and strives for union with that which is a bearer of value because of the value it embodies. These are found in nature, culture, and the divine source of these two. *Philia* and *eros* are polar, the latter a transpersonal pole, the former a personal pole. *Philia* therefore presupposes some equality and familiarity with its object and reaches it as a Thou, a personal center. *Agape,* the dominant quality of love in the New Testament, is love in relation to the ground of life; by it ultimate reality manifests itself and transforms love, cutting into the *libido, eros,* and *philia* qualities of love and elevating them beyond the ambiguities of their self-centeredness. Thus by *agape,* sexual desire is united to the *eros* and *philia* qualities and saved from distortion under the tyranny of the pleasure principle. By *agape,* cultural *eros* is saved from mere aestheticism and mystical *eros* from impersonalism. By *agape,* the preferential love of *philia* is purified of exclusiveness so that everyone is affirmed as a person (Tillich 1954, 5, 27-33, 116-19).

If the other three qualities need *agape* unless they are to be distortions, the *agape* quality in human love without desire is merely obedience to moral law (Tillich 1954, 31, 33; 1957,114-15). Nevertheless Tillich does not want to say that *agape* is dependent on the other qualities. *Agape,* he holds, is a manifestation of the "Spiritual Presence," possible only in unity with faith, able to unite with, to judge, and transform the other qualities (Tillich 1963, III, 137).

These four qualities are frequently spoken of by others as though each were a different type of love, differing in kind from the others. Even if those who speak this way were ready to assert an analogous core to love of every type, this core qualified in one of these ways in different acts, Tillich would not be in agreement. In his view, these qualities are not to be seen as essentially contrasted and opposed; all of them are in every love relation that is not distorted; all of them qualify the drive or movement to reunion. One can appear without the others, e.g., *libido* without *eros, eros* without *philia,* but it does so only as a perverted relation, a distortion which occurs in our human state of estrangement.

The unity of *agape* with *epithymia, eros,* and *philia,* and the unity of these three among themselves is underlined by Tillich in his assertion that we are justified in translating all these Greek words by "love." What justifies us in doing so is the one point of identity in all of them, the urge toward a reunion of the separated. Love as urge to reunion is the dynamics of life and is one and indivisible (Tillich 1963, III, 137).

Spinoza

Although it seems at first to be a notion of love far removed from the tendency or movement of Plato, Freud, and Tillich, Spinoza's notion of love as joy (*laetitia*), when understood within his philosophy, turns out to have a close kinship with these others.

The notion of love as joy is uncommon and is usually brushed aside without serious considerations. In fact, Spinoza stands as a famous and imposing but rather lonely figure in the history of thought on love. Some others do in a broad way of speaking or in a passing remark say that love is joy or rejoicing in the loved one without intending thereby to adopt any formal position such as that of Spinoza. For example: "But to love is…to will an object for itself, to rejoice in its beauty and goodness for themselves…" (Gilson, 1936, 280). Rollo May does insert "delight" and "joy" in his formal definition of love: "we define love as a delight in the presence of other persons and an affirming of their value and development as much as one's own. Thus there are always two elements to love that of the worth and good of other persons and that of one's own joy and happiness in relation with them" (May 1953, 241). Others speak of delight or happiness as a property, a necessary accompaniment or consequence of love. Thus Thomas Hobbes says: "All appetite, desire, and love is accompanied with some delight more or less" (Hobbes 1950, 40). So also Max Scheler says that "Even when love is 'unhappy' in the sense of being unrequited the act itself is still accompanied by a feeling of great happiness—and equally so when the loved one occasions pain and sorrow" (Scheler 1954, 147). To say that joy accompanies or even always accompanies love is not, however, the same as to say that love is joy or a mode of joy. Spinoza makes joy the very essence of love. In a philosophy as rigidly systematic as Spinoza's, no key concept can be understood in isolation. His concept of love is tightly embedded in his whole scheme of the affects (*affectus*) and takes its meaning from the primary affects. (On the difficulty of satisfactorily translating Spinoza's *affectus*, see Hallett 1957, 96-97.)

These in turn, take their meaning from the power or conatus (*potentia sive conatus*) which constitutes the human essence or of any individual human being. So, it is with conatus that we must begin in order to understand love. What does Spinoza mean by conatus? It is that by which anything endeavors to act either alone or with other things, i.e., to persevere in its own being. This is nothing else, says Spinoza, than the actual essence of the thing (Spinoza 1914, III, 7; all references to Spinoza will be to *Ethica* by Part and Proposition; all translations given are made from that text), and from it follows all that contributes to the being's preservation (Spinoza 1914, III, 6-9). When referred to mind and body together, it is called appetite (*appetitus*) (Spinoza 1914, III, 9, Scholium). When referred to mind alone, i.e., to the possession of ideas (adequate or inadequate) which constitutes the essence of the mind, this conatus is called will (*voluntas*) (Spinoza 1914, III, 9, Scholium; on the various usages of *voluntas* in Spinoza, see Wolfson 1934, II, 167-68). Now we are conscious of our appetite: and, insofar as our appetite is conscious, Spinoza calls it desire *(cupiditas)*: desire is conscious appetite. This is as much as to say that desire is our actual essence conceived as determined to a particular act by some modification of the essence (Spinoza 1914, III, 9, Scholium, and Affectuum Definitiones, 1).

In the following statement Spinoza speaks of the *mind's* passage to or from perfection (in the definitions at the end of *Pars* 3, he speaks of the *person's* passage): As desire is conatus reflected in consciousness, so joy (*laetitia*) and sorrow (*tristitia*) are the conscious emotional expressions of the passage to perfection or from it in accord with or disaccord with the conatus (Spinoza 1914, III, 11; *laetitia* is translated in a number of ways, sometimes by the same translator; some of the words used as equivalents are: joy, pleasure, delight, satisfaction, happiness; the first of these seems to me to carry Spinoza's meaning better than the others. Wolfson [1934, II, 206-07] gives his reasons for preferring "pleasure").

In his explanation, Spinoza insists that these affects consist in the activity of passage to or away from perfection, not in the perfection or lack of perfection. If one were born fully perfect, one would, according to Spinoza, never experience joy (Spinoza 1914, III, Affectuum Definitiones, 2-3, Explicatio). These three, then, are the primary affects according to Spinoza; desire, joy, sorrow. From them all other affections derive (Spinoza 1914, III, 11, Scholium). These three primary affects are grounded in conatus. All refer to the being's necessary striving for perseverance in being and for what conduces to persevering in being. Good is, then, understood as every sort of joy and whatever conduces to joy and especially what satisfies desire. Evil, on the contrary, is every sort of sorrow and whatever conduces to it and especially what frustrates desire (Spinoza 1914, III, 39, Scholium). So Spinoza concludes that we neither endeavor nor will nor have appetite for nor desire anything because it is good, but we judge it is good because we endeavor, will, have appetite for, desire it (Spinoza 1914, III, 9, Scholium). There is no discrimination of good and evil prior to desire nor any free choice to seek good before or after desire (Spinoza 1914, III, 9, Scholium, and see II, 48, on freedom).

If "power or conatus" is the ground of all affective life and if desire, joy, and sorrow are the primary affective expressions of conatus, and if love is an affect, then love will have to be understood in relation to these primary affects and to conatus. Love must be either a derivative of one of the three primary affects or a combination of more than one or else identical with one of them. Given that conatus is the essence of being for Spinoza, we might expect him to identify love with drive or desire, as Plato did before him or Freud and Tillich after. Spinoza does identify love with a primary affect, but surprisingly, not with desire. For him love is "joy with the concomitant idea of an external cause," just as hate is "sorrow with the concomitant idea of an external cause" (Spinoza 1914, III, 13, Scholium; see also Affectuum Definitiones 6).

Desire toward what is loved necessarily follows on love, desire for presence of the loved object or for conservation of presence (Spinoza 1914, III, 28, 37-38). However, will or desire for the presence of the object loved is no part of love itself; it is not even a property. Spinoza explicitly repudiates the thought of those who say that it is. Referring to his own definition, he says

> This definition conveys the essence of love with sufficient clarity. Those authors who define love as the will of the one loving to join oneself with what is loved express not the essence of love but its property. One point must be noted however. When I say it is proper to the one loving to join oneself by will to what is loved, I

understand by "will" neither consent nor deliberation of mind, that is, free decision (for this has been shown to be a fiction in proposition 48 of II). Neither do I understand a desire for joining oneself to what is loved when it is absent or of persevering in its presence when it is already present; for love can be conceived without including either of these desires. By "will" I do understand the contentment which is in the one loving on account of the loved one's presence, by which the joy of the one loving is strengthened or at least favored (Spinoza 1914, III, Affectuum Definitiones 6 Explicatio).

In this passage, two acts which others speak of as love are not only excluded from the essence of love by Spinoza but are even denied to be properties of love. Love is not nor does it involve a freely given consent to union with a loved object. Obviously, consistency alone would demand that Spinoza reject any notion of love which involves free choice once he has made his system such that it has no room for it. But neither is love a desire, not even a necessary and determined desire for union when the loved object is absent or for continuance of union with a present loved object. Love, says Spinoza, can be *conceived* without either of these. He does not say that love ever actually occurs in our experience without one or other of these desires; but the concept of love does not include either as of the essence of love or as a property. Contentment or satisfaction (*acquiescentia*) on account of the object's presence, is an affection Spinoza will allow as a property of love. But he will not say that it is of the essence of love. Love is prior to and independent of desire for or contentment in union.

What, then, is love essentially? It is a mode of joy. Recall that joy is the conscious emotional expression of the transition to perfection in accord with conatus. Now, love is joy when joy is accompanied by the idea of that which is an external cause of the transition. (The cause he is talking about can be an indirect or accidental cause. See III, 15-16). What is puzzling is his qualification of the cause as external. Elsewhere he speaks of someone loving self when one imagines affecting others with joy; for then one has joy with the concomitant idea of oneself as cause. Now, self is not an external cause. Spinoza is aware of the problem and so calls self-love "glory" (*gloria*) instead of love (*amor*) (Spinoza 1914, III, 30).

The reader is reminded here of Tillich's objection to the concept of self-love, for reasons other than those that cause Spinoza's difficulty. There are other and more important ways in which Spinoza's thought on love is allied with that of Tillich, Freud, and Plato. What sounds so strikingly different (and, as has been shown, is so in some ways) is on close inspection not so different after all. Love, for the authors we first studied, is drive, desire, tendency. For Spinoza it is joy as opposed to desire. But his joy is still bound up with tendency and movement. It is the conscious affective expression of transition to perfection with a concomitant idea of the cause. This notion of love necessarily leads to another conjunction with Plato, Freud, and Tillich; for Spinoza is forced to conclude that love ceases insofar as perfection is attained. Happiness is for all of them the end of love in both of the ambiguous meanings of that word "end": it is the goal and the point of cessation. Spinoza emphasizes the point by asserting that if one were born perfect, one could never experience joy (Spinoza 1914, III, Affectuum Definitiones 3 Explicatio); if one could not experience joy, one could never experience love.

The exposition of love in Spinoza's philosophy has to this point been based on Part III of his *Ethics.* It is noteworthy that in Part V the notion of love undergoes significant alteration in order to become what he speaks of as "intellectual love" in contrast to the "imaginational love" of Part III. For when he considers the one who has attained freedom or blessedness, he should logically exclude love in the measure that one is actualized in freedom and happiness. This Spinoza does not wish to do. Instead, he alters his notion of love to meet his need. He knows very well what he is doing and makes no apologies nor any retraction of his definition in Part III; nor does he attempt a more general definition which will fit both love as an affective expression of transition and love as an expression of perfection in act. The love which is ours in blessedness, insofar as we are blessed or free, is "intellectual love." Our intellectual love for God is "a part of the infinite love with which God loves the divine self" (Spinoza 1914, V, 35-36). Given that love has heretofore been defined as a *passio,* Spinoza admits that strictly speaking he cannot attribute love to God (Spinoza 1914, V, 17). Nevertheless, he continues speaking of God's love and of our human intellectual love as a part of it. This intellectual love in us cannot be joy, since joy involves transition to greater perfection, while our intellectual love is not transition to perfection. It is conscious perfection and is eternal. So Spinoza shifts from defining love as joy (*laetitia*) with an idea of external cause to defining it as blessedness *(beatitudo)* with a concomitant knowledge of God as the eternal cause (Spinoza 1914, V, 33; see also 27). The result of this revision is a notion of love that is active (Spinoza 1914, V, 36. 39. 40), that is no longer involved with tendency and transition, and that is not followed by desire.

In this respect, Spinoza's intellectual love departs radically from love in Plato, Freud, and Tillich, and takes on one aspect which we will find later as a basic aspect of love in human life according to Erich Fromm. For Fromm love is the goal of our most fundamental human desire and striving. In the love which is a *passio*, "imaginational love" as opposed to "intellectual love," there is another striking difference from Plato, Freud, and Tillich: such love, even though it involves movement and transition, is not desire but entails desire as a consequence. In this respect, if in no other, Spinoza's notion of love joins with that of many others who oppose love to desire as source to consequence. Let us now turn to this way of thinking about love.

3
LOVE AS SOURCE OF DESIRE AND JOY OR AS OBJECT OF DESIRE

However nicely Spinoza's definition of love may fit into his system, brilliantly contrived *modo geometrico,* it leaves most readers wondering if it accurately reflects the human experience of love. Max Scheler and Ortega y Gasset express the reaction of many. Scheler considers Spinoza's definition a "complete futility," and urges against it two facts: first, that through all the pain and grief a loved one may cause and through all the daily vicissitudes of joy and sorrow, love can remain unwavering; second, that hatred as well as love can bring joy, joy over the misery of the one hated (Scheler 1954, 147). Ortega with his characteristic rhetorical verve puts similar objections more strikingly;

> Who doubts that the lover can find happiness in the beloved? But it is no less certain that love is sometimes sad, as sad as death—a supreme and mortal torment. It is more: true love thus recognizes itself and, so to speak, measures and calculates itself by the pain and suffering of which it is capable. The woman in love prefers the anguish her beloved causes her to painless indifference....
> Spinoza did not observe carefully: loving is not happiness. Those who love their country may die for it, and the martyr may perish out of love. And conversely, there is a kind of hatred that derives pleasure from itself, that is transported with joy by the harm that befalls the hated person (Ortega y Gasset, 1957, 13-14).

Whether there is more to be said for the notion of love as joy than Scheler or Ortega would have us think (and perhaps more than Spinoza had to say) will be taken up later. Now, however, it should at least be noted in all fairness to Spinoza that the criticisms of his notion of love usually bear on imaginational love and not on his intellectual love. Perhaps the latter too can justly be criticized; but, if so, it will have to be for other reasons than those that are commonly brought against imaginational love. And what is more, Spinoza had already analyzed love so as to have an answer to the objections raised by Ortega and Scheler, though they do not seem to be aware of it (Spinoza, 1914, III, 14-17, 20-24, 35, 42, 47). If even imaginational love is to be impugned, it will have to be for better reasons than those with which Scheler and Ortega facilely dismiss the definition given by Spinoza.

Although love is not joy nor the only cause of joy, according to Ortega, both joy and desire do arise as consequences of love (Ortega, 1957, 11, 13, 191 n. 2). In holding this position, he joins at least partially a long tradition stemming from Augustine and finding its clearest and fullest formal statement in Thomas Aquinas. In the thought of Augustine and Thomas, love is seen as the source of all desire and joy. This is not to say that being a source of desire and joy is for all those in this tradition essential to love, so that love is unintelligible except in relation to desire and joy. What is meant is that whenever the latter arise they do so in dependence on love; that love, therefore, is distinct from and prior to both joy and desire. It will be clear from what follows, but it might be well to note it from the start, that for Augustine and Aquinas joy is not, as it is for Spinoza, an affective expression of passage or transition toward perfection; rather, it is the affective expression of fulfilment attained and rested in.

It is to Augustine and Thomas that Ortega refers when discussing the distinction between love and its consequences. Unfortunately, his interpretation of Augustine seems to be partly accurate only by a stroke of luck and his luck ran out when he spoke of Thomas. When citing Augustine, Ortega makes no reference to the classic text for understanding Augustine on this question. He seizes upon a famous but ambiguous text and exclaims that this is one of the few times Augustine freed himself from the interpretation which makes of love a desire (Ortega, 1957, 12). In the same context he makes the serious historical blunder of telling his readers that for Thomas love and hate are two forms of "desire or lust"! (Ortega, 1957, 10-11). As we shall see, it is Thomas more than any other who has formally argued for the distinction of love from desire, even of the kind of love which has the same object as desire. (This distinction is obscured when *amor concupiscentiae* is made the equivalent of "desire," as is done, for example, even by one with such a deep and accurate knowledge of Aquinas as Johann [1955, 10].)

Love As the Source of Desire and Joy:
Augustine and Aquinas

Before we begin looking at the pertinent Augustinian texts, we had better take account of another and opposite interpretation of Augustine. For he is sometimes interpreted as identifying love with desire. And he does give some grounds for such an interpretation in a num-

ber of passages on love as also by the ambiguity of the word he uses to
express the basic meaning of love in his thought, a "weight" (*pondus*)
(Augustine 1943, bk. 13, ch. 9; 1950, bk. 11, ch. 28). One of the
most famous interpretations of Augustine in this way can be found
in Anders Nygren's study, *Agape and Eros*. He asserts that to Augustine all love is acquisitive love (Nygren 1953, 476), and by acquisitive
love Nygren means desire (throughout his discussion of Augustine
this is clear; but see esp. 1953, 476-82). In the context, it is clear that
Nygren is speaking of Augustine's notion of *human* love: desire, he
says, in Augustine's thought is the mark of the creature. Nygren is
well aware that Augustine does not attribute desire to God (Nygren
1953, 479).

Nygren's assertion that all human love is acquisitive love according
to Augustine is debated by others. (Burnaby [1938] time and again
takes exception to Nygren's understanding of *agape* and *eros* in general and to his understanding of Augustine's doctrine in particular.
D'Arcy does the same [1956, ch. 2, "Eros and Christian Theology,"
esp. 74-78].) Without taking sides in that debate, I want to raise
another question, whether even acquisitive love grounded in the
creature's need should be identified with desire in Augustine's thought.
A careful effort to grasp the relationship of love to the other affections of the will in Augustine forces us to go slowly in making what
at first seems so patent an identification.

The classic text concerning the relationship of love and desire in
Augustine is found in *The City of God*.

> A right act of will is, therefore, good love, and a wrong act of will
> is evil love. Love, then, longing to have what is loved, is desire; but
> having and delighting in it is joy; shunning what is opposed to it
> is fear; and feeling what is opposed to it when it has happened is
> sorrow. And so these affections are evil if the love is evil; good if the
> love is good (trans. from Augustine [1900] XL, 13).

In this text, love (*amor*) is identified with willing (*voluntas*), i.e., the
basic unqualified act of will, which by reason of different relations to
objects becomes desire, joy, sadness, fear, and so on. Love is in a way
all these other affections; that is to say, they are love in a qualified
sense. Love simply speaking has to be really distinct from desire and
from joy and the other affections, because it is not limited to any one
of these qualified forms. There is some one underlying affection which
is the groundwork of all the others. It is this affection which as tending is called desire, as resting is called joy; it accounts for whatever

man desires and does, and it accounts for his resting with joy in what fulfils him.

For this reason Augustine speaks of his love (*amor*) as his weight (*pondus*) in the *Confessions*.

> Fire tends upward, a stone downward. By their weights they are driven, they seek their own places.... Not perfectly placed in the order of things, They are restless; put in order, they are at rest. My love is my weight; by it I am borne wherever I am borne (trans. from Augustine 1962, XIV, 440).

Now in this passage and in others like it, *amor* as *pondus* is readily taken to mean desiring or seeking one's "place." But closer inspection in the light of what is said in the literal statements of *The City of God* (see bk. 14, ch. 6-7) leads us to understand the metaphorical statement of the *Confessions* in a different way. For nothing in the latter's statement necessitates fully and simply identifying the *pondus* with psychic movement toward or rest in one's piece. *Pondus* by itself is what accounts for movement and rest, for desire and joy or peace. A distinction of love from desire fits more precisely with the text. Let movement in the metaphor parallel desire, and let rest parallel joy. Now, *by* my weight I am borne wherever I am borne, and *by* my weight I rest in my place. But it is not by desire that I rest any more than it is by joy that I move. It is by my weight, my love, that I move and rest. Thus, love is not simply identifiable with either movement or rest, with desire or joy. Nevertheless as explained above, desire and the joy must also be understood as love qualified by a certain relation to the object loved, its presence or its absence, a relation which is not essential to unqualified love, love in itself or simply.

This position of Augustine on the priority of love to desire and joy is also the position which Thomas Aquinas takes as his own in conscious dependence on Augustine. The arguments he elaborates to establish this position are so clearly and carefully worked out as to leave no doubt of what he means and why he means it.

The central text for understanding Thomas on love is that comprised by three questions in ST1-2, 26-28, where he treats of the nature of love, its causes, and its effects. Of these the first deals directly with our question, and all that is said here about Thomas' notion of love will be drawn principally from it, using other texts only as they throw light on this one. The reader should not be misled by the fact that these questions occur in the treatise *De passionibus* and that a *passio* in Thomas' strict meaning of the word cannot be found in the will or in any spiritual operative power. He explicitly and implicitly extends the treatise to include the spiritual affections of the will and, when speaking of love, is principally interested in these (see ST 1-2, q. 22, a. 3, where he discusses the more general problem of whether there is any passion in the will, and q. 26, aa. 1-2, where he distinguishes natural, sensuous, and intellectual love, the latter being a *passio* of the will; thereafter, he centers attention on love in the will.)

Two notions of love are developed. First, Thomas develops a notion of love as the principle of desire and delight, using the device of analogy with the Aristotelian physics of motion. Then he develops the notion of love as benevolence, willing good to someone, and employs this in the two following questions on the causes and effects of love. For the present, our interest is only in the first notion of love as related to desire and delight.

At the beginning of this treatise on love, Thomas brings up Augustine's famous passage from *The City of God* (bk. 14, ch. 7) in an objection against his own understanding of the affections. For in that passage, Augustine, so the objection runs, seems to be asserting that all the affections (*passiones*) are love (ST 1-2, q. 26, a. 1, obj. 2). Thomas' response is merely that love can be called fear, joy, desire, and so on, not essentially but causally (*non quidem essentialiter sed causaliter*). In other words, love is these only insofar as love is the source from which they arise (ST 1-2, q. 26, a. 1, reply to obj. 2). Whether this reply is meant as a correction or an interpretation of Augustine we may let pass. What alone is important in our discussion is the distinction of love from desire and from joy or delight, and its priority as the principle of both. This is his consistent opinion held to in a variety of contexts (ST 1, q. 20, a. 1; 1-2, q. 25, a. 2; q. 26, aa. 1-2; *In Divinis nominibus*, bk. 7, ch. 9).

Like Augustine he employs the comparison of love with the principle of movement and rest in Aristotelian physics, and does it in such a way as to leave no ambiguity about the priority of love as the root of all affective life.

> Now a natural agent produces a twofold effect on the patient; for in the first place it gives it the form; and secondly it gives it the movement that results from the form. Thus the generator gives the generated body both weight and the movement resulting from weight: so that weight, from being the principle of movement to the place which is natural to the body by reason of its weight, can in a way be called natural love. In the same way an appetible object

gives the appetite first a certain adaptation to itself, which consists in complacency in that object; and from this follows movement toward the appetible object. For the appetitive movement is circular, as stated in *De anima*, iii, 10; because the appetible object moves the appetite, introducing itself as it were into its intention; while the appetite moves toward the realization of the appetible object, so that the movement ends where it began. Accordingly the first change wrought in the appetite by the appetible object is called love and is nothing else than a complacency in that object, and from this complacency results a movement towards that same object, and this movement is desire; and lastly, there is rest which is joy (ST 1-2, q. 26, a. 2 c.; trans. from Aquinas 1941).

Again, as for Augustine, so for Thomas in this and in other texts, love, desire, and joy have the same object but under different formalities. The object of love is a good qualification as possessed or not possessed, whereas the object of desirers that same good inasmuch as it is not yet possessed, and the object of joy is that same good precisely as possessed is on this formal difference in their objects that Thomas bases his argument for the priority of love as the principle of the two other affections.

The line of reasoning runs this way (ST 1, q. 20, a. 1, c.): 1. good has a priority over evil (ST 1, q. 48, a. 1); 2. evil is the privation of a good that should be, and so can be, an object of will only if the will responds first to good; 3. therefore the affection toward good is prior to any affective response to evil, e.g., hate or fear. Among the affections toward good, that which is toward good without qualification, simply as good, has priority over those affections which are toward good qualified as not possessed and to be tended toward or as possessed and rested in.

In another text he argues from the nature of good as an end. Good has the character of an end. The end and therefore the good is first in the order of intention but last in the order of execution, of actual attainment. In the order of execution, then, desire for the end not yet attained precedes joy in the end attained, the good possessed. But there is and must be some affection toward this end which is prior to desire or joy and is the principle of both. This is the affection toward the object as good without qualification as absent or present, as possessed or unpossessed, attained or not yet attained (ST 1-2, q. 25, a. 2, c.). This basic act of the will toward good is love.

It is characterized by a series of terms scattered through Thomas' writing on love (*proportio, coaptatio, aptitudo, connaturalitas, conson-*

antia, immutatio, intentio, inclinatio, complacentia), all of which point to the general idea that by love the lover's will is put into harmony with the object loved, so that the latter is a good to him. Beyond this general meaning it is difficult to go with any assurance. Whether this harmony is to be thought of principally as quiescence in a good or as an active source whose meaning is understood only or principally in terms of psychic movement toward an end and rest in it when attained is a problem which seems unresolvable on the basis of Thomas' text (see Crowe 1959, no. 1, pp. 2-3). Love as a principle of desire and joy, movement and rest, is more in evidence throughout Thomas' writing, at least his later writings, than love as *complacentia*, as a quiescence in the reality of the loved object.

It is clear that in the texts we have considered, both Augustine and Aquinas leave us with a love that not only underlies desire as its source but also has the same object as desire. Further, although it underlies joy in the same way, joy itself as presented in these texts has the same object as desire. By the same object I mean the same *material* object; the affections are responses to the same material object under different aspects, different *formal* objects, good as good, good as not possessed and tended to, good as possessed and rested in. It is this material identity between the object of desire and love which can give rise to thinking that in Augustine's theory there is no room for any other love than acquisitive love, even after the distinction between love and desire is upheld. For then love is directed to that which the lover desires to have or rejoices in having. This is what confuses a reader of Thomas, who, after reading this account of love, is in the very same question of the ST suddenly told that love is benevolence, that benevolence involves a twofold love, and that only one of these loves is for an object that is materially the same as the object of desire to which it gives rise. The other love is love toward someone for whom a good is loved and desired. Thomas' notion of benevolence will be examined a little further on; for now it is enough to indicate that the above account of love gives an incomplete picture of his view as it is contained in this text.

Love As Benevolence: Aristotle and Aquinas

Besides Augustinian *pondus* and Thomist *complacentia,* there are many other notions of love which are either set in opposition to desire or are presented as sources of desire and joy. These usually turn out to be notions that tend to merge when explained. So true is this that there is reason to suspect that these notions may not merely represent closely related elements of a composite affective experience but represent aspects of one simple and basic element.

Among other things, love is said to be union, presence, coexistence, adherence, affirmation, concern, relating positively, benevolence, taking responsibility for someone, concern for someone, giving of self. Writers on love who reject the identification of love with desire or with joy ordinarily employ several of these notions, sometimes clearly integrating them, sometimes allowing them to stand as distinct descriptions of love without any effort to show whether they cohere as aspects of one reality or whether one is the cause of the other or the result of it. In most instances, we do find that one or another notion is dominant in any particular author and would most accurately characterize that author's thought on love, the other notions taking their place in relation to it. Sometimes one notion is dominant because it is made the center to which the other notions are integrated; sometimes the various notions are left unintegrated, but one of them more or less overshadows the others. We can, therefore, relate these notions and further underline the variety of notions about love by considering several theories with different dominant notions, theories which have more powerfully influenced the general thinking on love.

The task can be simplified if we note that some of these terms are so closely akin that for the purpose of this survey one illustration will suffice for several of them. Thus, presence, coexistence, adherence, are all ways of talking about love as union.

They do bring out different aspects of union; and, as they are treated by various authors, the difference is meaningful. But it is not necessary to expound all of them in order to illustrate this way of thinking about love. Similarly, affirmation can take in the notion of relating positively. Benevolence, concern for someone, taking responsibility for someone, giving, all these can be joined as notions of love which focus on preserving or promoting the loved one's well-being.

It is this last mentioned way of thinking about love that deserves first consideration inasmuch as it is, among all those opposed to seeing love as desire, the most commonly accepted opinion, the one with the longest and most illustrious tradition, and the one toward which most if not all the others verge and with which they ultimately tend to merge. The history of philosophy and theology as well as of contemporary writing is filled with descriptions of love in this vein, whether it be spoken of as care, concern, a will to promotion, availability, taking responsibility for, active leaning toward, giving of self to the beloved. Benevolence (well-wishing, willing good to someone) is a word with a long and respectable history and a word that expresses what most people are getting at in this notion of love. So, taken in its literal, etymological, sense, it will serve to name this notion of love. Scheler, when proposing reasons for rejecting benevolence as love says that a phenomenology reveals benevolence as seeking the material welfare of persons and also as including an element of remoteness, superiority, and condescension. This he opposes to "well-wishing" (Scheler 1954, 140-41).

Whether Scheler's phenomenology is true or not we may transmit and merely insist that as benevolence is used here, in its literal sense, it is equivalent to well-wishing, and there is no need to assume that people who wish well to others are concerned only about material welfare or are condescending.

Just as Plato's and Freud's statements are classical for love conceived as drive or desire for the lover's happiness, and Spinoza's statement is classical for the notion of love as joy, so also are those of Aristotle and Aquinas classical for love as benevolence.

Aristotle's analysis of benevolence appears principally in the treatise on friendship in the *Nicomachean Ethics* (=NE). The requirements for and characteristics of friendship as such do not concern us. What is of concern is the love that either friend has for the other and that either friend might have even prior to any return of love and any growth of friendship. However, since Aristotle nowhere else discusses love so fully and clearly as he does here, we have to look for his thought on love as it is embedded in his thought on the mutual love in the life of friendship.

In this discussion he distinguishes three types of friendship, i.e., three relationships of mutual love, three relationships of good-will (NE, 8, 2-3). The distinction arises from three grounds of friendship: pleasure, usefulness, goodness (i.e., nobility, intellectual and moral). Some are friends because they find pleasure in each other; when the pleasure ceases, the friendship then ceases. Some are friends because they are useful to each other; when utility ceases, so does the friendship. These are imperfect forms of friendship, according to Aristotle, not friendship in the proper sense of the word but merely likenesses to it. Perfect friendship, friendship properly speaking, is between those who love one another because each sees the nobility of the other's mind and heart and each loves the other for the other's own sake. If there are three sorts of friendship, there are three sorts of mutual love, good-will. And if two of these friendships are called such only by likeness to the third, then the proper meaning of love or good-will is to be found in this third or perfect type. In what does this love consist? It is first of all for Aristotle the attitude of a someone to oneself; love of a friend is an extension of the attitude we have toward ourselves (NE 9, 4).

It would be a grievous distortion of Aristotle's thought to think that he is talking about something such as Fromm calls symbiotic love. There is a vast difference. While Aristotle conceives of friends extending toward others the attitude they have toward themselves, it is not in such a way as to incorporate or dominate others nor to submit themselves irrationally to others. The love for friends he is talking about consists in "wishing for them what you believe to be good things, not for your sake but for theirs, and being inclined, so far as you can, to bring these things about" (*Rhetoric* 2, 4[1380b35–1381a1). This sort of love in friendship, Aristotle insists, can arise only between equals or creates equality in order that friendship should be (NE 8, 7-8). And no true friend will ever do evil for the sake of the other or even willingly allow others to do evil to themselves (NE 9, 12). As a matter of fact, Aristotle says that love can only be fully realized in a good persons. For evil persons (and others insofar as they are evil) is divided against themselves, willing what *is* harmful, and what they even *know* is harmful to themselves. So, they are hateful to themselves, want to be distracted from themselves and may even destroy themselves. A good person, on the contrary, is a unity. Good persons will themselves (especially that which is most themselves, their minds) to be, to continue in being, and to realize in action what is most fitting and fulfilling to them as intellectual beings. So also they will the same for their friends. And for this reason the friend can be called another self (NE 9, 4). When this good will towards another is superficial and lacking in intensity, as it is with strangers, it is only the beginning of love which arises in friendship of the perfect sort. Not until it becomes intense and is accompanied by a desire for presence and a sharing of life does it become the love which constitutes friendship (NE 9, 4-5). The good will that arises in the imperfect forms of friendship, grounded only in the hope of gain for the lover's self, is in ultimate analysis love or benevolence properly speaking towards self; to be love of the other in the proper sense of the word, benevolence has to be a response to the other for the other's own sake and grounded in some noble quality in the person who is loved.

The notion that love is willing good to someone (self or the other), is confirmed and clarified in Aristotle's response to the question whether a we should love our friends more than ourselves (NE 9, 8). The answer, he says, hinges upon the meaning attached to self-love; and he distinguishes two forms of self-love by distinguishing two types of goods that one can wish for oneself or for one's friend. The whole discussion, then, whether good persons should love themselves more than their friends centers around and is resolved in terms of the good I should will to myself or to my friend. There is a common and censurable form of self-love which seeks for self more than a fair share of money, honors, pleasures, etc.—what we would speak of as selfishness. There is another form of self-love which is rare and noble, which wishes for self what is noblest, that is, excellence of intellect and moral character, excellence of intellectual and moral activity. This kind of self-love leads to great generosity and magnanimity in one's dealing with others. Now good persons do love themselves more than they love any other in this way. But not in the former way of self-love, the vulgar, selfish way. They will gladly sacrifice wealth and honor and pleasure so that their friends may have them. They will even forgo opportunities to do noble deeds if by so doing they yield the opportunity to their friends. But in doing this they are really claiming for themselves a greater and nobler act. If, then, good persons do love themselves more than any other loves them, since they will the greater good to themselves, then they ought to love themselves most. For they ought to love most the one who loves them most, i.e., the one who wills them the greatest good. That one is oneself. So, whether we are speaking of self-love or love of the other, a friend, love in every instance is, for Aristotle, an act of willing good to the one loved.

This Aristotelian notion of love as benevolence appears quite generally in the writing of Thomas and particularly in the questions of the ST where he addresses himself formally and explicitly to analyzing love, its nature and causes and effects, and where he discusses the right moral ordering of love. (There is one text where Thomas explicitly declares that benevolence is not love [ST 2-2, q. 27, a. 2 c.], but this is a unique instance.) However, as noted above, the sudden turning to this notion is surprising after his other (Augustinian) analysis of love as an affection underlying desire and having the same material object.

The following text is so important as to be worth quoting in full.

> It must be said that, as the philosopher says in *Rhetoric* II, "to love is to will good to someone." Therefore the motion of love tends toward two objects, namely, toward the good that is willed for someone, either for self or for another, and toward that for which the good is willed. Therefore, one has love of concupiscence (*amor concupiscentiae*) in relation to the good which is willed to the other;

but in relation to the one for whom one wills the good, one has love of friendship (*amor amicitiae*). Now the members of this division are related as primary and secondary. For what is loved with a love of friendship is loved simply and *per se*; while what is loved with love of concupiscence is not loved simply and *per se*, but is loved for the other. For just as being *per se* is what has *esse* simply, but qualified being is what is in another, so also good, since it is convertible with being is good simply if it has good itself, but is good relatively if it is the good of another. Consequently the love with which something is loved so that it may have a good is loved simply; whereas the love with which something is loved so that it may be the good of another is loved relatively (ST 1-2, q. 26, a. 4 c.).

Clearly Thomas' analysis here introduces a much more complex notion than what he was speaking about before. As it is described, love in the concrete is twofold; there is a primary love and a secondary love. Each implies the other: the primary, love of someone for whom a good is willed, implies the secondary as flowing from it; the secondary, love of some good for someone, implies the primary as its source. The object of the secondary is lovable wholly by relation to the object of primary love and so it is a relative love, whereas the primary love is love simply or absolutely. The two together constitute the full act of love defined as "willing good to someone."

Thomas uses another set of terms as equivalents of love simply and love relatively in this text and in many other places: these are love of friendship and love of concupiscence. And as an equivalent of love of friendship, he also uses love of benevolence (*amor benevolentiae*; ST 1-2, q. 27, a. 3 c.). These terms, although the common terms used by Thomas and Thomists, would better give place to 'love simply' (or absolutely) and 'love relatively.' Love of friendship gets confused with friendship; love of concupiscence gets confused with desire or even with morally evil desire; and love of benevolence can be confused with benevolence (of which it is only the primary love of the twofold love). That is to say, these notions get confused in Thomas' commentators and in those who adopt his terminology for discussing the subject; there is no confusion discernible in Thomas himself.

This primary love (love absolutely or simply speaking) is clearly love in a more proper sense than relative love. Nevertheless, it is the latter that fits in all ways the love that Thomas described in the preceding articles as a principle of desire (ST 1-2, q. 26, a. 1 c. and a. 2 c.; also ST 1, q. 20, a. 1 c. and ST 1-2, a. 25, a. 2 c.). It is true that the primary love is also a principle of desire, but only as mediated by the secondary and relative love that is the immediate principle of desire. And further, it will be remembered that the love of which he spoke as the immediate principle of desire had the same object materially as desire itself and as the delight which comes of desire satisfied. Its object was said to be a good as good in contrast with the objects of desire and delight, which were good as absent or present. Only the secondary or relative love in benevolence as Thomas defines it has such an object. The object of the primary love is someone relative to whom a good is loved and who is loved simply or absolutely.

In fact, strictly speaking, the Aristotelian formula which Thomas uses, to will good to someone, is a definition only of relative love. It implies a love for someone to whom the good is willed but does not mention it explicitly, much less define it. By noting this love in his explanation of benevolence, Thomas takes us more deeply into love than he does in his previous analysis. But beyond indicating that this is primary, that its object is someone for whom a good is willed, what does he tell us about it? Not about its object but about the act of love which has that object. In the following questions where he deals with the causes and effects of love, it comes out that this love is a response to someone as to another self. Good is willed for someone else as for self (ST 1-2, q. 27, a. 3 c.; also q. 28, a. 1 c.). When speaking of union as an effect of love, he distinguishes it from the union which *is* love, a union of affection (ST q. 28, a. 1 c. and reply to obj. 2). This latter union, he says, is "a union by adaptation of affection" (ST q. 28, a. 1, reply to obj. 2). The meaning of this is made clearer when he speaks of the beloved as in the lover inasmuch as the beloved is impressed on the lover's affection by a certain complacency (ST 1, q. 28, a. 2 c. and reply to obj. 1; strictly speaking, Thomas calls this complacency an effect of love in this text, but it seems clear that it is a "formal effect," which is identical with love; see q. 28, a. 1 c. where he distinguishes the union which love causes effectively and formally). In short, love simply (love of friendship) is a fitting of the lover's affectivity to the beloved as to one for whom as to another self the lover wills (with a relative love) the goods which fulfil him.

When we have finished drawing out what is explicitly or implicitly contained in Thomas' brief and not altogether coherently expressed exposition of the nature of love and filled it out from passing remarks in texts where he is dealing with causes or effects of love, we find he has led us to a love that underlies desire, joy, and all relative loves, and has indicated something of its character as an affective union which differs from the union which is a cause of love and the unions which are effects of love. We could, perhaps, add a few strokes to the notion of love by gathering hints here and there in the many pages where Thomas speaks about love. But it is clear that he did not take the question about the nature of the act of love nearly so seriously as he did the moral ordering of its objects, the development of the virtues which enable us to love well morally, the effects of love in human life.

Love As Affirmation: Ortega y Gasset

If we were to seek for some common note to all the notions of love so far discussed or merely mentioned in passing, we could find it in this, that all of them are affirmative of the object loved, whether of the object in itself or in relation to someone or something other than the object. So it is that love is sometimes spoken of as an affirmation. Without explanation of what this term means, it is not very enlightening. It could mean nothing more than that love is not a negative affection. Positively, it could mean any of a number of things which the writer may or may not have in mind. Rarely, however, can one find any attempt at describing or explaining what this loving affirmation consists in. In the writing of Ortega y Gasset, affirmation becomes the dominant notion of love, and he does say at some length what he means.

We have already noted his agreement with Spinoza in opposing any identification of love with desire, his opposition to Spinoza when the latter identifies love with joy, his agreement with Augustine and (contrary to his own understanding) with Aquinas in making love the source of both desire and joy. The opposition between love and desire is a constantly recurring theme with Ortega and even seems sometimes to determine his way of thinking on love (Ortega 1957, 11-12, 46-47, 191, n. 2). So also but to a lesser degree, the opposition between love and joy. The opposition between love and desire is clear, but the reasons are somewhat confusing. Love is said to be eternally unsatisfied, while desire can be satisfied and die. Love is said to be active while desire is passive, despite the fact that he describes desire in such terms as pulling or seeking. Love is said to be centered on the other while desire is egocentric. The question how an egocentric sentiment can have its source in an other-centered one is not brought up, much less answered.

Ortega is at pains to make clear that he is answering the very question with which this study is concerned. In his essay on "The Features of Love," he says that he wants to "enumerate the most general and abstract characteristics" of the act of love, any act of love whatsoever (Ortega 1957, 14). And in his essay of "Love in Stendahl," he further seeks to find the "one identical ingredient" in all love which alone deserves the name love, a "common denominator" of every love for persons or for things (Ortega 1957, 45, 47).

Before studying these passages, a word of warning is in order for those having some familiarity with Ortega's work on love. Much or most of what Ortega says about love is concerned with romantic love or with the experience of falling in love (which he insistently sets apart from romantic love). To read his analysis of falling in love or even of romantic love as if these were to throw light on the essential core of all loves would seriously distort his thought. The "enchantment" and "surrender" of romantic love and all the sensational symptoms of what he styles the "frantic zone" preceding and not always arriving at romantic love are peculiar to these experiences and not to be looked for in other forms of love. Ortega himself warns us:

> The immense variety and the disparity of the objects into which love enters will make us cautious in considering certain attributes and qualities as integral to love which emanate instead from the diverse objects which may be loved (Ortega 1957, 10).

It is next to impossible to restate Ortega's thought on the features of love in any other way than by gathering up and regrouping his metaphors. For his thought is expressed in a cloud of fluttering tropes that will not easily allow themselves to be pinned down to a clearly defined and fixed meaning. Love, he says, is a centrifugal act, a virtual going forth to the object loved, a being on the march from one's inner being out to the loved one, a migration. He is not talking about attaining any spatial closeness or external intimacy. These may result from love, but love itself is in the psychic realm (Ortega 1957, 15). And this psychic going out to the beloved object is a flow, "a stream of spiritual matter" (whatever that may be), a fountain, a current, a psychic radiation—as opposed to a discharge or explosion or a series of sudden movements (Ortega 1957, 15-16). Love streams out to the object and envelops it with its ardor, with warm, active corroboration (Ortega 1957, 17-18).

None of these features of love can be truly understood without stressing one characteristic which colors them all. For, oddly enough, hate also can be described by all these features: hate also is a psychic going out to its object in a steady flow to envelop the object with its ardor. It is a scorching, unfavorable, active but negative force, which tends to separate and to destroy. What characterizes love, on the contrary, is that it is affirmatively and unitively active. Of its unitive character Ortega says little, of its affirmative character he says very much. Because love is essentially affirmative, its going out is on behalf of the object; its ardor is a life-giving warmth, an active force, even almost "an effort" which brings hearts together which is intentionally creative and preservative of the loved object (Ortega 1957, 16-20). The more one rereads Ortega's brilliant but not altogether precise nor self-consistent flood of metaphors and his contrasts of love with other sentiments or psychic acts by which he strives to give expression to his notion of affirmative activity, the more it seems at times to verge towards or even merge with those notions of love defined in terms of benevolence, of concern for the loved one's wellbeing. A number of explanatory phrases make it look very much like benevolence, a sentiment underlying desires and the "physical or spiritual, movements which love incites" for the preservation and vivification of its object. Love is said to give life to what depends upon us, to be an intentional preservation of the object, an exerting of self on behalf of what is loved (Ortega 1957, 20, 47). Still, it must be noted that his affirmation has a warmth about it that need not be found in benevolence, a warmth and a continuity. And at least in one passage his expression could be taken to suggest a sentiment deeper than benevolence.

> Love . . . reaches out to the object in a visual expansion and is involved in an invisible but divine task of the most active kind that there is; it is involved in the affirmation of its object. Think of what it is to love art or your country: it consists of never doubting for an instant their right to exist; it is like recognizing and confirming at each moment that they are worthy of existence. This, not in a manner of a judge who coldly passes a sentence in recognition of a right, but in such a way that the favorable decision is, at the same time, participation in and enactment of that right (Ortega 1957, 19).

Passing over the careless confusion of love with such acts as recognizing or being certain ("never doubting"), his descriptive phrase about love as a "participation in and enactment of" the beloved's right to exist suggests some meaning for love as affirmation which is deeper,, more radical, than willing what is preservative or fulfilling for the loved one. Just what it means to participate in and enact another's right to existence is not clear to me. If he had said that love participates in and enacts the other's existence, that would still call for some explanation but would be more nearly understandable. What was in his mind we cannot know, since, unfortunately, he does not develop the idea flashed off in this brief and enigmatic phrase which suggests rather than states a momentary insight more penetrating than what is stated with more care and clarity elsewhere.

One place we might hope to find some illumination would be in the pages where, instead of drawing up the features of love, he wants to isolate in thought the common denominator, the one identical ingredient of every act of love. He does think that there is such an ingredient, which is joined with many other ingredients in the total state of a person who is loving. It is this one ingredient which is alone to be called love strictly speaking. He tries to catch this love in a formula: "Love, strictly speaking, is pure sentimental activity toward an object, which can be anything—person, or thing" (Ortega 1957, 46).

It is a striking defect in the formula itself that it fails to encompass what his previous description showed to be the essential feature of love, its affirmative character. As he was at pains to point out, hate is also a sentiment that has ardor and desire. Strictly speaking, Ortega's formula could apply to hate as well as to love. What is omitted in the definition, however, is made up for in his explanation of what he means by sentimental activity. On the one hand, he wishes to call the activity of love *sentimental* in order to set it apart from all intellectual function (perception, thought, memory, imagination) and from desire (Ortega 1957, 46). On the other hand, he wishes to insist on the sentiment of love as *activity* in order to set it apart from inactive sentiments such as joy or sadness. Love "is not simply being but acting toward that which is loved." It is an "act in which we exert ourselves on behalf of the beloved" (Ortega 1957, 46-47). These expressions are joined with others that are not very clearly expressing the same psychological reality; thus love is said to be "an indefinable flow of a warm and affirmative nature," or "a cordial affirmative interest," or an "affirmation" (Ortega 1957, 47-48).

On the whole, Ortega gives the impression of trying out one formula after another to express an insight, never quite satisfied with any of them, not concerned to make them coherent with one another, but hoping that through them all the reader will see what he sees. If I may be allowed to put into a definition for him what does come through, I would say that for Ortega, love is an *affirmative sentimental activity.* It is *sentimental* as opposed to all intellectual functions. It is *activity* as opposed to passive sentimental states (joy or sadness). It is *affirmative* as opposed to the negative sentimental activity of hate. These several elements of the definition, if kept together, are adequate to set off this affirmation which is love from all other acts or passions. If we press for any further delineation of what this sentimental activity of affirmation is in itself, almost all that is said sounds like benevolence, with one possible exception where he speaks of participating in and enacting the loved one's right to exist. What the "right to exist" means and how the lover participates in or enacts it, however, is never so clarified as to give any certain and precise meaning to the phrase.

Love As Union and Goal of Desire: Erich Fromm

Ortega's effort to explicate love viewed in its essential character as affirmation ends up for the most part with what seems to differ little, if at all, from the benevolence of Aristotle and Aquinas. There is no question here of Ortega's contribution to a study of romantic love and the experience of falling in love, which encompass by far the greater part of his writings on love. Certainly, to pass over these contributions as ending up with benevolence would be ridiculous. But, on the other hand, to confuse as some do what he says about these with his endeavor to seize on the essential character of any and every sort of love is equally misleading. Like Ortega, although beginning with a view of love dominated by a different notion than affirmation, others end up pretty much as he does. One interesting and famous instance is Erich Fromm.

Among all those whose dominant notion of love is union, Fromm is the most valuable for this study. His treatment of love is more than others explicitly and emphatically centered on union. He incorporates into his explanation a series of common notions of love, such as giving, care, concern, responsibility. Further, he makes explicit and emphatic and basic to his theory a conception of love in contrast with love as desire and with love as the source of desire: for Fromm love is the most important object or goal of our most fundamental human desire. Finally, there is another extrinsic but very important reason for discussing Fromm. His writing on love is probably more widely known in this country and generally well received than that of any other of our contemporaries. When I discuss the problem with which we are concerned I find that people assume Fromm (if not others) has provided a thorough answer. Let us see whether this is so.

Fromm's theory of love is worked out from a clinical and ethical perspective. (See Fromm 1947 for his ethical theory; for a condensed account of his main positions, with critical comment, see McGlynn and Toner 1961.)

The basic problem of human life, as Fromm sees it, is to overcome aloneness and separation and the disharmonies of life that are consequent on separation and loneliness. The only adequate solution for that problem is the union that is love. (This problem is treated in most of Fromm's major works under some such rubric as "the human situation" or "the condition of human existence," and is formative of his thinking; see Fromm 1947, 38-50; 1956, 7-10; 1955, 22-66).

It is our power of reason and self-awareness which gives rise to the problem. For we alone of all beings on earth can feel cast out of paradise, uprooted, alone, a separate entity. This experience of separateness gives rise in turn to anxiety, shame, and guilt (Fromm 1956, 8-9). While one or another point is treated more fully or clearly in his other works, chapter 2 of *The Art of Loving* is Fromm's most complete and mature statement of his theory of love (Fromm 1956, xx).

Obviously, the solution to the basic problem of human life, as Fromm sees it, is some sort of union with the rest of reality; and all the efforts to which we have been driven by our existential condition have been efforts to achieve union. One of the most common ways of trying to achieve this union, according to Fromm, has been orgiastic states produced by auto-induced trance with the help of drugs, alcohol, sex, and primitive ritual (Fromm 1956, 11-12). Another is conformity with customs, practices, beliefs, and the work and pleasure routine of the group, a union of "herd conformity" (Fromm 1956, 12-17). Less common but one of the principal ways of union, nevertheless, is union achieved in creative activity, productive work, in which artists and workers become one with the material upon which they toil and in this material one with the world which is represented to them by their material (Fromm 1956, 17). All these ways of achieving union and escaping separateness have their relative advantages and disadvantages for that purpose (Fromm 1956, 12, 16), but Fromm thinks none of them is an adequate answer to the problem imposed on us by the human condition. The only full answer to our problem is the fusion achieved in love (Fromm 1956, 18).

However, not every kind of love gives a full and satisfactory answer to our problem. Fromm distinguishes union of mature love from what he calls symbiotic union of immature love. He chooses to restrict the word love to mature love while speaking of immature love as symbiotic union (Fromm 1956, 18). This choice of vocabulary can frustrate our intent unless we hold firmly in mind that for Fromm symbiotic union has been said to be love, however perverse or immature the love may be. What we want to lay hold of is Fromm's essential notion of love, what he thinks is the common or core component in every experience of love, whether mature or immature. It is of course in mature love, which achieves the fullest union of persons on the personal level, that we expect to see best what love is; but we must not forget that there are lower, imperfect, even perverse forms of love.

Symbiotic union or fusion of immature love is a union based on mutual needs. Passively it is achieved, according to Fromm, in submission, in the sacrifice of independence, of integrity, in order to escape aloneness, decision, risk. Put in technical terms this is masochism. Actively, symbiotic union or fusion is achieved by inflating self, by incorporating another person, exploiting, commanding him and so escaping aloneness. In technical terms he speaks of this as sadism. In either case there is fusion without integrity (Fromm 1956, 19-20). The union of mature love differs from immature love in this, that in it the integrity of the persons in union is preserved: "Mature love is union under the condition of preserving one's integrity, one's individuality" (Fromm 1956, 20).

The important question to be put to Fromm at this point is: what constitutes this union? For if the love is union, then whatever constitutes union constitutes the love. To say love is union is already to distinguish this view of love from love as tendency to union; but there are many forms of union other than love, as Fromm himself has pointed out in leading up to his description of love. The question he must answer is this: What is the union which is love as distinct from every other form of union?

Symbiotic union is constituted by submission to or domination of the other; it is in the very masochistic submitting and sadistic dominating that the two are joined. Is immature love, then, the very submitting and dominating? Fromm does not say this in so many words, but I see no other way of understanding what he says. If love is union and if this union of immature love is constituted by domination and submission, then domination and submission are the love. If submission and domination are not constitutive of immature love but effects or prior conditions, then we still have to ask what the union is which is such love.

Turning to mature love, what is it that constitutes the union with preservation of integrity which is this love? This love is, Fromm says, an activity. It is not merely an external activity, the use of energy to produce external effects; rather it is the "use of our inherent human powers" whether externally effective or not (Fromm 1956, 21). In a most general way, this active character of love is described as the lovers giving, not merely material possessions, but of themselves, "of our own joy, sadness, knowledge, humor, in short of all that is alive in us, of our life" (Fromm 1956, 22-24). It is noteworthy that in this passage lovers gives of themselves. Fromm does not, as others do, say that the lover give themselves and supply no explanation of what it means to give oneself and how this can be done. What Fromm means by giving of self is clear. Further, the active character implies care, responsibility, respect, knowledge (Fromm 1956, 26-32). These Fromm shows to be mutually interdependent and form, as it were, a "syndrome of attitudes which are to be found in the mature person" (Fromm 1956, 32). One who loves has concern, care, for that which one loves. Love, says Fromm, "is active concern for the life and growth of that which we love" (Fromm 1956, 26) and without such care or concern there is really no love. To have such concern one must be responsible, i.e., able and ready to respond to others. But responsibility without respect can easily deteriorate into domination. And without knowledge of the person lovers cannot respect nor guide their care and responsibility; even as, in turn, knowledge without concern is empty and without the penetrating power of love never reaches the secret of the person.

Within the syndrome of maturity, care or active concern for the life and growth of the loved one is central. One sort of knowledge and responsibility is said to be necessary for the sake of making this concern possible. Respect is necessary to safeguard it. Another sort of knowledge flows from it. And it is not difficult to see the close relationship between active concern for the loved one and the giving which Fromm puts as the first characteristic of love. He does not tell us how they are related but only that they are both characteristics of the active, mature love. In any case the love he began speaking of as union has turned out to be giving and caring, something very like benevolence.

Such are the main lines of Fromm's answer to the question, what is love? Given the framework within which he places love in order to understand it, his answer is surprising and interesting. For he sees the human condition as Plato and Tillich see it. Man is estranged, his basic problem is how to overcome separation and loneliness, his basic tendency is to achieve union. We would expect that such a view of the human condition would prompt Fromm to join Plato and Tillich in conceiving of love as the drive toward reunion of the separated or to join Spinoza in conceiving of love as an affective expression of man's passage from imperfection and separation to union and perfection. On the contrary, he says that love is union itself. But he does not mean it is a union which is the root of desire and transition as it is for Augustine and Aquinas. Rather it is a union toward which our human drive is directed, the goal of passage to perfection, the object of our "most fundamental passion" springing from our "deepest need." There is a further surprise. For once Fromm has made love the goal of a drive and the fulfilment of a need from which the drive springs, it is surprising to find that instead of being an act by which our striving is in some way brought to rest, love is explained as a starting point of striving, an active concern for the life and growth of the loved one. How love so conceived constitutes a union with the loved one so as to resolve our human existential problem of estrangement, of separation, this Fromm does not explain. To put that question to him leads to a critical evaluation which is not in place here; we take it up in chapter 6.

Part 2

Descriptive Analysis of Experience

4
RADICAL LOVE

The approach taken in this study assumes until proven otherwise that every one of the notions stated by the reputable thinkers considered in the preceding chapters is pointing to some reality in our experience which, if it is not what another calls love, is in some way to be found in the full experience of human love. If it does not truly express the basic and proper notion of love which is central to that experience, it is nevertheless in the unreflected concrete experience as the condition or cause or accompaniment or consequence of what is basic or central. That is why any of the notions of love noted in the preceding pages can appeal to common speech and thought for some justification, and why whatever genuine insights the authors give us have some value for understanding the full concrete experience of love.

✳ The Starting Point
The appropriate starting point for any effort to evaluate the multiplicity of opinions about love and to uncover what may have been left covered is indicated by the foregoing consideration. We need to bring attention to bear on our lived experience of love in an intense, disciplined, and orderly way, using fully whatever others have said as far as we can to assist our reflection on experience but not to replace it. All these opinions have to be evaluated in terms of the experience itself. But what has been said can be of great value in directing our search. Beginning with the total concrete experience, a rich but confused multiplicity, we shall try to arrive at what is central or radical, the core or root of the experience, that on which all the other elements depend for their meaning precisely as parts of the experience of love. Whatever reality they have in other ways, independently of

this experience and so of this core element in the experience of love, is not of interest to us.

We can get at the core through an analysis of the experience, an analysis which tries to penetrate more and more deeply, always keeping hold of the total experience by seeing the analyzed elements in the whole, distinguished but not separated from one another. Analysis such as is to be done here must not be understood after a model of an operation necessarily involving a separation of parts from a whole which then have to be put back together again—as if our task were comparable to dissecting a specimen in the biology laboratory or dismantling an engine in a shop. There is no need to fear that the achievement of clarity about human psychic life has to lead to mechanistically separating the elements in that way.

On the other hand, since a human person is not a simple being, only two courses are open: to advocate obscurity as a method or to analyze by distinguishing within unity—for there is no need to re-unite what is distinguished but never separated. It is only a matter of seeing in detail and with precision what is first seen as a blurred and indiscriminate whole. It is a reflection on conscious experience in order to see each part precisely as a part, which means to see it within the whole, with all the other parts. However, to distinguish the parts requires focusing our attention now on one and now on another and now on the relations between these as, for example, one may in ordinary observation note the color and the contour of the face, the arch of the eyebrows, the curve of the lips, and the relation between these. This does not require isolating the parts. Rather, each part is attended to precisely as a part within a whole which we desire to apprehend, the human face.

It would be a mistake to think that our main problem is to lay hold of what is not in conscious experience, whether to bring it into consciousness or to reason to it as the necessary condition for or the necessary consequence of what is explicitly in consciousness. Such is not the case. What is brought to light by this mode of reflection on experience is not brought into the light of consciousness for the first time. It is in consciousness but usually escapes clear awareness because our attention is focused elsewhere. As far as any clear and discriminating awareness goes, most of what is in our consciousness is as unknown to us as what is in the unconscious, and sometimes much harder to get into the focus of a discriminating attention than it is to bring into consciousness the content of the unconscious. No free association will do it, only relentless effort at attention, exact description, and analysis of experience, supplemented but not replaced by hypothesis and analysis of concepts. Our principal effort is not therefore to suggest what experience might imply nor what it demands for its intelligibility, but to bring the obscure because profound elements of conscious experience into the light of attention. Or it might be more accurate to say the effort is to bring the light of methodically moving attention to bear on the obscure depths of the experience of love. When conceptual analysis or hypothesis are used, it is ordinarily to suggest directions for the movement of attention or to confirm what has been discerned by showing that what we have seen is what we should have expected to see since the intelligibility of what we started with would not allow it to be otherwise.

Before beginning any reflective analysis of our experience it is important to remove a possible misunderstanding about the meaning of experience. First of all, let me disengage the word "experience" from two assumptions which were characteristic of the nineteenth century and are still common enough today, namely the empiricist assumption and the positivistic assumption. Both of these are, to use Gabriel Marcel's phrase in speaking of the former, prejudices which have tried to assume the status of principles (Marcel 1960, I, 60; see 57-69 for Marcel's discussion of experience). The empiricist would have us limit experience to our internal states, the positivists to what is sensibly verifiable. Experience as used in this discussion of love is not to be arbitrarily limited in either of these ways. Our experience is of the world as much as of self, of the two in correlation, and of the suprasensible (which is not sensibly verifiable in the positivistic sense) as well as the sensible and the sensibly verifiable.

Now, human experience of self-existing-in-the-world is complex and unified, and reveals the complexity and unity of both self and the world. In my experience I find an interaction, an interdependence, and even an interpenetration, of manifold elements; but all these are integrated in what I refer to as my experience. This experience is the conscious encounter of my being with the world in which my unitary self is acted on and responded to by many other beings and responds to and acts on other beings in many ways at once. Every one of these acts and responses is influenced by my other acts and responses and influences them in turn. Within this unified manifold I can discern really distinct (albeit inseparable) elements and to some extent understand their relationship. Thus, in the experience of human love, I respond to reality in manifold ways: knowledge and affection, spirit and flesh, nature and freedom, are all interacting, cooperating or conflicting, intensifying or subduing each other, resonating and giving fuller expression to or smothering each other. No act or passion arises in isolation uninfluenced by my other acts and passions or without influencing the others. The experience is to un- reflected consciousness a rich, confused, mass of interpenetrating parts, each coloring and colored by the other parts and taking on meaning from the whole.

This experience is our starting point. It is necessary to put aside all ready-made definitions of love, all abstracting or prescinding, and bring attention to bear on some concrete moment of actual love. We cannot avoid prescinding and abstracting in the process of working toward an understanding of the concrete and ultimately toward a generalized notion of the central, essential, element in the experi- ence. But we must, on pain of certain failure, refuse to begin with anything but the concrete experience of love, a beginning to which we must constantly return. Or rather, we should try never to lose contact with this starting point, but to see all our abstract and precise notions grounded in this experience of love. In this way we can reach a universal understanding without departing from the concrete.

In this effort, all that the writer can do is to stimulate reader to recall their own concrete experience and to see if what is being said is justified by it and helps them to see clearly what was not attended to before. To assume that by presenting in a few large descriptive strokes some common situations of human life a writer actually conveys that the concrete is an illusion. Some remarks by contemporary practitio- ners of phenomenology in the broad sense of the word or of "con- crete philosophy" give the impression of laboring under that illusion. Concreteness in the sense that composition and rhetoric textbooks speak of it is possible in philosophical writing: the writer can supply some details for the imagination of readers to recreate. But the de- scription itself is only less abstract than most philosophical writing. To refer to a table with an apple on it in the sunlight or to someone visiting a friend who is sick in bed is only less abstract than talking of a table, or an apple, or a person. But it is still abstract and universal. Only you the reader, at the writer's suggestion, can turn to your own personal experience for the concrete, strictly speaking. The only in- telligible meaning of concrete philosophical writing is that in which the writer keeps an eye on experience instead of merely analyzing concepts and keeps referring the reader to the latter's own concrete experience. Therefore, while I shall refer to the concrete, sometimes in less abstract ways of speaking, I have to depend on you to follow my description with reference to your own concrete experience of love even as I have to have mine in view while writing.

The Total Concrete Experience

In the full concrete experience of love, our whole being, spirit and flesh, is involved: cognitive acts, feelings and affections, freedom, bodily reactions—all these are influencing each other and all are continually fluctuating in such a way as to change the structure and intensity of the experience.

By *cognition*, I refer to all acts of sense and intelligence: sensations, perception, insight, conceptualization, imagination, judgment, memory.

By *affection* I mean what some mean by emotion, passion, or feeling, whether sensuous or spiritual, but not what some others mean by these words. Among these words I choose the word affection as being less ambiguous than any of the others. For feeling can refer to a sensation of touch or to an experience of pain or pleasure, as well as to what we call emotion or passion. Emotion is sometimes limited in meaning to a response at the sensuous rather than at the spiritual level. Passion can be limited to mean only a very strong emotion or even only sexual emotion. And, on the other hand, it can be broadened to mean any reception of influence from another reality, the opposite of action. Affection, however, is not as liable to these ambiguities; its meaning is broad enough to include the experiences of joy and sorrow, love and hate, desire, hope, fear, etc., both mild as well as intense, spiritual as well as sensuous; but it is not commonly broadened out into a meaning such as that which passion has in its broadest sense. Another word sometimes employed is sentiment: this can refer to an opinion charged with affection rather than to the affection itself and can also easily connote artificial or exaggerated affection.

The word affection, of course, has its own difficulties. However, I hope to be understood if I say that by affection I mean the *act of affectivity* in contrast to a purely passive feeling, as of pleasure or of pain. I mean a *spontaneous response* which is neither a free act in the sense of a self-determined, chosen act nor a merely passive state of being, a feeling. An affection, as I use the word, is passive in as much as it is called forth by its object without the subject's free choice; but it is an act in which the subject responds to that object. For instance, loving or hating someone is an affection, so also sorrowing or rejoicing over someone or something which has happened to someone as contrasted with merely feeling depressed or exuberant; desiring something is an affection as opposed to merely feeling a need. Although affections are immanent acts, they can mediately be effective of external results. And once in act, they are to some degree subject to control by free choice. All this will be developed at length with regard to the affection of love as the description progresses.

By *freedom* I mean power of self-determination by choice which is not determined by any condition or cause whether extrinsic to the agent or intrinsic to the agent but extrinsic to the act of choosing. It is the power by which I can responsibly approve or disapprove, affirm or negate, my spontaneous affective responses. All these have some unity in as much as they are all responses of this one personal subject. But they rarely form anything approaching a unity in the sense of being harmoniously integrated. Rather, there are usually tensions and collisions and confusions among them. Limited in what we can sense or understand of the object at any one moment and apprehending the object now under one aspect and now under another; reacting with ambivalent affections to the object under different aspects; influenced in our perception, understanding, and affections, by our temperament and by the effects of our education, environment, experiences, and past decisions; drawn one way by spirit and another way by sensuality, one way in spirit by generous aspirations and another by selfishness—caught in all these conflicts, we have to bring into play the act of freedom by which we (more or less in possession of ourselves, depending on the degree of effective freedom at the moment) accept one of the conflicting alternatives and affirm it as the chosen expression of our free and responsible selves.

Finally, by *bodily reactions*, I refer to those elements in the experience such as accelerated heart beat, blushing and tears, constriction of the throat, sexual (that is, physical vs. emotional) excitement, sighs, gestures, smiles. These appear most obviously in very intense experiences, but some of them are readily noticeable to some degree in any experience of love.

This manifold of psychic and somatic elements insofar as they form a unity in consciousness can be called love in the sense of the total concrete experience of love. All the views of love we have seen in the dialectical survey of opinions can find some justifying evidence within this total experience—at least in the experience as it usually arises. And there are many elements there besides these, which no one calls love. For instance, while experiencing love, a man may also be experiencing the warmth of the sun, the sweetness of the wind, the glory of light and movement in the trees. These can be distractions from attending to and loving someone. But they can also be integrated into the experience. Thus the glory of a beautiful day may be to the lover a symbol of the loved one or something to rejoice in for the sake of the loved one. To one loving God, it may be accepted as a gift of God's love. So also hunger and tiredness can be merely concurrent experiences, distracting from and so in conflict with the experience of love. Or they can be taken into the full experience of love, as when they are with conscious freedom chosen and gladly endured in serving the loved one. In this way they are made an expression of love. But who would say that experiencing the beauty of the day or being tired is by itself an experience of love?

☆ The Unifying Center of the Total Experience

Further investigation will show us that among all the elements integral to the experience of love, even among those called love, some can be left out (in the experience or in thought about it) without the experience ceasing to be (or thought to be) an experience of love. Among those which seem necessary in order to have the experience at all, some can appear outside the experience of love in experiences which are not commonly, if ever, thought of as love. Clearly these two classes of elements require to be joined with some other element or elements in the experience in order to belong to what we call the experience of love; that is, they must be joined to some element or elements which can neither be omitted from nor appear apart from the experience of love. These latter are essential to, the core or root of, the total experience. The other elements are conditions or consequences or accompaniments of love properly speaking. But if the essential elements are multiple and if one is reducible to another, then the latter is love more properly speaking.

What that fundamental or core part of the total experience is remains obscure in unreflected experience. There is, however, some undefined insight which enables us up to a certain point to generally agree what it is *not*. Here we all find ourselves in a position similar to that of the philosopher whom Bergson describes as having that first basic intuition. The philosopher cannot communicate it positively, cannot even grasp it in reflection. It shows itself in its "negative power." Strangely, in the light of it, the philosopher knows with clarity and certainty that this or that philosophical or scientific position cannot be held, that this or that way of putting the insight really does not express it (Bergson 1946, 109-10). Artists have a similar experience when trying to express an inspiration in some medium. They have not yet formulated it to themselves and do not quite know what it is until they give it expression. But they know when they have not been faithful to it. So with our experience of love. We know very well up *to a point* what within the total experience is *not* the vivifying root that makes the experience of love.

We know, for example, that it is not the somatic element nor knowledge. No human love occurs without physiological manifestations or without the influence of the physiological factors. But there is no doubt that love properly speaking is not any of these. Cognition is the necessary condition for the possibility of human love and gives form to love. On the other hand, attention, perception, conceptualizing, judgment (speculative, aesthetic, moral) are all profoundly influenced by love; a certain kind of knowledge is made possible by love. But there is no doubt that love properly speaking is not an act of knowing. Knowing and bodily reactions are in the experience of love by relation to something else which is love in itself.

Bergson points out that philosophers can turn away from their intuitions and say what they have to deny when they turn back to it. So also, one who allows one's attention to the experience of love to slacken can fall into confusion about choice and freedom in the experience. Thus, for instance, we find love called "motiveless choice" (Plattel 1965, 81). Leaving aside the question whether choice can be motiveless, when we keep attention focused carefully on love, we know choice is not the radical element in the experience. Love is not identical with choice any more than hate is identical with it. We can choose to love or hate, to love in this way or that, to hate in this way or that. Both love and hate can to some extent be controlled by free choice, but neither is an act of choice.

Others avoid this confusion of two acts but still include free choice in the essence of love. Such a formula as "a free gift of self" is used. This is wholly arbitrary and eliminates many if not most of the experiences which almost everyone refers to as love and is clearly an illustration of the error, not uncommon in speaking about love, of confusing the adjectival with the substantial. Love is not substantively a free act in the sense of a self-determined act any more than other psychic acts. Only free choice itself is *per se* free. We experience ourselves loving and hating, doing kind acts or harmful ones without reflection or choice. And we find ourselves making free decisions about our spontaneous responses of love and hate. Free choice, as seen above, changes spontaneous love from a merely necessary response into a chosen love and so renders it a fully human, personally responsible, self-possessed, act of the person. Nevertheless, love is not itself the free choice nor in essence freely chosen. If it were, we would not find ourselves making a free decision in opposition to spontaneous love. But this is a very common experience. Of course, anyone can say that what they want to mean by love does involve free choice, that without freedom the act "isn't worthy to be called love"

or "isn't really love." This way of proceeding, however, gives no understanding of experience and makes intelligent discussion about the experience difficult or impossible. For, if love is essentially a freely chosen act, the question remains, what is the act which is freely chosen? Is it freely chosen desire or joy or benevolence or what? The fundamental question remains unanswered, and it is this we are trying to answer.

Love is not free choice nor a cognitive act nor a physiological reaction. By the above process of elimination, we have readily arrived at the conclusion that the radical element among all those elements noted in the concrete experience of love is to be found in the affective acts. As a matter, of fact, the principal reason for attending to the other elements of the concrete experience is to enable us to keep the affections in a concrete perspective and also to set up the framework within which we can work out a coherent picture of love's relation with the other elements within the totality, All writers on love whom we have considered above are in agreement in looking for love properly speaking among the affections. Some of them do make love an ontological energy running through all of reality; when, however, they speak of love as it appears in conscious human experience, they speak of some affection, whether desire or joy, or concern or benevolence, etc. Some also, as we saw, do speak of love as union, presence, co-existence. But such notions remain vague and of little help in understanding love unless the act which constitutes the union is identified. Not all take this further step. When it is taken the act turns out to be some affective response.

When we get to the affections, our insight begins to lose its negative power. This indicates that here we are getting close to that which is love properly speaking. The negative affections are still readily eliminated, e.g., hate, fear, anger, despair. But when we arrive at the affirmative affections, confusion sets in and we find not only dull minds but astute and careful ones asserting positively that love is many different affections: desire, joy, benevolence, complacency, affirmation, adherence, reverence, respect, taking responsibility for someone, self-giving, accepting, and so on.

Reductive Analysis of Affections

At this point, therefore, we must undertake the difficult problem of analyzing the affective side of the concrete experience. Is the word love simply an equivocal name for several different and irreducible affections so that there is no generally common meaning for its various uses? Or is it a name for what is analogous to several affections?

Or is love some one unique affection? If so, is it identical with some affection which goes by another name, such as desire, or joy, or an affection which has no other name?

How should we go about looking for that radical element? The problem suggests the method. That which is radical is as such irreducible. Whatever affection is seen to be rooted in another which is within the total concrete experience of love, from which it arises and which it presupposes for its very possibility as a part of that experience, is by that very fact excluded from being the affective act which is love most radically and most properly. Therefore, an appropriate method is a reductive analysis of affections, not in the sense of reducing them to what is more easily understood or less sublime but in the sense of going back to the roots which may well turn out to be more profound, sublime, and mysterious.

But where to make a start among the multitudinous affections? Here the dialectical survey we have already made can give direction to the inquiry. This survey has equipped us with a set of the affections which have the most reasonable claims to be considered. If there are important opinions we have omitted which would be included in a more complete survey, there is still reason to hope that what is to be done now will provide an adequate framework within which other opinions on love can be fitted without necessitating any change in the final insight to which the following analysis leads. And what is more, this survey also indicates an order for testing the several affections. The human experience of love is so permeated by desire that many consider it the core or root of the experience. We have seen that at least *prima facie* a strong case can be made for saying that it is so. We have also seen that many deny desire is love and want to put some one of several other affections as the root or goal of desire and call this affection love. Before considering these, we first considered Spinoza's notion of love as joy. We did so because his notion of joy bears some close affinity with the psychic tendency or movement which is called desire and also because those who make love the principle of desire in affective experience usually make it a principle of joy as well. We can, then, make a start by putting desire and joy to the test of reductive analysis to see if this reveals either or both of them as underived and irreducible affections or as rooted in some other affection which may more properly be called love because it is more radical in the whole experience.

✴ Reductive Analysis of Desire

In any act of desire, there is an affective tendency or movement toward some end which is for someone or toward some means to that end. We desire food for ourselves or for our children, for our own health or pleasure or for theirs. We desire books or the company of intelligent friends for ourselves or for others, for our delight or growth in learning or others'. We desire medical training for the sake of those who are suffering, to ease their pain and to heal them. Or we desire it for ourselves as a way to money and prestige. We do not, in these acts (we may in other acts), desire ourselves or our children or those who suffer. We desire something for them, either as an end for them or as a means to an end for them. This is the very structure of desire, that it have an object tended to and that it implies someone for whom the object tended to is desired.

Several questions arise. If the one for where the object is desired as an end or as a means to the end is not desired (neither as an end nor as a means), how should we express our relation with the end desired? And what is the affection which the one desiring the end has for us? Finally, what is the relationship of this latter affection to the affection of desire?

First of all take the question about the relation between this one for whom an end is desired and the desired end. The desired end is desired for someone. It has its character as an end by relation to that person; and it immediately loses its end-value, ceases to be desired, when dissociated from that person. The one for whom the end is desired appears, therefore, as an end for the desired-end—an end which is not an object of desire.

But how justify calling the desired end an end at all? It is a relative end. Within a series of desired objects it is the final or terminal object to which all others in that series are ordered and from which the others derive their desirability as means. An object may be desired both as an end and as a means. Insofar as it is desired without reference to some further desired object, it is desired as an end. For example, a I may desire to read a book because I want to gain some useful information from it to be applied in my work; or I may desire to read it just because reading the book is itself fulfilling. Within any context of desired objects, the ultimately desired object is an end. But the whole order of desired objects, means and end, is for someone. Thus, for example, a father desires work to get money to send his child to college so that the she can become a lawyer. His daughter's position in society as a lawyer is the end within this context, work

and money and college are means. But the end is for the daughter—
or perhaps for the father, for the sake of his vicarious success, and
then the daughter is a means also. Let us call the one for whom the
end and means are desired a radical or fundamental end, an underived
end. And let us call the desired end a derivative or relative end.

A difficulty comes to mind, occasioned by an ordinary phrase: we
do speak of desiring something for its own sake and even define an
end in opposition to a means as something desired "for its own sake"
or more simply "for itself." It would seem that such a way of speaking
is in conflict with what we have just observed about desire. Either
common speech and thought are mistaken, or else our description of
desire is faulty. Really the difficulty arises only from the ambiguity of
such phrases as "for its own sake" or "for itself." If desiring something for its own sake should mean that the object of desire can be
absolutely terminal, without subordination to any radical end, then
the phrase does contradict the very nature of desire and has no intelligible meaning. If on the other hand it signifies something relatively
terminal, that is, the last within the order of desired objects, the ultimately desired to which the means and what are sometimes referred
to as proximate or intermediate ends are referred, then in that case it
carries an intelligible meaning fully in accord with the preceding analysis of desire.

If the relation between the object desired and the radical end for
whom it is desired is now clear, the question concerning the affection
toward the radical end can be attended to. That affection is not desire. What then is it? It is certainly a positive or affirmative affection,
since it gives rise to desire for a relative end to fulfil some need of one
who is a radical end. This sort of affective act is what we commonly
refer to as concern for or care for or taking responsibility for someone. To be more precise we should call it a radical or fundamental
care. For clearly I can care for something which is only a relative end,
as when I care for my neighbors' house or dog while they are away on
a trip. But I do so because of a care for a radical end, my neighbors in
the above illustration. So it is necessary to distinguish between radical and derivative care. Our interest now is in what is radical.

It is precisely one who I think is in some need that I am concerned
for, have care for: to say that I have care for or take responsibility for
people who are utterly fulfilled and secure in their being and need
nothing in any way at all seems meaningless. It is only for those in
need that I desire what will fill their needs. But if I did not care at all
about them, then their need would not give rise to my desire to fill
the need. If I desire something for these persons, it is presupposed

that I care for them; if I care for them, it necessarily follows that I desire what I think they need. (I presume that the reader will make the necessary reservations here without my delaying over them and distracting from the main movement of thought. Surely if I care for my friends I will not desire what they think they need but is really harmful for them, etc.) Care, then, is an affirmative affection toward someone precisely as in need. It is not the need nor what is needed that is the object of radical care; radical care is of the one who has the need, under the aspect of needing. For example, I have an affection of care toward anyone who needs food or friendly words or a listener or instruction. As a consequence of care, I desire food for them, or friendly words and so on. If I have a care or concern for the food or words or instruction, etc., it is only the relative and derivative care of which we spoke above. But even that is not desire.

However, need understood in too narrow a meaning will exclude many acts that are ordinarily and justly thought of as care. The most obvious meaning, it is true, implies some lack in the those who are in need and cared for, some defect in their being: they are ignorant or sick or indigent or lonely or powerless against danger. Nevertheless, there is another way of being truly in need without any lack, without any defect of being. Suppose A, who is full and secure in being, loves B, who is in need according to the obvious meaning just noted above. Without our as yet having arrived at a philosophical understanding of love, we know by common experience and observation that in some sense B's need and deficiency becomes A's by reason of A's love for B. As a consequence, C can care for A inasmuch as C can be concerned to fulfil B's needs for the sake of A, as if they were A's own needs.

Still there does seem to be a lack in A's very being insofar as A seems to lack the power to fulfil B and so needs C to do so. If that is the case, then we are back to the first and obvious meaning of need. But two considerations occur which prevent reducing every instance of need to that meaning. Take the case in which A wants B to grow as a free being in time, to achieve some goal by B's own exercise of freedom and enduring efforts rather than have it done for him by A. The fact that A because of love for B needs that B make such effort implies no lack of power on A's side, but only a wise and delicate respect for B's dignity as a person with freedom. And further, suppose A also loves C. Then A might freely choose to need C's help in accomplishing the task of encouraging B to freely grow, a task that A could very well do alone. A chooses to need C in order that C might have the honor and joy of accomplishing the task with A. What A cannot do in the very nature of the case, even if A's power were infinite, is to make C have that honor and that joy unless A does let C help. Take the simple case of a mother who chooses to need the help of a child to do a job she could very well do alone. In a true sense she really does need the child for the purpose she has in mind; for without the child's help, she would do the task alone, not with her child as she chooses it should be. And yet her need implies no lack of capacity in the mother.

It will help to avoid a possible misunderstanding if we note that care is not necessarily of someone under the aspect of a particular need clearly understood and attended to by the one who cares. Care can be merely a generalized care for one known to share the common human condition of neediness. Sometimes care arises first of all only because someone is injured or in danger or starving, that is, only because of some particular need. Before that we may not even notice someone. Thus, a man crossing the street was of no concern to others until they saw him in danger of being run down by a car. But we do have a generalized care for some persons which is particularized as we attend now to one and now to another particular need. Pastors care for one who comes to them inasmuch as they are ready to fulfil this one's needs whatever they are. Then as they unfold to them, the loneliness and financial need and ignorance of religious truth, their general care becomes care for this one specifically as lonely, as indigent, as ignorant.

We have seen that when we desire something, the someone for whom it is desired is to us a radical end as distinct from a derivative or implemental end. The latter is an object of desire, not the former. The affection toward the radical end is radical care. Now, what is the relation between care and desire? Desire is distinct from but derivative from and dependent on care. One reason for saying it is distinct from care is that it has a different object. This has already been noted. Another reason is that desire is a tendency-affection, whereas care is not a tendency to its object; to care for persons is not to tend to them but to have a principle of tendency toward that which is for them. It could be called a being-affection. (This notion of being-affection vs. tendency-affection will become more meaningful after the analysis of radical love, of which radical care is a mode).

To insist on the distinction between care and desire should not lead to thinking that desire can be an autonomous affection. To think of desire as conditioned in its origin by care but able to endure without care is to fail to see the significance of what we observed before about the structure of desire and to miss the profound unity of the distinct elements in human affective life. We noted above that desire is in every instance a psychic tendency to something for someone. Remove the care for someone and desire ceases. This is a matter of fact. It is also a necessity; the observable structure of desire makes a desire without care impossible and unintelligible. It might at first seem otherwise. For whether through change of affection or mere forgetfulness, I do find myself ceasing to care for the one for whom I have been desiring something, and yet continuing to desire what I was desiring. A close observation of what happens, however, reveals that I have only substituted a different object of care. There is still a care underlying the desire. What began, for example, as an act expressing a desire to do something for a friend turns into a selfish act done because I desire some satisfaction for myself. Sometimes it can happen the other way around. For affections slide around with such rapidity and subtlety as to escape our ordinary attention. At every moment of its life, desire is flowing out of care for someone. Even the metaphor implied in the adjective "radical" as applied to care is not adequate to express the dependence here: a plant cut off from its root will die slowly; desire cut off from care ceases to be immediately. We are reaching deeply into the experience of human love when we arrive at care or taking responsibility for someone. With good reason, this affection appears to many as the core of love, love properly speaking. The weight of responsibility, of care, seems to be indistinguishable from the weight of love—in a meaning of weight different from that which it has in Augustine's *pondus meum amor meus*. The sense of love as indistinguishable from responsibility or care is powerful in those intense moments when we experience the call of a loved one in great and manifest need. But human life being what it is, the same experience at low key runs through most of our experiences of love. When is a loved one not in need—at the very least in need of the fulfilment of being loved and having the love manifested? How often do we respond with love without attending to any need? We must beware here of thinking of the frequent instances when we "love" others with no thought of their need, but only of our own satisfaction in the other's beauty or wisdom or sympathy. In these experiences, the care is for ourselves; and if we are to call the act toward the other love at all, it is only as desire or relative love for the desirable object that it can it be called love: the others are derivative or implemental ends or sometimes merely means, not radical or fundamental ends, not ends in and for themselves—the radical end is, in these instances of love, the lover's own self.

The mention of relative love recalls the analysis of the affections in Augustine and Thomas. They thought to discover an affection, *amor* (*pondus, complacentia,*) which is distinct from and underlies desire and yet has the same material object as desire. Whether there is such an affection and, if there is, whether it should be called love, are questions we can put off to be answered later. For now it is sufficient to point out that any such affection, if real, is also distinct from care and derivative from it, for the same reasons that desire is. It could be only a "willing some good" which is for someone; whereas care is, if I may so put it, "willing the someone" who is in need of that good and for whom it is willed. The affection toward someone is certainly not the same as that toward the relative good.

Although care underlies desire (and relative love), there are serious reasons for doubting whether we have yet laid hold of the fundamental affection we are trying to bring into the focus of attention. For suppose that I am asked why I am concerned about this person in need. Without being thought tautological or going in a circle, I could answer, "Because I love him." If it is possible for me to respond in this way, then the love expressed in the phrase, "Because I love him," is more fundamental than the concern for him, more fundamental than taking responsibility for him.

That this mode of speaking is pointing to something in reality more fundamental than care can be seen if we recall that the latter affection necessarily implies need in the one cared for. Now, if this is so, then it is impossible for me to take responsibility for someone, to have a care for someone, unless here and now I am actually and explicitly attending to the fact of some need. And so, if love is basically caring or taking responsibility for persons, then it is never possible to love them unless I think they are in need. Nor is it even possible to love those whom I know are in need unless I am here and now considering their need. Neither of these consequences fits the facts. Therefore, it cannot be true that love is in its most proper sense care or responsibility for another. Some people do love God, in God's infinite fulness of reality and beauty, for God's own sake. People do love others who are as a matter of fact in need but not always with advertence to the fact of the other's need—rather sometimes with a mind altogether absorbed in and overwhelmed by the beauty of the other's actuality.

Consider some actual moments of intense human love: for example, a mother loving her child in a moment of joyful security and careless playfulness; a man and his bride in a moment of joyful union; a saint in a moment of ecstatic, desireless, love for God; a moment of exultation in one's own existence, springing from self-love. To say that the deepest reality of these moments from which all the rest of the experience derives its significance is that these lovers are taking responsibility for or are concerned about the welfare of the loved one— to say this seems to fall far short of expressing the heart of the reality. It not only falls short; but in some instances, caring or taking responsibility for the loved one does not appear as being any part of the present conscious experience of love. Certainly, love without care will also become care or concern when the lover adverts to the loved one's need. The point here is just this, that one can love without presently considering the need of the loved one and so can love at this moment without care.

If so, then this affection toward someone as a radical end without regard for need has a priority over care. It can be in act without care; yet, whenever care is in act, it is this very affection just insofar as it is modified by relation to the loved one under the aspect of being in need. And when need and care cease, love does not cease. If all need were to be fulfilled in the loved one, that would not mean the death of love. Care is only the form love takes when the lover is attentive to the beloved's need.

What should we call the prior affection of which care is a modification? In order to distinguish it from any other affection called love which is derivative from it, let us call it fundamental or radical love. It has not yet been established that this affection toward the radical end is the ultimate affective root or core in the total experience of love. Whether it is cannot be settled until analysis has shown what it is. However, for the sake of referring to it without circumlocutions, I shall tentatively name it fundamental or radical love. To call it fundamental love implies that all else in the experience of love so depends on it as to collapse without it. To call it radical love implies that all other affections in the experience of love grow out of it, have one life from it.

Now this affective act of radical love which can be before care and endure after care, has as its object the actuality of the person whether in need or not. The relation between radical love and care could be stated in a proportionality. Radical love is to care as the person is to the person in need. To say this is to exclude saying that the relation parallels that between care and desire. In this latter relationship, desire has a different object from care, and they are distinct acts even though inseparable. Care is to desire as a radical end is to a derivative end. But radical love and radical care are not fully distinct acts. They have the same object, the radical end, the person; and radical care is really only a qualified form of radical love.

Reductive Analysis of Joy

Is this radical love perhaps the same as joy? Spinoza thought so. However, if Ortega and Scheler are right, then Spinoza's view is not really worth considering seriously, nor any other view which makes love the same as joy. On their evaluation, this idea so plainly runs counter to the facts of human experience that it is odd anyone should suggest it.

On the other hand Scheler himself makes a concession which leaves the reader wondering why he did not treat Spinoza less gingerly. All love, he says, even "unhappy" (i.e., unrequited) love or love which for other reasons is sad and painful, is accompanied by a feeling of happiness (Scheler 1954, 148). He simply asserts the fact and makes no effort to understand this paradoxical phenomenon. One wonders whether, if Scheler had pushed further in the direction his concession points, he might not have found the notion of love as joy worthy of respect, even if he still thought it mistaken. For, if radical love is not joy, it so resembles it or at least is so closely and (as will be shown) necessarily bound up with it that they cannot be distinguished without careful reflection on experience. It is, perhaps, a less careful reflection which easily disposes of the problem without seeing the real difficulty.

It appears that a serious effort at a reductive analysis of joy is called for. If such an analysis leads to rejecting any identification of radical love with joy, it may nevertheless lead also to better understanding the structure of the total concrete experience of love and help us close in with greater precision of attention on the affective root of that experience.

For reasons other than those offered in Spinoza's writing and using a lived, common-sense understanding of joy as a point of departure, a plausible case can be made for affirming that the very essential core of the total human experience of love either is joy or necessarily includes it as a property. It is best to leave aside for the moment those instances of love which will cause trouble and to which appeal is made by those who facilely reject the identification of joy with love. More generally our experiences of love, whenever they are intense enough to call attention to themselves, seem to be joyful ones. Even when they are tinged with sadness, anxiety, anger, etc., they do involve a deep, subtle, delight or satisfaction, which is bound up with a sense of fulness in being. Paradoxically this is so sometimes even in moments when emotional loneliness is also experienced. For example, in time of separation from a loved one, in a moment of shame for having failed a loved one, as a lover I still feel that I exist more fully than when I have a pleasant life with less love. Something that is or is like joy is still present in the experience. The joy that is felt in the ordinary experience of love is or can be joy in the reality and well-being of the loved one for the latter's own sake as well as delight in the beloved as fulfilling the lover. In one way or another, all our ordinary experiences of love seem to involve joy in some broad and deep sense of the word, as something which, if it is not love itself, is at least a necessary accompaniment, something integral if not essential to love.

What then of those experiences of love in which joy seems to be altogether absent even though love is very great, experiences in which love seems to be divorced from joy and to be instead permeated by sorrow and bitterness and despair? After what we have observed in the more common experiences, we should go carefully here rather than jump to the conclusion that love has no necessary connection with joy. The total experience is a manifold of many affections of varying intensity. Our conscious attention is drawn to and held by the more intense ones. Is it not possible that one very intense affection or several together could "drown out" a more subtle and quiet affection, which nevertheless is still actual in conscious affectivity— as a soft note of an oboe could be drowned out by a symphonic crescendo or the rustle of a single leaf by a wind through a forest? Could not joy be drowned out by dread or sorrow and still be actual? If so the appeal to experiences of love in which sadness predominates is pertinent to our discussion but by itself altogether inconclusive. It does give some grounds for calling into question any definition of love as joy and even any thought of joy as a necessary accompaniment of love. But something more than a simple appeal to sad or painful experiences of love is required to settle the issue. What is required is a careful inspection of the experience of joy.

In reflecting on the experience of joy, confusion will surely ensue unless two kinds of joy are clearly distinguished. There is a joy that has as its object the very actuality of the one rejoiced over, and there is another derivative and relative joy in what is for the object of the first sort of joy. With joy of the first kind I rejoice over you, my friend, who are a beautiful personality, wise, brave, and kind, who are healthy and at peace in your own being. I rejoice over you for your own sake inasmuch as your being is actualized and your life happy (I may also rejoice because such a splendid person as you is my friend and fulfils me; but this is joy of the first type with myself as object and you as object of the second sort of joy.) The more you are actualized and happy the more I rejoice; the less you are so, the less I rejoice. Insofar as you are harmed or stunted in your being, I am saddened. But I also have joy of the second kind when I rejoice over your possessions, friends, position, honors, inasmuch as these are yours and tend to preserve or increase your actuality as a personal being.

Joy in the secondary meaning can easily be eliminated as claimant to identification with love. Such joy, like desire, is relative. Just as desire is of an object for someone who is not desired but cared for, so joy in the secondary meaning is over an object for someone. All that was said above to show how desire implies a prior affection toward someone could be paralleled here to show that joy in the second meaning also implies a prior affection. If I am delighted over an honor bestowed on you or a danger removed from your life, clearly I have some affection toward you on which this delight over your honor or safety depends. There may be others who were honored or saved from danger and this fact caused me no delight.

What about joy in the first and primary meaning, joy in the happy actualization of those we rejoice over for and in themselves? This joy is not merely a parallel of desire. We are mistaken here if we think of the their qualities and acts as though they were things they had as they have wealth or honor or friends. We say someone has wisdom or courage, or that a person's acts wisely or courageously. But these are not extrinsic to a person's reality. Persons *are* wise and courageous: these are actuations of their reality as a person. And when they acts, they are in their acts. Their acts are actuations of their personal being. When I have joy in your qualities or your thoughts, affections, etc., I have joy in *you* as existing and acting; my joy is not merely in something for you. Therefore, the analysis of desire and joy in the secondary sense will not apply here. If we are to refuse the claim of primary joy to be identical with radical love, it will have to be on other grounds.

That there are other grounds for doing so is pointed to by the same phenomenon which pointed to an affection grounding care. If I am asked why I rejoice over the fulness and splendor of your personal reality, even without regard for my own benefit, I readily answer, "Because I love you." And I do not think that I am being tautological, as would be the case if joy were love. An inspection of affective experience will, I think, justify giving this answer.

We noticed that in the total concrete experience of love there are manifold affections which are integral to the experience/ They do not appear to be merely irrelevant concomitants, contemporaneous with love but not part of the experience of love, We could, if we had to, even admit that there are some affections going on at the same time that we are experiencing love which have nothing to do with the experience of love—that is, we could admit this without prejudicing the case being made now. All that we need to see is that some affections of desire, fear, sadness, etc., along with joy, are integrally bound up in the experience precisely as a love-experience. What is worthy of the name love in the radical and most proper sense is the affection which is at the heart of the integral experience, the affection from which the other elements that are integrated into the experience as an experience of love derive and to which they are relative. We have already shown that desire and relative love are so related to a distinct but as yet undefined radical love that takes the form of care when the beloved is apprehended as in need. Can this affection be identified as joy?

Let us make trial of it. Suppose my experience of love is colored by sadness because of my loved one's loss of mental vigor, moral virtue, or peace of heart. (What we say now would hold *mutatis mutandis* if the affections were fear that these ills would happen to my loved ones or hope that they would escape them.) Does joy give rise to sorrow, joy I mean in whatever actuality my beloved one still has? I am glad that you are still alive, still able to recognize and converse with me, still have some aspiration to moral greatness. But surely there is no reason for seeing this joy as the source, the ground, of my sorrow. The sorrow and the joy are not directly interrelated; their union in one total experience is by reason of a common source, a love for you, my friend, from which arises both joy and sorrow. Remove the love and both joy and sorrow would cease. Diminish the love and both joy and sorrow diminish. Increase the love and they increase.

But notice how joy and sorrow can increase or decrease with inverse proportion to each other while love stays constant. As a friend's life grows fuller, one's joy increases and one's sorrow decreases. Do we have to say that our love has increased? Whenever my friend grows worse, my joy decreases while sorrow increases. Is my love then less? We know by experience that it is not so. Furthermore, if joy were the radical constituent in the experience of love, how would we explain the resonance of the lover's other affections with the beloved's affections? How does joy in the your being explain that your fear and hope and hate and anger and sorrow and desire tend to resonate in my affections as one who loves you? Joy in your being offers no clue. But all these resonances, as we shall see, can be understood in terms of a deeper affective response.

These observations seem to make overwhelmingly certain that love underlies both joy (even in its primary meaning) and sorrow. To reject joy as love, it is not enough to point out that the experience of love can be shot through with sadness. By itself that proves nothing. When, however, we examine the relation of joy to the other affections in the experience of love, the impossibility of identifying joy with radical love appears clearly. Nevertheless, when the claim of joy to be radical love has been rejected, it still remains that joy has a better apparent claim than desire and even a better claim than care in one respect. Those who claim that love is joy are nearer the truth than they are sometimes given credit for being by their critics. For we have seen that desire is of its very nature relative, in the sense that an object of desire is always for someone or something really distinct from it. This is not necessarily true of joy. Joy can be relative in this way: for example, I rejoice in a book or music or a meal which brings me or a friend some enlightenment, pleasure, or health. But joy can also be in an object for its own sake: for example, I rejoice that I am I, that my friend is and is happy.

There is a certain, absolute character to this latter joying or rejoicing. This absolute joy (not absolute in the sense of unqualified or unlimited, but only in the sense of terminating in an object for itself) opens up the possibility of joy as a primitive, fundamental affection such as desire could never be. It seems to be more like care, a mode of fundamental love. When the object of radical love is in need, care arises; when and insofar as the loved object is actualized, joy arises. But the relation of this joy to love differs from the relation of care to love. Care arises only insofar as need is attended to and is sometimes not in the experience of love. Since anything that is has some degree of actuality—and this is necessarily attended to when I love, whenever I love—there will always be some joy, even if it is drowned out of attention by other affections such as fear or sadness. This joy is not merely an incidental aspect of love but a *necessary* one. It is therefore in every experience of love. However, for the reasons given above, we have to say that it is not the fundamental or radical element in the whole experience of love.

5
RADICAL LOVE AS RESPONSE

Now our attention must be focused and steadily held on an affection so deep as to escape all clear-sighted awareness of ordinary attention. Only a prolonged and intense reflection can hope to yield some intelligible insight into it.

Until now, the movement of thought has been from one more evident act in our total, complex experience of love to another less evident but more radical act, always understanding that these acts flow one from another in a living unity of distinct but not separate acts. Now that we have reached the act which holds promise of being the ultimate root in conscious affectivity, we will not look for distinct and more fundamental acts. What we must do now is try to understand this one act by clarifying its various aspects, moving from the more evident and more superficial to the more obscure because more profound, bringing into the light of attention a spectrum of related aspects and seeking to discover whether there is one in which all the others are rooted and joined coherently to one another. If we succeed, we may well find intrinsic to this affection the evidence of its radical character. If not, we will in any case have gone as far as we can go by reflection towards understanding what radical love is. We shall have understood and expressed insofar as we can understand and express conceptually what is ultimately a mystery to be lived beyond the reach of all reflective analysis.

A Preliminary Question
Before beginning this new stage of analysis, there is a question to be cleared up. The answer to it will determine how we are to proceed with the descriptive analysis of radical love. Since the question arises from the confusing multiplicity of conflicting opinions about the objects of love, before trying to say what the question is, let me show what the opinions are.

Some say that love properly speaking can be had only toward persons and is extended to non-personal objects only by projecting personal characteristics into them. Aquinas limits the object of love in the proper sense to beings with rationality and freedom (ST 1, q. 20, a. 2, reply to obj. 2.; ST 1-2, q. 25, a. 3 c). For irrational creatures, the only fitting love is relative love by which they are loved for persons, not for themselves. Johann goes so far as to require a direct knowledge of the other's unique personality concretely experienced: no abstract certainty that this individual person has such a unique personality as yet not experienced by me can make possible love that is really love (Johann 1955, 34; in fact he further requires [36] reciprocal knowledge and love in order to make possible love properly speaking). Buber's definition of love, "responsibility of an I for a Thou" (Buber 1958, 15), could lead the unwary into thinking he limits the object of love to the realm of persons. His doctrine of the "three spheres" of relation, however, along with his explanation of the "thou" and the "it" as constituted by the attitude of the "I" rather than by any personal or non-personal characteristic of the other, makes clear that the "thou" could be God, a human being, a work of art, a cat, a tree, a stone. But if Buber's I-Thou relation still leaves room for love of beings other than persons, his position does not allow love for an "it" as an "it." For Buber, love can endure outside the I-Thou relation, but love arises only within that relation and consists in taking responsibility for the "thou." Thus, if he is to be consistent within this framework, the rather universal practice of speaking about love for food, drink, tools, and so on, as objects for use, would be meaningless.

On the other hand, some assure us that love without becoming equivocal can be of God, science, a woman, art, a piece of land, sports, etc. This is the position of Ortega y Gasset (Ortega 1957, 44-48). Scheler vigorously attacks those who "claim that another human is the sole original object of human love, and that it can be extended to other things inasmuch as they are accredited with human ways of life by virtue of the 'pathetic fallacy.'" He has in mind such theories as those of the British moralists, of Feuerbach, and of Freud. Love, Scheler insists, is clearly of other objects than humans. We love spontaneously, he says, all sorts of other things whose values have nothing to do with humans, as for example, the organic forms of nature for their own sake, so also art and above all God (Scheler 1954, 155-56; see also the whole of ch. 6 in that work). C. S. Lewis holds for love of non-personal objects and discusses it at length with his usual charm and clarity (Lewis 1960, ch. 2-3).

The question which arises from these conflicting opinions whether we can love non-personal objects, once raised, can be put aside—not as without significance, but as a question which has no bearing on how we proceed at this point. It is raised and put aside so that it will not be confusing the question which does bear on our procedure. This question arises from conflicting opinions about what person or

persons we can love. Even those who insist that we can love non-
personal beings would agree, I think, that love is found in its fullest
and clearest form in love for persons. Therefore, even if love properly
speaking can be for nonpersonal realities, we can limit our description to love for persons and still bring out all that is essential to radical love. But love for what person? For self? For the other? Or for
both?

However strange it may sound to most of us, there are those who
refuse to allow that self can be an object of love properly speaking,
i.e., the lover's self. We saw that Tillich, for instance, urges that we
drop the term self-love altogether. He questions whether it can be
really meaningful and finds that at best it is not a genuine concept
but a confusing metaphor (Tillich 1954, 33-34, 51, 69-70). Macmurray identifies self-love with an egocentric attitude, a negative attitude
toward the other as a danger to myself, and says that "self-love is self-
contradictory. Love is necessarily for the other, and self-love would
mean self-alienation" (Macmurray 1961, 94). There are other writers
who do not explicitly take up this problem but, whether by intent or
oversight, define love in such a way as to make it always of the other
than self. Thus Rollo May writes: "We define love as a delight in the
presence of the other person and as affirming of another's value and
development as much as one's own (May 1953, 241). Obviously, if
love is defined in terms of the other, love cannot be of self. As we saw,
Spinoza runs into this difficulty when he defines love as "joy with a
concomitant idea of the external cause'" (Spinoza 1914, III, 13 and
Affectuum Definitiones 6). When he speaks of self-love he has no
external cause and so he concedes that he ought to use a name other
than love (Spinoza 1914, III, 30).

To say that self-love is meaningless or a contradiction sounds very
odd and unreal to most people. Some do not approve of self-love
(see, e.g., Nygren's account of Luther's condemnation of all self-love
as evil: 1953, 709-16), but that is another matter. What many are
likely to consider a real question is whether we have any love for
others which is not in the ultimate analysis love for self. Those who
adopt the position that all love is reductively self-love are by no means
a majority among those who write on love, but they are more numer-
ous than those who refuse the name love to any self-centered act.
"Psychological egoists," as they are called, do not necessarily urge the
value of self-love for moral or clinical reasons. If they do, they can be
joined by many of those who hold firmly to the reality and value of
irreducible love for others. Psychological egoists think they are merely
showing a fact. Whether we like it or not, whether we approve it or

not, the fact is, they say, that all our love is egoistic and cannot be otherwise. That is the very nature of love. Thus, for instance, Jeremy Bentham begins a book on morals by telling us that pain and pleasure are the two sovereign masters of humankind. Everyone's own pleasure and pain determine what they do. Whatever we love or hate, we are drawn to or repulsed from because of ourselves, to gain pleasure and to avoid pain; and no one lifts a finger except for their own advantage. This is simply a *fact,* he thinks, and so we must build our moral thought on this fact (Bentham 1948, 1, i, 1).

Now if it be true that all love is reductively self-love, egoistic love, then nothing but self-love could ever validly lay claim to the title of radical, and a description of any other love could be at best only a preliminary step, one we might even dispense with here. On the other hand, if those who deny that self-love is an intelligible notion are right, any description of a psychic act called self-love will be a description of some thing other than love. The more common opinion, allowing for both self-love and love of others without the necessity of reducing the latter to the former or of denying the former, permits us to describe either radical love for self or the other. The question then is: which of these loves should be described? If both, with which should we begin?

Do we, in order to answer this question and begin our analysis of radical love, have to settle our minds on the reality of self-love and on the reducibility of other-love to self-love? If so, we can begin only by making an arbitrary decision; for the solution to these problems depends on the conclusion of the analysis which is being made. However, there is no need to make any such arbitrary decision. The claims of psychological egoists and of those who deny self-love can justly be held in abeyance. Psychological egoists have never made a convincing case, but only, ultimately, an assumption. It is not therefore to be declared false; it is only unproved, and must wait on evidence. (Arguments against psychological egoism that do have great force have been advanced, but this is not the place to call upon them; see Broad 1952, 218-31, and his discussion [1930, ch. 3, esp. 63-66] of Bishop Joseph Butler's ethics.) Similarly, the denial of self-love rests on an assumed definition of love by which self-love is ruled out of the realm of intelligibility. Whether the assumed definition is right or wrong waits on the evidence. Those who propose it do not support it with convincing argument. And so far in this study, no evidence has appeared requiring a denial of self-love or a reduction of all love to self-love. On the contrary, the fact that care and primary joy can have as objects either self or the other person suggests that the simpler and more fundamental affection that grounds them can also have self or the other as object. If so, and if this affection turns out to be worthy of the name tentatively given it, i.e., radical love, then both psychological egoism and the negation of egoistic love will be proved wrong.

Without assuming the truth of the third position which asserts the reality of an irreducible love for self and for the other person, we can at least say that the evidence so far makes it more probable, and that by allowing for the possibility of its truth we avoid any illegitimate prejudgments. If either of the other two positions is correct, this should show up as we proceed.

Should we then begin with self-love or with love for another person? For several reasons the latter seems preferable. First of all, no one holds that self-love is reductively love of the other; whereas some do hold that all love of other persons reduces to self-love. So, if either of these extreme positions is true, we can find out more readily by analyzing love of the other person than by analyzing self-love. If love of the other turns out to be always reducible to self-love, then psychological egoism is true. If not, psychological egoism is false. We still, of course, in that case have to show whether or not self-love is intelligible at all. But that should emerge from our analysis of the nature of love.

The answer to the question raised above is, therefore: we shall begin our examination of radical love by allowing for the intelligible reality of self-love until evidence requires otherwise; we shall allow for the irreducibility to self-love of our love for others until evidence requires otherwise; and we shall center our description of radical love on love of one person for another rather than on self-love.

◁ Preliminary Cautions

Besides answering this question, another matter requires attention before beginning a description of radical love. There are several dangers of error against which anyone undertaking this description is to be forewarned. Failures in accuracy or in comprehensiveness of vision resulting from a lack of sensitivity to these dangers are commonplace in discussions of love. The first of these errors is one which is already partly brought to light by the foregoing analysis of affective experience. It is that of confusing love, properly speaking, with its consequences, its conditions, or its accompaniments. One of the subtlest forms of this error is a constant temptation at this point of our investigation, when we are not trying to discriminate between affections but between aspects of one affection. Here we will find that a word used to describe some aspect of radical love has a range of re-

lated but different meanings, one or the other of which applies to
some condition or consequence of radical love as well as to radical
love itself. We are easily liable to confuse these meanings and to think
we have noted an aspect of radical love when we are really describing
a condition or consequence of it.

To illustrate, consider such a word as "union." There is a cognitive
union which is a condition for the very possibility of affective union
that is love, and there is another cognitive union which is a consequence of and is conditioned by love. There is also a union of affections which is a consequence of love, the resonance of the beloved's
affections in the lover's affection that we spoke about above. This is
what some mean when they talk about the affective union of love.
None of these unions is the union that is love. When love is said to
be union or unitive without delicate care to distinguish and describe
these various unions, the union that is an essential aspect of radical
love can be missed altogether. It can be mistaken for one or a combination of the other ways of union between the lover and the loved
one in the concrete experience. Similar problems, as we shall see,
occur when speaking of presence, giving, identification, affirmation.

A second danger of error in describing radical love is that of excluding one of two apparently contradictory aspects of love, both of
which are commonly considered to be involved in love, and doing so
just because they appear to be in conflict. In doing this, two things
are overlooked: first, the value to be placed on the spontaneous testimony of those who experience love, especially those who are generally considered to love most intensely and most maturely; and second,
the inadequacy of our language and concepts when we try to express
the highest and deepest realities.

What is generally found explicitly or implicitly in spontaneous
expressions of love, especially when it is expressed by those who love
best, cannot easily be put aside by theoreticians on the ground that
they have already found an aspect of love that seems to contradict
what even they who love best say. The theoreticians may possibly be
right and they may be mistaken; but they had better go cautiously
and with respect for the testimony of those who love. Yet we do find
it said, for example, that one who loves does not possess nor seek to
possess the beloved since love respects the reality of the other just for
the beloved's own sake. We are told that love is giving and not receiving, that love is a going out to the loved one in contrast to the taking
in of an object known. Yet those who love and directly and spontaneously express their love speak of possessing the loved one, of receiving and taking the loved one into their hearts. We are even told by

the learned that love is not union, that it is a tendency toward union or is unselfishly unconcerned about union and possession. But who of us, when giving expression to our love instead of subjecting it to psychological or philosophical study, ever said such a thing—and even if we did, our testimony is surely drowned by the voices of those who proclaim otherwise. It may be said that the lover and the theoreticians are differing only in words, the latter trying to be more precise. And they may succeed. But they are in danger of leaving out some aspects of the reality in attaining their precision by merely negating the lover's expression instead of explaining and integrating it into their theories. Even those who themselves love greatly and well can fall into error here when they also play the role of philosopher or psychologist.

The truth is that when we get beyond the more superficial aspects of reality we find that the reality overflows and breaks through our concepts and language. We are forced to express our insights in *apparently* contradictory concepts. (Maslow [1962, 86] notes that "self-actualizing" people and others during "peak experiences" see the resolution of dichotomies and contradictions. To see the resolution of dichotomies and contradictions is not yet to be able to express the resolution conceptually or in language.) Jean Mouroux's treatment of love in his *The Meaning of Man* is an excellent example of awareness of and conscious striving to avoid the danger we are speaking of here. His very method is to "try to seize love's inner reality through a series of paradoxes" (Mouroux 1948, 202). Thus he says that love is passivity and activity, union and movement, affectivity and liberty, spirit and flesh, desire and gift (Mouroux 1948, 201-09). However, it is only his awareness that paradox is necessarily involved in a description of love that I wish to note and commend. His paradoxes, as he expounds them, are paradoxes only of love in the full concrete experience, including the consequences of love in its root meaning, its modifications by freedom, and its sensible accompaniments. They are not paradoxical aspects of love in its root meaning. To take them as such would be to fall into the first danger noted above and also into a third one.

3) The third error into which a description of radical love can easily slide is that of confusing it with love as modified, qualified, in some important but accidental way. It is a confusion of the accidental with the essential, of the adjectival with the substantival. For instance, I read or hear from time to time that love is a total self-giving. Now, assuming for the moment that love is a giving of self to another, does it have to be a *total* giving in order to be love? If so, how many people

ever love? How much of what everybody calls love now and what everybody has called love throughout human history is or was love? Almost none of it. This way of thinking is, I find, frequently bound up with a larger error of the same sort, that of making the I-Thou relation as described by Buber and others coincidental with love—despite the fact that Buber himself is sure that love endures outside such relation (Buber 1958, 17, 98-99. Paul Ramsey criticizes Reinhold Neibuhr and Daniel Williams for erring in this manner, the former for making self-sacrifice and the latter for making mutuality essential to love or, more precisely, to Christian love (Ramsey 1962,131-36). My intention is not at present to take sides; whether or not Ramsey is correctly criticizing these men, the sort of error he attributes to them is illustrative of the sort of error to which I am calling attention here.

Passive-Active Response

With these warnings in mind, we can now turn to our task of uncovering and ordering the aspects of radical love. An initial insight and direction for further investigation can be gotten by observing how radical love arises. Radical love originates in human experience as a response which, if not entirely dependent on the object of love, is so to some extent. Language is deceptive here. The "beloved" or "loved" is a passive form, indicating the object of an act of "loving" which is active in form. But in the realm of observable evidence, there is no direct effect of love on the loved one. Rather, the love is an act immanent to the lover, a response made possible by the object of love which in some way influences the subject of love. In what way it does so will appear as our analysis proceeds.

The response is, of course, an act from the lover's side; it has the character of a passion, but the lover is also immanently active in love. Love involves passivity and spontaneous activity. The beloved calls and the lover answers from the lover's own inner power of love. Love arises in an encounter or meeting. By encounter or meeting we need not and should not understand here an experience of mutual love. We are talking only about the love of one person for another. If the love is mutual, what we say has to be said from the other side also. And the point I am making now is that love in just one direction involves some sort of meeting or encounter of two persons, even though not an encounter of two loves. The active-passive character of radical love at its origin is evident in two aspects of the response: in this response the lover has the experience of being liberated and of being taken a willing captive, both at once but in different respects and both involving activity and passivity in the lover.

Before considering these two aspects of the response, however, we had better show that the response that is radical love is in its origin not immanently active in the sense of being a free act. Otherwise some of the things said about it will be objected to on false grounds and some things not said will be desiderated as omitted essentials. Some insist that love is a freely chosen response to an appeal from the loved one. Without doubt love can be that; and, until it is that, it will not be a completely human love. But without doubt also, radical love does not originate as a free response, if that means a response given by a deliberate act of free choice in the ordinary meaning of free choice, i.e., an act of self-determination to one of several really possible alternatives. If by free is meant unhindered, the statement that radical love is always a free response poses no problem in our present discussion. It is irrelevant, and rather obviously contrary to facts. Radical love begins in an indeliberate, unfree response. Once in act, this unfree love can be brought to a free decision and in choice can be negated or ratified and transformed into a freely given, fully human love.

The point can be highlighted by noting the difference between two meanings of appeal to which the lover responds: the appeal which is responded to by indeliberate love and the appeal to which free choice is a response. To be persons is to be, in our ontological reality, appeals for love. In this sense we can be "appealing" without being at all *aware* of that appeal. A person can also appeal to another for love by words, gestures, looks, etc. In this sense, the ones appealing are aware of their own need and consciously appeal for love by trying to bring it to the attention of others. In either case the one appealed to may or may not be aware of the appeal. When others do become aware of the appeal, they may immediately and spontaneously, without deliberation or free choice, respond with a genuine radical love. But now, whether for selfish or unselfish reasons, they can choose to ratify or negate this spontaneous response. The one loved precisely inasmuch *as loved* now appeals to the other's freedom to ratify the continuance of this love as an expression of that other as a free person. The lover finds the beloved "appealing." But the lover also, on the other hand, may find the love unappealing, and may not want to get involved, to bear the responsibility that love entails. The appeal, in this last meaning, is not an appeal merely of a person for the response of love but the appeal of a person already spontaneously loved by the one appealed to. The lover's own spontaneous love is an ap-

peal for an act of freedom to ratify the love, to transform it by raising
it to the level of freedom and to ensure its continuance. To speak as
though radical love of a person were essentially a free response is to
fall into the error of confusing the adjectival with the essential.

With the foregoing clarification about freedom in mind, we can
take up those aspects of the experience that reveal the passive-active
character of the response as a meeting. Love begins at the touch of
the loved one upon the lover's affectivity. Wonderfully, at that touch
the power of love within the lover's being is energized. It is not as
though the beloved created what was not there, but rather as though
a deeply hidden energy pressing from within were suddenly released
into full conscious life. Whether it comes slowly, almost imperceptibly, or whether it comes in a sudden and dazzling shock, it always
gives the sense of liberated life flowing or flashing from the subject's
personal center.

It would, then, be a serious misunderstanding of what the response
of radical love is if the sense of being liberated were taken to mean
that love is merely passive, caused by the unilateral influence of its
active object, or that love *cannot* be an expression of a person as free
and self-possessed, a gift properly speaking. Radical love, as an unfree spontaneous response depends on its object; it is a response to
someone. But the someone who is object does not cause the existential reality of the love. That comes forth from the lover's own being,
rushing into consciousness, as it were, in response to the call of the
object's reality. Lover and loved meet in the experience of love.

There is another aspect to the experience of liberation that is closely
bound up with the experience of a generalized urge to love. In the
response of radical love the subject not only experiences a release of
energy but also a liberation from the confines of individual life, from
the prison of affective solipsism. (Radical love of another person always flatly denies and mocks the academic posture that questions the
reality of the other or the possibility of sharing another's life. One
who is capable of and actually experiences radical love for another
may hold on to an academic posture, but only at the price of splitting it from life; what one says in one's books and in the classroom,
one cannot live, and *vice versa*. And what one says in books and in
the classroom is based on what is infinitely less certain than a loving
experience of the other—even if it be rationally more manipulat-
able.) There is a sense of exultation at liberation from individual limits made possible by the beloved—and confirmed by the inevitable
accompanying affection of gratitude. But the exultation is also an
exultation in the lover's victory, in the lover's own active bursting

through the confines of one's ego to experience a new world. Of this there will be much to say later. For now, let us turn to a paradoxical opposite aspect of the experience.

At the same time that the response of love is experienced as a release, it is also experienced as being captured by the loved one. This is most obvious when with a divided affectivity we respond with several conflicting loves to several different objects. For then we feel constrained by each in opposition to the other. It is precisely because each has some hold on us that we find it difficult to respond to one if it means turning away from the other. Clearly then, when we respond without conflict, without sense of constraint, it is because our love is captivated by one object or by several without any conflict between them. But we are captive with or without an experience of constraint. The fact that we do not always feel constrained does not argue against the aspect of captivity as an essential aspect of the response. The point to note is that although we do not in some particular response experience constraint, we would experience it if we for any reason attempted to escape the binding force—more or less, as the intensity of the love varied. For the intensity of the love and the constraint (when the situation is such as to make constraint felt) are experienced in direct proportion, varying from the hardly noticeable to what is impossible to overcome.

The explanation of the fact that the captive feels no constraint unless some conflict of loves is set up can be found in the active, spontaneous aspect of this passive-active experience noted above. It is in the very nature of the case that the lover is not only captured but also actively surrenders and remains a willing captive of the loved one, and this also in direct proportion to the intensity of the love. When there is a conflict of loves, then one's affectivity is in tension, and one is both a willing and an unwilling captive to each object of love, surrendering and revolting, but doing neither fully.

The Object of Response

We have been looking at the origin of love with our attention concentrated directly and almost exclusively on the subject's experience Of the love, on the object only obliquely. Still looking from the subject's side let us shift attention to the object and ask what it is in the object which accounts for the response. To what in the object is radical love a response?

The object of radical love will differ formally from the object of any of the other affections from which that love was distinguished in our analysis. Love as desire is for an object which meets the lover's need or the loved one's need. Love as care is for the one who needs precisely as needing. But what we have called radical love is not explicitly a response to the lover's need nor to the beloved's need nor even to the beloved as in need. It is not even the object as in need of my love to which radical love is responding. Some present the call for love as a plea or appeal of a person's very being to be confirmed in the person's subjectivity as tending toward an unfulfilled destiny. But this way of thinking fails of precision. What I am responding to is you, an actual person, here and now incomplete in your actuality— destined to completeness, to be sure—but lovable now for what you are *actually* not merely for what you are potentially or for your destiny, which I can help you to achieve. It is precisely because I respond to your present actuality that I also want the preservation and increase of your actuality in the future. As you are here and now, you are to me an actual, radical end value. As a consequence I am interested in your destiny. If I did not respond to you as an actual, radical end, I would not respond with a radical care for you in your need. I might attend to your needs for other reasons: because it is my professional work to do so, because it makes me feel creative and important to do so. But to respond in these ways is to make the other an object for my use. The radical care is for my actual self in need of further actualization.

When, therefore, it is said that love is a response to the beloved's actuality as a person, does that mean a response to you insofar as you have actualized certain lovable qualities of a person, insofar as you are, for example, kind, brave, wise? If so, we could not love new-born infants as persons, nor adults who are harsh, cowardly, ignorant. Yet we do love infants and adults with very unlovable qualities, and we love them with radical love as ends for themselves and in themselves. What is the actuality we are responding to? Any intelligent and unrelenting effort to understand the experience of love eventually forces us to face up to what we are talking about when we talk of a human person, when we say "I" and "you."

That I have any personal qualities at all is manifest only in my acts. It is because by my intellect and affectivity and freedom I respond in wise or stupid, brave or cowardly ways, that I can be known to be a wise or stupid, brave or cowardly person. Now, in every conscious act I am aware not just of an act; I am aware of myself in act. Hume assured us that when he entered intimately into what he called "himself," he came upon nothing but a bundle of perceptions, succeeding one another with inconceivable rapidity. This was all the self he could find. Try to enter into yourself without an assumed phenomenalistic theory of knowledge to blind you and you will find not merely a collection of different perceptions, but a flow of acts, all of which are *your* acts, or rather *yourself* in act. For these acts are neither independent of you, nor fundamentally constitutive of yourself, nor yet an addition accruing to yourself, but are your fundamental self in act. You will find nothing which has any reality apart from yourself; and you will find yourself fundamentally as an act of being enduring through all your changing acts of intelligence, affectivity, and freedom, giving actuality to all these, being the actuality of all actualities in your flowing personal reality. Putting aside all assumptions and theories and looking at the experience to be explained by theory, you will find that, while remaining fundamentally stable, the act of being that is constitutive of self is also a dynamic energy, seeking expression in the flow of your acts. In these acts, you interact with the world so as to persevere in reality, to grow by union with the rest of reality, to expand self's actuality into others. The personal self is in all these acts; they are self in act. No one nor all of these acts gives full expression to the actuality of the act of being, which seems to be a source inexhaustible in the number and variety and novelty of acts in which it can transiently express itself. And as human persons we always experience ourselves as more or less confined, unrealized, with the energy of a fundamental, self-constitutive act of dynamic being reaching for fuller realization of its virtuality.

Nothing in consciousness is more all-pervasive and more certain than the fundamental act of personal being. But just because it is so deep and pervasive and grounds all partial expressions on the surface of consciousness, it can be missed—especially if one comes to it with a theory which assumes it is an impossibility.

Now this fundamental act of personal being shows in its modes of acting that it has certain relatively lasting qualities, dispositions for acting. These account for one and the same person spontaneously responding to others in harsh, cowardly, stupid ways at one period of life and in kind, brave, wise ways at another period. There are ways of being that account for ways of acting. These ways of being, like the acts which reveal them, are actual by reason of the fundamental act of personal being, the actuality of their actuality. No more than the acts for which they dispose a person are they mere accretions overlaying some unknown and unknowable Lockean substance. It is I, constituted by my act of being, who am kind or harsh, brave or cowardly. It is I, the enduring personal actuality, who am modified by qualities and revealed in them as they appear in my acts. My fundamental act of being is never fully known nor entirely unknown.

When, therefore, radical love is said to be a response to the loved one's actuality, does "actuality" mean the other's fundamental actuality, the act of being a person, or the other's implemental actuality, the set of qualities that can change for better or worse while the person remains the same person fundamentally? To answer this question adequately it is necessary to distinguish several ways in which we respond to others, all of which are commonly spoken of as love. Thus, I can respond to others: 1) as bearers of certain qualities that make them pleasing or displeasing to me, useful or a hindrance to me; 2) as personal beings revealed through certain lovable qualities; 3) as personal beings whose qualities are unknown to me.

The first kind of response cannot be radical love. No response of mine, if it is only for others as bearers of qualities pleasant or useful to me, is such; for then they are loved not for themselves but for the use or delight they afford me. The radical affection here is for myself. I am the radical end; others are the means or, at best, implemental ends.

The second mode of response, to persons glimpsed in and through certain acts and qualities, is such that it reaches to the inexhaustible actualizing center of all acts and of all qualities, which is always lovable, whether beautifully realized in action and character (moral and psychological) or not. This second mode of response (to others as personal beings revealed in their acts and qualities) can take two forms. At one time, I can respond to someone as this unique person *experienced* in uniqueness. At other times, I respond to the same person as revealed in certain acts or qualities characteristic of a "lovable *sort*" of person, knowing *that* this person is a unique value but without the inexpressible experience of that person in very uniqueness. The first of these responses is the fuller, deeper mode of response by radical love. For most of us the moments when we are able to respond to others in their experienced unique personalities with a full and intense response are relatively rare and of brief duration. The love that arises in those moments can endure without actual experience of the beloved's unique splendor of being enduring. That experience can come and go again, leaving only a memory of having had the experience. To make the love endure this way demands a belief in the validity of the experience when it was had, a fidelity to the seen glory of the loved one when the vision has faded, a refusal to let the drabness of what appears in ordinary experience lay claim to being "reality" or the passing vision decline to the status of a dream.

The call to which we respond more commonly is the call of the other simply as *a* person—a being whom we judge to be a "lovable sort of person" by reason of certain qualities exhibited in act now or at an earlier time. In this response there is no experiential knowledge of the person's unique personality as we have in those privileged moments of interpersonal revelation and insight. It is true that everything we experience is individual; but we rarely catch the individuality, feel the "stress and stroke" (Gerard Manley Hopkins) of someone's individuality. More rarely do we encounter the unique person with experiential awareness of and affective response to each one's personal unicity—even though each person is unique and we know that each one is such.

As a matter of fact, although the call that brings forth radical love is usually mediated by knowledge of certain qualities or acts, we find that we can and do respond to those who are known to us only as human beings in a situation, without seeing them act or having knowledge of their qualities. This is the third manner of responding listed above. For instance, suppose I come upon a traffic accident and see only someone lying crumpled on the ground, or suppose I hear about some person, otherwise unknown to me, who is suffering or in danger. My response can be love of these people as radical ends without knowledge or concern about their qualities. I do not know whether they are morally good or evil, savants or boors. I can, without any such knowledge, respond to them as persons, as beings of inestimable value for and in themselves. As a consequence, my radical love issues in radical care for them, for and in themselves, and so issues in acts to help them. If the situation in which I come upon such persons or about which I hear is a joyful one, I can find myself rejoicing over their well-being, with a joy which is for them, for and in them as persons. To say that I have to have some experience of them in their uniqueness, or even some experience of their qualities in order to love them, is a completely arbitrary, a priori limitation put upon love to make it fit an assumed definition.

To sum up, radical love is a response to the fundamental actuality of whomever we love, to their radical acts of personal being. It is also a response to their lovable qualities and actions insofar as these are expressions of their personal being in which they are realized and revealed. These qualities revealed in acts need not be included in the object of radical love, but our observations show that it is altogether contrary to experience to say that these qualities can be no part of what genuine personal love responds to. It is true that a love fails to be radical love of others if in the others' qualities the lover fails to love the persons for and in themselves. Nevertheless, it is obviously easier to respond to persons for themselves when they show the beauty of their personal acts of being in gentleness and generosity rather than when they distort it by harshness and avarice.

Conditional and Unconditional Response

But what if others' gentleness and generosity are made a condition for loving them, so that without these lovable qualities in them radical love would cease? Can such love be personal love of others for themselves? Or does personal, radical love have to be truly unconditional loved? (There are many ways in which human love is conditioned by both positive and negative conditions; there is no need to discuss these ways here. "Conditioned love" in the present context will mean a love conditioned by the loved one having certain desirable qualities, and "unconditioned love" will mean a love that does not depend on the beloved having these qualities.) If the response is made to the other as a person, even though on condition of being realized in these ways, I see no reason for denying the name of personal or radical love to it. It is a *conditioned* radical love. Some speak as if to love in this way could not be genuine love of persons for and in themselves. Now, there is no doubt that love conditioned in this way is justly suspect as perhaps a love that is for the loved one only as enriching the life of the lover, as useful, pleasant or even ennobling to the lover. But it need not be so, for it can be a response to persons as realized in those qualities which make them useful, pleasant, ennobling, and which reveal their lovableness for themselves, making it easy to love them. Granted that when it is love for the other as a person, it is still not as complete as unconditioned love, nevertheless it can be a radical love for the other, without any ulterior selfish motivation. The loved persons have realized certain human potentialities in such a way as to manifest in and through them the lovable actuality of their personal being. The one loving has responded to them so actualized. It is a fact that people who love in this way are so limited in their understanding of personal value and in their love that, if the loved one ceased to realize these capacities, they intend to cease loving. This fact does not negate the fact that they *do here and now* love these others as radical ends for and in themselves and intends to continue loving so without end, if only these other continues as they are. They are not loving merely the qualities; they love the persons who has the qualities, but only on condition that they have them. This is very different from loving them merely as bearers of qualities by which they are beneficial or pleasant to the ones loving them. Certain limiting conditions are set for responding to the other with love for them as persons. These conditions are met and there is a response which could even lead a lover to sacrifice one's life for the loved one. It is entirely arbitrary to insist that this is not genuine love of a person. It is a radical affective response to a person precisely as a person who is gentle, brave, generous.

This is very different from the response to someone merely as capable of performing certain functions which answer to the purposes of the one loving without regard for the personal worth of the one who is loved. In this sort of response the qualities upon which the response is conditioned are not viewed as intrinsically ennobling the ones loved nor as revealing their personal acts of being by which they are radically lovable. Rather they are regarded and valued merely as rendering the loved one beneficial or enjoyable to the lover; and the loved one is valued merely as beneficial or enjoyable to the lover precisely because of these qualities. The object is responded to as an instrument, as functional for implementing the goals which the lover has in mind. Such love is not personal and is not radical. (A nuance is relevant: loving the other as useful or enjoyable is not necessarily opposed to or exclusive of radical love for the same person; in fact, it can be an expression of radical love if the lover loves in this way because it gives joy to the loved one to be useful and enjoyable.)

Another sort of limiting condition appears when one loves someone not on condition of having any special personal qualities or modes of action, but on condition of having a certain relationship with another person and exclusively because of that relationship—not because of any intrinsic lovable qualities or any useful or beneficial ones. The relation may be to the one loving, for example, when the latter loves the former because of being a blood relative. It may be a relationship with a third party who is loved with radical love, as when I love the daughter of my friend just because she is the daughter of my friend. In this sort of response, the person is not loved as a person, or as a person with certain desirable qualities actualized. She is not loved because of anything which constitutes her as a person, actualizes any potentiality of her personal being, or reveals anything of the lovableness of that being. The lovable reality which accounts for her being loved is the one to whom she is related. She is, therefore, loved not in herself but in the other. She is regarded and loved as an extension of the other; her whole value is derived from the other.

Nevertheless, it is possible, given the relationship that conditions the love, that the daughter is loved as a radical end—for herself— even though not in herself. I who affirm her do not regard her merely as useful or as pleasant either for her own purposes or for those of a third party for love of whom I love the second. This can appear in the care I may have for the latter's welfare when there is no gain for herself or for the third party, when I think the latter is not even aware perhaps of what is ensuing. To take another example, I might make great sacrifices for the sake of one very dear to a friend who has died, for no other reason than that he was beloved by my friend. I do what I think my friend would have done if he had lived to make his loved one happy. But cut off the relationship with my deceased friend and I have no interest in the other at all. Nothing intrinsic to him calls forth my love. Is this conditional love of the other for himself a conditional radical love? It has one characteristic of radical love: it is an affective response to someone as a radical end, that is, as lovable for himself. On the other hand, it is not a *radical affection* toward him as a radical end. The response is radically to another and only derivatively to him. He is loved not by reason of his personal being but by association with one who is so loved. A dog or an old hat or a photograph could be loved in this way. Such love is not a conditioned radical love, but at best a quasi-radical love.

Such quasi-radical love can become genuine radical love, even though still in dependence on love for a third person. Take the illustration just given above. Suppose it should dawn upon me that if this man were so dear to my friend there must be some lovableness in him, even if I do not see it and respond to it. My friend's judgment that this man is worthy of love is taken on faith. Or I observe my friend's love for this man and something of the intrinsic value of the man is mirrored to me in my friend's love. Now my radical love can begin to be a genuine radical love for this man, for himself, *and in* himself. Even though I do not respond to his intrinsic worth as directly known, I do respond to it. I do love him *in* as well as for himself. In this way Christians may love even those who repel them in other ways. They believe that these creatures are in their personal being images of God and loved by Christ, whose love creates some seeds of Christlike lovableness in them. So they loves them with radical love along with Christ. This is very different from loving them for themselves because Christ loves them, but with no regard for them as having intrinsic value as persons, as images of God, their own very acts of personal being given a Christlike splendor by union with Christ. In one who has faith in and love for Christ, a response of genuinely radical love can arise quite spontaneously even toward those who under other aspects call forth a contrary response of hatred.

Clarification and Summary

Till now we have been speaking of a response to the loved ones' actuality, distinguishing fundamental actuality from secondary, qualitative actuality, from their "facticity," if you will. Allowing the description of radical love's object to stand without any mention of other implicit elements in that object would be an inadequate way to describe it and could easily be misleading. To say that the object of radical love is the *actuality* of the ones loved does not mean that the loved ones' *potentiality*, their dynamism to fulfilment, their needs and destiny, are excluded from the object of radical love. Stated accurately, radical love is a response to the *total reality* of these loved ones. Potentiality, need, dynamism, destiny—all are real. Their reality, however, is not radical in the total reality of the loved ones; they are *of* their personal actuality. As actually existing personalities constituted as real by their personal acts of being, they are able to be more fully realized, have needs and drives to fulness of being. Remove the actuality of their personal being, and all else ceases to be real. It is to loved ones constituted as a personal actuality by their radical acts of personal being that radical love always responds *directly* and *explicitly*; it is to these same loved ones insofar as they are in need that radical love responds indirectly and implicitly. Sometimes, even most of the time in human life, our love explicitly responds to the loved ones precisely as incomplete actualities, in need of our love and of the action flowing from our love to help them achieve fuller actuality. The response may also be to need in the broad sense, explained above, which implies no defect of actuality in the one who needs in this way. Consequently, radical love rarely appears in its unmodified form; it ordinarily modulates into care and issues into implemented love and into desire.

What we have been able to note about love upon reflection on our experience of it as it arises in response to the beloved can be summarized in this way: It is my response to your total reality. It is directly and explicitly a response to your actuality, primarily and in every instance to your fundamental actuality as a personal act of being; secondarily, to your qualitative actuality revealed in your acts and partially revealing your act of being. It is indirectly and implicitly a response to your potentiality, dynamism, and need. This response is experienced as liberation of the subject's energy for love and liberation from the confinement of individual being. It is at the same time experienced as a willing captivity to the beloved.

6
RADICAL LOVE AS UNION

If we now try to bring to light some essential aspects or features of the relation between the lover and the loved in the response of radical love, the most obvious aspect calling for attention is that of union. Anyone who loves another with radical love has an experience of union. Lovers have a lived certainty that they are in some way one with those they love. What this union is, how it is constituted, remains hidden and can be brought to light only with great difficulty.

Erich Fromm on Union

Since Fromm has spoken more fully than others of love as union, we might expect to find help from him in describing the union constituted by love. So long as Fromm's description of mature love is taken as a description of the total concrete experience of love, it is an illuminating and practically helpful account of some of the most important elements in that whole experience. But if we should press him to render his account internally coherent and to tell us what within that total experience is love properly speaking, what is the interpersonal union, therefore, in which our fundamental human need and dynamism for union is achieved, then ambiguities arise on all sides and crucial questions are left unanswered if not unanswerable.

First of all, Fromm says that whether we call the symbiotic forms of fusion or union by the name love is merely a semantic problem and like all such problems is resolved arbitrarily by a decision. So he decides to use the word love only for mature love. This is a perilous decision which leads to the later decision (it is no more than that) that selfishness is not self-love (Fromm 1956, 60-61). Unless the symbiotic forms of love are only equivocally love, then to make such a decision as Fromm makes results in a legitimate but dangerously confusing figure of speech. Understood as a rhetorical device, it is serviceable for exhortation but solves no questions about the nature of love. Taken as a literal non-normative statement about psychic acts, it is not to be taken seriously—except by one who has assumed that love is always mature and perfectly rational. To adopt such a rhetorical device when trying to discover the nature of love, not just the nature of morally or clinically commendable love, endangers the en-

terprise by omitting from consideration much of the data to be covered by any definition or description of love in an unqualified sense.
In fact, one might, without appearing cynical, fear that it omits the
greater part of love as it appears in human life. Whether that be so or
not, if neurotic or immoral love is still love, then anyone who is going to tell us what love is, love without qualification, will have to
reveal what is common in some way to mature love and symbiotic
love. It is true that the nature of love will show more clearly in the
more perfect instances. But if in the perfect instance we see what is
essential to love as such, then it is found, however defectively, even in
defective instances. To say that the common note is union is of little
help. There are many modes of union other than love, which Fromm
himself points out. What is it that distinguishes the union called love
from any of these other unions and is common to both mature and
immature love, to irrational and rational self-love? Fromm does not
tell us. Now, suppose Fromm were going to tell us what the act of
judgment is or some other affection than love, say fear. And suppose
he eliminated from consideration all acts of false judgment and all
unreasonable fears and produced a definition or description of judgment or fear that could not include erroneous judgments or unreasonable fears. We might find that he had given us something of value,
but he would certainly not have given us a description or definition
of judgment or of fear. An author may, of course, decide not to include in the category of love any act that is not mature, rational,
productive. Then we know what that author is discussing when speaking of love. But then also we have to admit that our author has avoided
a real problem, not solved it.

Even if we allow the assumption to stand that love is what Fromm
calls mature love, it must be said that any coherent statement of what
love is cannot be found in his explanation. Love, he says, is a union,
a fusion, with another person. What is love that it should constitute
an interpersonal union? Love, he says, is active, i.e., it is the exercise
of an inherent power—with or without any external change effected.
This active character is described as giving: giving of the lover's possessions, giving of what is alive in oneself, of one's joy, one's interest,
knowledge, humor. Now giving in these ways can effect some sort of
bond between lover and loved: they then have some possession or
joys or jokes or knowledge, in common. But this is an effect, a consequence of giving. Love is said to be giving. Is the giving itself a
union? I hand over a gift to the other. I communicate in words, smiles,
tears, gestures, deeds of service, what is alive in me. It is by such acts
of handing over or communicating that I give to the other. But these

are neither union nor love. The love is not the giving but is expressed in the giving—i.e., the kind of giving Fromm speaks of.

In fact, this sort of giving can go on without mature love for the one to whom I give, and mature love can arise without this sort of giving. We may share our wit and knowledge to gain fame or money; we may share our sorrow because we are weak and need a lot of sympathy. And on the other hand, there are situations in which we love maturely and are frustrated because we cannot succeed in giving: we lack material means, or the loved one will not accept what we offer, or we are misunderstood. We desire to give and share but cannot. Is the love, then, the desire to give, the tendency to union? Fromm does not want to say this, and it has already been shown to be wrong. So we are still left wondering what love is which constitutes union.

Can we perhaps get further with Fromm's syndrome of maturity? The active character appears also, he says, in the fact that it implies certain fundamental elements common to all forms of love: care, responsibility, respect, knowledge. There is much ambiguity in this statement and in the whole discussion of these elements or components, as he calls them, of love. However, he does seem to make care the most fundamental one of the three affective "attitudes," with knowledge and the other two attitudes (responsibility and respect) as conditions or consequences of care. This care is active concern for the beloved's life and growth. In saying this Fromm is getting near the radical element in the experience of love; but he fails to even suggest how care constitutes a union.

What is more, if the analysis of desire made in chapter 4 is valid, then to say, as Fromm does, that love is the union that answers to our most basic human need and to the yearning that arises from that need, still leaves unmentioned the more fundamental love living at the root of all yearning and all tendency for fulfilment. It is because one loves oneself or another that one desires interpersonal union as one's fulfilment or the other's. (Within the context of Fromm's thought, there can be no hesitance in speaking of self-love.) Union of love is the source of all conscious desiring and striving for more perfect union of many sorts, but above all of perfect love. If love is union and giving, what are the union and giving that constitute that love which is both prior to desire and the goal of desire?

In summary, love is union, love is giving, love is active concern— these three things Fromm has asserted without ever showing how giving or active concern (care) constitute a union with the beloved or ever showing how the union which is love differs from union which is a condition for love, from unions which are consequences of love, from other unions which are not directly related to love at all. He has, rather, confused two modes of giving which follow on love with the union which is love itself. And finally, whatever that union may be which is love itself, Fromm has failed to note that it is the source as well as the goal of human yearning and striving, that the desire for union of love is always a desire for greater union of love springing from an initial imperfect love. If affective separation, estrangement, were ever complete, desire for union would be impossible.

To point these limitations in what Fromm has done is not necessarily a criticism of him in terms of his own aims. Perhaps his purpose did not require any greater precision of thought and expression than he gives us. In fact, it is possible that it would have defeated his purpose of teaching the art of loving to a wide audience if he had attempted to achieve any greater precision. His own purposes seem to have been remarkably achieved, if one is to judge by the impact of the book on the reading public. (Insofar as he writes on matters within his own field of competence, Fromm's success is richly deserved. When, however, he takes up metaphysical and theological questions, his performance can be embarrassing to those who admire and are grateful for his work in psychology.) All I am doing is pointing out a fact and clearing away a misconception, namely that Fromm has done what he has not even seriously attempted to do. That he not only noted union as an aspect of love itself but even made it central to his view of love shows a deeper insight into the full experience than is had by those who never get deeper than desire or drive in conscious affective experience. But when he says that love is union, he has, like most others who write on love, assumed the validity of his insight which singles out some element in the total experience of love as his basic notion. It fits very well with his whole understanding of the human condition and with his understanding of what we, in that human condition, need in order to be psychologically healthy and happy. He never *establishes* that love, properly speaking, *is* union, nor ever provides a coherent exposition of what the union is which is love. But, on the other hand, who has done so? Perhaps what is to be done now in this descriptive analysis will be no more successful than Fromm or others. But let us try.

A Test Question Concerning Union

In order to guard against the mistake that plagues the history of thought on love, the confusion of love with its consequences, it might be well to begin our inspection of radical love as union by setting up one way of testing any union to see whether it is love or whether it is a consequence of love. Can the proposed union be sacrificed for the sake of the loved one? The answer to this question may not tell us with certainty what the union of love is, but it will enable us to eliminate many specious claimants. The sign of union which is fundamental love is that it cannot be sacrificed here and now as an expression of the love. I say here and now, because one might even out of love decide to stop loving in the future; but that very act here and now arises from and expresses a present union of love. Any of the unions that follow on love as its consequences can be sacrificed precisely on account of love. One may sacrifice physical union because of love, as when one leaves a loved one for the sake of doing a service or refrains from sexual union out of consideration for the beloved's well-being. Radical love may force the lover to sacrifice union of other affections with the loved one's when convinced that the loved one desires what would be harmful (to the loved one) or fears for what is necessary for the preservation of life or fulfilment as a person: only think of a father whose friend or son is embarking on a career of crime. Even the union which comes of the beloved knowing the lover and returning the love can in certain situations be sacrificed out of love: think of a mother who discovers a lost child now grown up happily in another's family with no knowledge of the mishap and whose life would be completely disrupted by learning the truth. So with other forms of union which follow on love or conduce to love but are not love. What could lead our thinking astray in this matter is the fact that the *tendency* to these forms of union cannot be sacrificed. The lover will always have a spontaneous tendency toward them. Love itself, however, will render the tendency a mere velleity if the beloved's well-being demands it.

The Fact of Union

A first approach to the union that is love can be made from the side of some obvious and characteristic elements in the total concrete experience of love that point to it as a fact because they cannot be understood without it. They not only point to it but, when studied closely, reveal it as their conscious ground. We are not forced at this point to posit some hypothetical factor that is not in consciousness. The union spoken of is conscious, an aspect of love as a lived experience prior to reflection; but it is so deep and undefined that we can only bring our reflective attention to bear on it with the greatest difficulty.

Some radical affective union with the loved one is required by experience and can be noted in careful reflection on experience as grounding the lover's sense of increased fulness of being (whether accompanied by joy or sorrow, pleasure or pain) according to the measure of the love. Such union is vaguely seen as the ground of the lover's participation in the loved one's thoughts, emotions, moods, deeds, suffering, success, failure; for these are experienced as the lover's own by as much as one loves. So also with the care which the lover has for the loved one as for one's own self, as if one's being and life were the lover's. So also with the consequent tendency to action for the sake of the loved one, which springs from care. Even the tendency to further union in all the ways in which the lover seeks union with the loved one is a tendency much like the tendency to unify one's own being and life: a tendency to more fully unify what is already one but not as fully and intensely one as is possible. All these elements in the full experience of love reveal radical love as a radical union that grounds them all and yet is distinct from them all.

Union As Presence

If we try to say more accurately what is the nature of the union that is radical love, the aspect of *presence* readily offers itself: the lover is present to the loved one and has the loved one present to oneself. And this is so by love itself, not merely as a consequence of love. There are modes of presence that one who loves seeks to effect, but love itself *is* a being present to the beloved and a having the beloved present to the lover. This is so even when one loves another without the other returning the love. There is no implication here of mutual love, but only a noting of two inseparable sides of one reality, the reality of the presential union which is love. This point must be kept in mind and will be clarified in our discussion of the ways of presence.

What is presence ? The least that can be said of presence is that it is a being-with, a co-existing. However, to say that love as presence is a being-with, is true but not very helpful unless the modes of being with another are specified. For there is a scale of meanings to be attached to the word presence. In fact, to say without any further elucidation that to love is to-be-present-to or to-be-with could be misleading insofar as such a way of speaking could be taken to imply that without love there is no presence to or being-with. The truth is that to-be is to-be-with and as being is fuller so also is presence fuller— or, perhaps, it is more accurate to say that as presence is fuller, being is fuller. So, to get the significance of loving presence it will be necessary to run up the ascending scale of presence. There is no pretension to doing more here than giving some principal forms of presence in order to bring out its meaning for fundamental love.

At the bottom of the scale we can put mere physical presence, presence by spatial-temporal proximity, a being-there-with or here-with. In this way one is present to another when one is in the same room with another but without being aware of the other. The other may even be touching but doing so without attention to or affective response to the other.

Clearly the presence constituted by cognition and affection is a fuller mode of presence, with or without physical presence. Cognitive presence comes to be with any awareness of the other whether by perception, memory, or thought. It increases with fuller knowledge of or with more concentrated attention to the object. Within the field of consciousness an object may be on the outmost fringes where things are hardly real to us, where the object just barely enters cognitional presence; or it may be the center of attention where things are intensely real to us or anywhere in between.

By affective response to the object, a mode of presence is achieved that surpasses not only physical but also merely cognitive presence though as a conscious act it presupposes cognitive presence as a condition for its possibility and even includes it. That there is fuller presence with affective response can readily be seen if we only look at the experience of presence with one who is physically present and attended to but not responded to affectively and compare that with the experience of presence with one to whom we do respond affectively, even if the latter is physically absent and less known than the other. For instance, you may be in a group and become aware of someone you don't know but be quite uninterested, altogether indifferent. Or the thought of someone you know who is physically absent may pass through your mind without a flicker of affective response. In either of these cases, you are certainly not present with either one in as full a sense as you are when there is a deep affective response, even if the affective response is a negative one, hate or fear or anger; for then your very being is more completely present to the other, more wholly with the other.

To speak of cognitive and affective presence as being-with does not, however, express its inwardness with adequate force or clarity. By knowledge and love the knower and lover is *in* the object. Such presence is a *being-in* as well as a being-with. It is a *presence-in* as well as a presence-to. Borrowing a striking verbal form from Dante, when I know or love you, I "in-you me" (*Paradiso*, Canto 9, lines 80-81).

And it must be added, I "in-me you." For there is a two-fold in-being established, an interpenetration of distinct persons. In knowledge or in love, the reality known or loved is in the mind or affectivity of the subject and the mind or affectivity of the subject is yielded to that reality. Each is in the other, each present in the other. The two-fold in-being is one union with two sides, not two unions, and is constituted by the one act, not requiring two acts of one agent nor reciprocal acts of two agents. If I "in-you me" by knowledge and love, at the same time and in the same act I necessarily in that very act "in-me you"; and conversely, if I "in-me you," I necessarily in that very act "in-you me." Although these are two sides of one union, it is necessary to insist that presence in each other does not mean presence in each other in the same way. That occurs only when there is mutual knowledge and love. To be present as known and loved is not the same as to be present as knower and lover, even though being known and loved is a being-in the knower and lover, and knowing and loving a being-in the known and loved. To fail to see the double but different presence of subject and object in one-directional knowledge or love closes off any vision of the fulness of union and presence when knowledge and love are reciprocal and the two-fold inward presence is doubled. (Speaking in a metaphysical context rather than in a psychological one, Thomas makes the point in response to those who argue that God is not in creatures because creatures are not in God: "It must be said that although bodily realities are said to be in something as in a container, spiritual realities contain those things in which they are, as the soul contains the body. So also God is in things as containing them" (trans. of ST 1, q. 8, a. 1, reply to obj. 2).)

We are all impeded in seeing the full reality of inward presence by our natural tendency to spatial meanings of "in" and "outside" or "contained in." These cannot apply at this level of reality. At this level I am in that which is in me, and contained in that which contains me. We interpenetrate without loss of distinction between us. The reality here is so full and many-sided for conceptual knowledge that in philosophical reflection something of it is usually left out. Knowledge is thought of as having the other in the knower without noting that it is also a penetrating of the known. And love can be thought of as ecstatic, being out of self in the beloved, without noting that it is also having the loved in the lover. Or presence is frequently described exclusively or almost exclusively in terms of the knowledge which precedes and makes love possible and of the knowledge that love makes possible, omitting or barely mentioning in passing the presence which is love. Some of those who do discuss the union or presence that is love, alternate between a view of love as presence and a view of love as a tendency to presence or union. For anyone who conceives of love as tendency to union or presence, these will logically have to be constituted by some act other than love itself. The tendency is not itself union or presence. Nevertheless, we frequently find writers who speak of love in both ways with no sign that they are aware of a difficulty. (Gilleman's beautiful chapter on love [1959, ch. 2 of part 2] is marred by this confusion; it must be said that the confusion is derived from the source of his thought, Thomas Aquinas.) Radical love is not a tendency-affection but a *being-affection* by which I *am* in union with, *am* present with the loved one. By being-affection I do not mean a passive inert affection as Ortega y Gasset does when he contrasts "being" sad or joyful to the activity of love (Ortega 1957, 46). Being is active: to be is to perform the act of being, to affirm or posit self in the universe. To affirm self in the universe is not to move or tend: it is the source and goal of tending and movement. So also a being-affection is the source and goal of tendency affection. The being-affection which I call radical love is itself an act of being in union that presupposes a union of knowledge with the loved one and makes possible a deeper union of knowledge. It takes up the union of knowledge into its own reality and surpasses all merely cognitive union by the union which it alone constitutes.

Description of the union constituted by radical love as an affective mutual presence is still ambiguous. Such a description is not proper to love: it can fit other affections, even hatred! One who hates is obviously present with the object of hate by cognitive union. What is more, to hate is to have the hated other in one's affection of hate; and by that affection, one is in the other. But is it not true, at least, that hate is *a principle of disunion* with its object? Perhaps this would distinguish hate from love. Even this cannot be said without qualification. Truly, hate can issue in aversion and so in avoidance of external presence by keeping one's distance and avoidance of inward presence by cutting off thought of the hated one. And it usually issues in disunion of desires, fears, and other affections between the one who hates and the one who is hated. But it can also issue in a tendency to certain types of closer union and presence in order to more effectively cause pain to the one hated. One who hates can even become obsessed with the hated one, so one's whole conscious life is permeated with the latter. One may want in ultimate analysis to be present to the other in order to destroy the other and so effect disunity forever; but one may also want to preserve the other's existence, to preserve one's own hatred, to cause pain without ceasing. Hatred can become a way of life, the meaning of a life that loses its meaning when the object of hate is lost. Thus, being a source of disunity cannot serve adequately to distinguish the presence of hatred from that of love.

What can, however, serve for that purpose is the radically dissonant character of the presence constituted by hatred: the more intense the presence, the worse the affective discord with the reality of its object. Love, by contrast, is a *consonant* presence. If hate is dissonant, this is what we would expect. And this is exactly what we experience. Radical love is experienced as being in accord with the loved one, vibrating as it were, in harmony with the beloved's act of being and so with the whole melody of the beloved's life. It is a welcoming of the loved one into the lover's self and life-world, as fitting there, making a harmony with the lover's being and life. Because it is consonant, harmonious, the presence constituted by love can reach to depths of presence beyond what is possible to hatred, to depths of the lover that would be closed even to the lover if hate rather than love were the affective response, to depths of the beloved that are closed to one who hates.

The consonance or harmony of love must not be confused with the affective harmony that can follow on love: the harmony of desires, joys, fears, sorrows, and so on, between those who love. The latter sort of union is a union of likeness, of conformation, which of itself does not involve loving presence. It can be real even between those who are indifferent to or hate each other radically. For two people who have a common interest but no radical love for each other may still have like hopes, fears, joys or sorrows, with the same objects. Consider, for example, political allies or business associates. In short, it is possible to have consonance of other affections than love without the consonance of radical love, or even to have it with the dissonance of radical hate. So also it is possible to have the consonance of radical love along with dissonance of other affections, as when you, the beloved, desire for yourself what I, the lover, fear because I think it would be destructive of you and bring you misery. When, therefore, conformation of the lover's affections to the beloved's does appear as integrated into the total experience of love, it is not itself a union of presence but only of similitude, which is a consequence flowing from the radical consonant presence that radical love is. The latter is an *act of union,* not merely an act that may or may not be in union with another by conformation or similitude. It is an act by which the lover is in consonance with the loved one's reality as a person, not merely with the loved one's thoughts or affections.

This description of love and hatred as consonant and dissonant affective presence is confirmed by and in turn throws light on what at first glance is a puzzling fact, namely, that hate is psychologically nearer to love than is indifference. A merely logical analysis notes that indifference is only a negation of love, while hate is more than a negation, it is the contrary extreme. But living experience shows hate as psychologically closer to love. Religious teachers, for example, have told us and religious experience has verified their saying that a tepid person is harder to convert to love of God than is a grave sinner. Marriage counselors find that there is sound hope of reviving love between marriage partners who hate each other; but when indifference has set in, reviving love is almost like raising the dead (Lepp 1963, 131, 184). The reason for these surprising facts can be found in the common factor of love and hate which is missing in indifference. Love and hate are both unions by affective presence with their objects; indifference is affective absence. It is easier to change a dissonant presence to a consonant one than to change affective absence to presence. Hatred at least takes its object seriously.

The question occurs whether what has been designated as affective presence is "real." The question has already been answered at least implicitly, I think, by what has been said above; but it is so important that it calls for explicitation. We do find that sometimes union or presence by knowledge and love is spoken of as intentional in contrast with "real union" and "real presence," union and presence by proximity or contact in space and time. (It is surprising to find those who would never knowingly accept the implications of this terminology nevertheless using it; see, e.g., Aquinas, ST 1-2, aa. 1-2.)

Perhaps these modes of union are the only real ones. Perhaps the union we have spoken of as the lover being in the beloved and having the beloved in oneself is only a wish. Proximity and contact are real, but they are not enough to satisfy love, at least intense love. The lover wants to be in the beloved, to have the beloved in oneself, to interpenetrate with the other without loss of either self. Perhaps it is just because we so much want to be in such union that lovers feel as though they *are* by love somehow mysteriously in each other. Is there anything more to the experience of love as mutual in-being? Is it merely a lover's dream expressing a lover's desire?

The root of the difficulty is one we spoke of above. There we noted how our natural drift toward spatial modes of thought set a false limit to the meaning of "in" and so put an obstacle to understanding that realities can be within each other. Uncritical yielding to that drift of human thought can account for accepting what to careful reflection is clearly false, that physical presence is more real than spiritual presence by knowledge and love. As we noted, mere physical proximity or even contact hardly deserves to be called presence without conscious attention and affective response: its reality as personal presence is totally derived from the latter. The ordinary illusion in understanding presence, then, is as a matter of fact quite the contrary of that proposed in the above reduction of affective presence to the lover's dream expressing heart's desire. It is because presence by knowledge and love is not enough to meet the need and the tendency of incarnate spirits, embodied persons, who need physical union as well as spiritual, that we are so readily subject to the drift of spatialized thinking and uncritically fall into the illusion of judging that a needed and wonderfully satisfying but relatively superficial element in the total experience of presence is the "real" as opposed to the deepest and most real elements, i.e., knowledge and love.

Presence by Giving and Accepting

Presence of the lover in the loved and of the loved in the lover seems to involve in some way two other common notions of love, self-giving and the acceptance of the loved one. Both in language expressive of love and in language descriptive of love, in colloquial speech and in learned writing, loving is spoken of as giving self and being loved as being accepted. Are self-giving and accepting the other acts within the total concrete experience of love which are distinct from the act of radical love? If so are they its conditions or its consequences? Or are they only aspects of radical love itself? If so, how are they related with presence and with each other? Before answering these questions, there is a prior question that must be answered. For whether these acts are distinct from radical love or aspects of it we cannot say unless we know what the reality is in our experience to which self-giving and acceptance refer. What can it mean to say that a person gives oneself to another or accepts another?

Consider giving first. This much is obvious—giving is characteristic of love. Love does make lovers give of their possessions to loved ones. Giving in this context means transferring something into the possession of the loved ones for their use or joy. Lovers give in this way according to the measure of their love, their capacity to give, and the benefit that will come to the loved one. Who love little give little of what they have. Who love greatly want to give all they have. But they may have little to give, or the loved one may not receive the offered gifts, or they may understand that what they are inclined to give may only harm the beloved and so they withhold it. Such giving cannot of itself be called self-giving. It can be a sign of self-giving, but not necessarily so. For even those who do not love can give to another what they possess, to fulfil a contract or to gain a favor in return or to maintain self-respect or reputation. And even if the giving does express love, the expression is not the self-giving. The question remains—what is the self-giving and how is it done?

There is another sort of giving that is more likely to be a sign of self-giving and is even a giving *of* self (as distinct from giving self). In this sort of giving the giver shares something of what the give *is*: wisdom, wit, strength, joyfulness. What is shared are the qualities of the lover's own being. These are expressed in one's acts and communicated to the other's own being to enrich the other's life. The lover communicates the lover's own joy, tranquillity, courage to the loved one. Or it can be that the lover's qualities are put at the service of the loved one. Thus you may use your bodily strength to earn a living for your family or endures pain courageously in defense of your country. Since there is here a giving *of* self, i.e., of what self is in qualified ways, we could easily think that such giving constitutes the self-giving of love. But such giving is not giving self simply, and it is not love. That sharing one's wit and wisdom and strength and so on with the other is not itself love is evident from the fact that just as we can give our external possessions with or without love so also we can share in this way with or without radical love for the one with whom we share. We all find ourselves doing this for the sake of praise or gain or living up to our own self image. If then it is done with radical love for the other, it is still only an implementation or expression of radical love.

This expression of love along with and usually even more than the giving of possessions points to the truth of the insight which arises in the lived experience of loving and being loved, namely, that to love others in and for themselves is in some way to give self to them. Whatever may constitute the act of self-giving, however it is done, it is implied by the giving which expresses love. Giving self explains why lovers, according to the measure of their love for the other and according to the circumstances of the situation, tend to give of their possessions and of themselves without concern for their own gain or satisfaction. The beloved's gain or satisfaction is to them as their own. Further, radical love as self-giving is implied by several otherwise very strange ways that we have of responding to objects which are gifts. In certain situations, the acceptance or rejection of a gift meant to express love is, without any reflection, felt as an acceptance or rejection of the giver's self. This is not so when the giver is only giving a payment or a bribe. A gift accepted is often treated with reverence and tenderness as one would the person who gave it: somehow, the implication is, the person is in the gift. And this is implied also in the joy with which a gift can be accepted when that which is given has in itself no value at all to the receiver.

Let it be clear what has emerged so far. We have not yet succeeded in saying what it means to give self as distinct from giving one's possessions or giving what is *of* self, that is, sharing one's own joy, wisdom, courage, etc. Certainly when these ways of giving are expressions of love, self is given. But what does it mean to say that? What is the self-giving which is manifested in these acts but which can be without them even as they can be without it? So far we have only been able to see that there is a self-giving underlying and distinct from these expressions. Nevertheless, just to know the fact, even without understanding it as yet, is already of value. For to see radical love under the aspect of self-giving throws light on the aspect of love we have already seen, love as a union of personal presence by mutual in-being. This is what we might expect, if both self-giving and presence are aspects of the one affective response, that they would throw light on each other. To understand love as a gift of self fills out the meaning of love as being-in the loved one. Nevertheless being-in does not by itself bring out what we previously noted in the experience, that the lover is in the loved by an *act,* the act of giving self. And so we see also that by this act the lover is in the beloved as a gift to the beloved. Dante's phrase could not be better to express the active aspect of the experience: I "in-you myself." But this does not by itself express the further truth, that I "in-you myself" as a gift, that the "in-youing" is a gift-giving. Radical love is an act by which the lover is constituted gift.

Conversely, what we have established about love as giving self to the beloved is confirmed and even deepened and clarified by love as presence in the loved one. For the giving that is love is not merely a giving to someone for the other to possess and use. The giving that is an act of radical love is a giving *into,* so that by it the gift is *in* the loved. Neither is it a giving into someone a gift other than myself as a symbol of myself and my love. It is not even a giving into the beloved something *of* self. It is a giving *self,* for it is myself who am in the loved one by my love, not merely my possessions or even my thoughts, my wit, my joy, my wisdom, my strength. It is I myself.

It would be a serious mistake and one we could easily fall into here to think of this self-giving as that which terminates in presence so that the giving is preliminary to presence and ends when the presence, the in-being, is achieved. In this way of thinking the self-giving looks forward to presence and presence looks back to self-giving. But if so, then both cannot be radical love: either love is the presence and giving self the condition for it, or giving self is the love and presence a consequence. If the latter is the case, then we are back with a love that is a movement, a process or tending, with all the insuperable objections to that notion. If presence is love and self-giving is a condition, then we could have self-giving which is not love and radical love which is not self-giving. Both of these conclusions are in conflict with our experience of love.

What is needed is an understanding of love as giving freed from the false connotations that cling to it by reason of our more superficial modes of giving, the modes that are more obvious, more easily described, and in terms of which we almost always understand self-giving. In these modes of giving, some sort of movement is involved, some sort of process with successive moments (even if continuous), tending toward and terminating in the one to whom something is given. Something belonging to the giver is transferred to the receiver. Even if what is given is of the giver's self, e.g., my knowledge, there is the process of communicating through speech, gesture, facial expression, etc. Only when the process is terminated is there really anything given. And as soon as there is something given, the giving of that which is given ceases. The one giving can continue to give more, even more of the same, but I cannot give what has been given.

The giving that is radical love, the giving self, is very different. It is an act by which lovers in their very reality as persons are constituted gifts from the very first instant of loving and at every instant thereafter. There is no connotation of movement toward completion of the act, at which point the lover's self could first be said to be given: radical love is from its inception an accomplished giving by which self is a gift given. The act can continue. It can grow into greater love and so to a fuller, more intense self-giving. But, according to the measure of the love, the giving at any instant is an accomplished fact. The lover is already gift, not merely in process of becoming the gift. With this understanding of giving, there is no conflict between self-giving and actual presence by in-being as different aspects of one and the same act of radical love.

In the light of the foregoing examination of giving, it will be relatively easy to speak about radical love as accepting. Radical love as accepting the loved will leave us with problems even as giving does, and these will be noted in a moment. But we can quickly get as far with describing accepting that is radical love as we were able to go with giving. First of all, the accepting that is radical love is not an accepting of what others have nor even an accepting merely of the others' qualities expressed and communicated in action. It is an accepting of them in their actuality as personal beings. Second, the accepting that is radical love is not a movement during which the beloved has not yet been accepted but is in process of being accepted into the lover. If that were so, the accepting would cease when love begins or love would end when the loved is accepted. Accepting by love is from its inception and at every instant an accomplished acceptance. Finally, love as accepting and love as presence confirm and illuminate each other. Accepting the beloved makes explicit that the latter is present in the lover by the lover's own act. To use Dante's phrase again, by love I "in-me you." So the beloved is not just present in me, but is in me as interiorized to me by my act of accepting the beloved. On the other hand, the beloved's being-in the lover shows that the latter's accepting is an accepting of the beloved *into* the lover's self, accepting the beloved's very self, not merely what is of that self. For it is the beloved who is present in the lover, not just something from or of the beloved.

Union As Affective Identification

So profound is the mutual in-being, the self-giving and acceptance, by radical love that when we let the evidence within the total concrete experience of love lead us where it will, we find ourselves led to look for some kind of identification between the lover and the loved one in order to make the whole experience intelligible. In some way the lover *is* the loved.

Before attempting to show what there is in the total experience of love that points to a radical affective identification of the lover with the loved, it will be advisable to note and remove two likely mental blocks to recognizing the reality we are talking about. Some refuse to think of love in terms of identification because the sort of identification they think of involves an irrational subjection of the lover's self to the loved or an irrational domination of the loved by the lover. Identification in this meaning involves a diminishment of the distinct, individual, personalities. It is for this reason that Gabriel Madinier says it flows from "objectivistic thinking" and excludes it from love (Madinier 1938, 93-98). Hasty repudiation of identification without any qualification closes off one of the deepest aspects of radical love and leaves other elements of the total experience unexplainable. As we shall see, affective identification need not assume irrational forms and instead of diminishing the uniqueness of the lover and the loved, it accentuates and increases it.

Again, it would lead to grave misunderstanding if the reader should not distinguish affective identification as used here from the psychoanalytic usage that refers to an unconscious mechanism influencing one to pattern oneself after another. One can identify with another in the psychoanalytical sense out of fear and jealousy without any fundamental love for the one identified with and certainly without that experience which is the sign of affective identification as it is meant here.

Leaving aside, then, any misleading preconceptions about the meaning of identification, there are two main steps to be taken toward a positive showing of its reality as an aspect of radical love. First, it is necessary to point out and clarify the more obvious experience which is a sign of identification because it demands the latter for its intelligibility. Second, the nature of this identification must be brought to light so far as it can be.

This is the sign that directs our attention to radical love as an affective identification with the loved one; one who loves another with radical love consciously participates in the life of the loved one in the sense of experiencing the other's life as one's own, and this experience is proportioned to the intensity of the love. Before describing the experience of participation in another's life, let us first of all be clear what is meant by "life" in this context. I do not wish to mean merely a state of being, a mode of existence. Rather I refer to the activities and the sufferings of living beings, to their actions and passions, to whatever they do and whatever happens to them and in them. So, by participation in another's life I mean participation in another's thoughts, affections, suffering, choices, deeds, in another's successes and failures, good and evil fortunes, and so on.

Now what is meant by participation? First of all let us be clear what it is not. This participation in the loved one's life on which we are focusing is not just a sort of knowledge; it is not even just knowledge from within, such as might be had by an all-knowing but uninvolved spectator or such as can be attained to some slight degree by anyone with intuitive and imaginative power. Some are able to a degree to enter into another's mind and see things from another's point of view, to understand another's pain or pleasure, joy or sorrow, fear or desire. Anyone can, for instance, on the basis of oral past experience, project oneself by an act of the mind into the other's thoughts and feelings as a parallel of one's own. Or one can bracket one's own attitudes and beliefs and by an effort of the imagination put oneself into the other's shoes: if I believed thus and so, as you do, and if I were in this or that situation which you are in, this is the way I would think or feel. Such knowledge is a sort of participation in your life, but it is certainly not a participation in your life *as mine* in yours. Therefore, it does not require any affective identification by radical love with the one known. A diplomat trying to out-guess an opponent, a detective trying to reconstruct a crime, can do this, and sometimes understand what is going on in the other's mind and heart more accurately than someone else who loves that other.

If participation in the other's life by knowledge alone does not require affective identification as its ground, neither does conformity or similitude of affections that can follow on such knowledge and can in turn deepen it. To have like desires and fears, joys and sorrows, is usually a consequence of radical love; but it can be without radical love and without any sharing of the other's life *as mine.* Such knowledge and affection, therefore, even when it is rooted in radical love, may suggest but does not necessarily direct attention to the aspect of radical love that I have called affective identification. If the participation we are talking about is not merely knowledge of the other's life nor the resonance of the lover's affections with those of the beloved, what is it? Perhaps Buber's description of what he calls "inclusion" *(Umfassung)* will help.

> Its elements are, first, a relation, of no matter what kind, between two persons, second, an event experienced by them in common, in which at least one of them actively participates, and third, the fact that this one person without forfeiting any of the felt reality of his or her activity, at the same time lives through the common event from the standpoint of the other (Buber 1955, 97).

To live through the common event from the other's side is not necessarily to live through the other's side of it as mine. Even if it should mean this, inclusion is only a small part of what I am pointing to as conscious participation in the other's life. Buber's inclusion is described in terms of a common event in which at least one participant is active and the other receptive of the action. The active one experiences the event from the side of the receptive one as well as from the active one's own side. The examples Buber gives are all of this sort: he speaks of one man striking another, a man caressing a woman, a teacher instructing a pupil, a doctor healing a patient (Buber 1955, 96, 98-101). It is the man, the teacher, the doctor, who experiences the inclusion. I am concerned with a realm of experience which includes what Buber calls inclusion but also goes beyond it to include experiences that can arise independently of a common event in which one acts upon the other and experiences one's own action from the other's side. In the experience I am talking about the loved one could be active and the lover who participates be passive. The lover could be the pupil, the patient, the recipient of caresses. Or the loved one could be acting on someone other than the lover so that there is no common event in Buber's sense at all.

Further, if Maurice Friedman's interpretation of Buber's inclusion is correct, then I would have to disagree very strongly with Buber on one point. Friedman says, "Experiencing the other side is the essence of all genuine love (Friedman 1955, 88). As I have stressed above, this conscious participation in the life of the other, including this experience of a common event from the other side, is most certainly not the essence of radical love. It is a consequence and a sign of radical love. One might say it is essential to the total concrete experience of love necessarily following on radical love. Whether Buber would agree to this distinction depends on what love itself means to him. This is never very clear. (Perhaps D'Arcy [1956, 230] was correct in what at first hearing is a very surprising statement: "Buber, despite the many imaginative and fascinating things he has to say, tells us very little about the nature of love.")

In his treatise on friendship in the *Nicomachean Ethics* Aristotle points out an experience of participation in the friend's life that is broader than Buber's inclusion and that is a consequence rather than an essential note of love for the friend. In doing so, he touches on a characteristic of the experience which Buber does not, namely, that the lover experiences the loved one's life not only from the other side but experiences it as the lover's own. This aspect of the experience, which may not have been important in the context of Buber's discussion, is crucial in Aristotle's context where he is asking whether friendship is necessary for happiness. Despite the fact that such participation is crucial to Aristotle's argument, the *Nicomachean Ethics* touches only lightly and briefly on the experience to which I am referring. A hurried reader could pass it by without getting the point at all. He seems to be assuming its reality and implies the nature of it rather than explicates it. What he says, however, is clear and penetrating when read carefully.

He is responding to the question whether friends are necessary for the happiness of a good person, and his argument runs in this vein (NE 9, 9). Life is activity; for us persons, life is human activity, activity of moral virtue and especially of thought. To be aware of our acts and to be aware of them as our own is pleasant. But we can contemplate another's activity better than our own; and when the activities we contemplate are those of a friend, then they are that friend's own. The meaning is that life is doubled by love for the friend: I can be aware of my friend's life and the friend's life can in some real way be mine. This interpretation is confirmed by Aristotle's conclusion that one needs to live with one's friend, sharing the friend's thoughts, and so come to participate in the other's existence (NE 1170b 11-13).

One reservation and one addition to Aristotle's observations are necessary. Aristotle is talking about friendship. Friendship involves mutual love. Thus, the lover Aristotle is talking about is experiencing the life of the one who loves that lover. In our discussion we are restricting attention to a unilateral love. Nevertheless, what Aristotle finds within the context of friendship can be found to some extent (not as perfectly) in any experience of radical love, however minimal, i.e., a conscious sharing of the loved one's life with an awareness of the loved one's life as the lover's own. Whether it occurs in reciprocal love of friendship or in unilateral love, there is an aspect of this participation that Aristotle does not stress but which is of crucial importance. To say that I experience the other's life as mine without immediately adding that the experience is of the beloved's life as the *other's life* leaves us in danger of falsifying the whole experience. For without both aspects held firmly together, the essential character of the experience escapes us and becomes confused with affective absorption by submission or domination. The experience we are talking about is of the other's life as the lover's own without it ceasing to be experienced as the other's. It is the other's life, your life, that I experience as my life when I love you.

The point I am making here can be easily seen in those experiences in which a loved one's success is more satisfying than the same success for self. If I did not experience my loved one's success as mine it would not be a participation in your life; if I did not experience it as yours it would be impossible for me to find more satisfaction in your success than my own. Even when I do not find more joy or sorrow in the other's good or evil fortune than in my own, there is still this double aspect to the experience of participation in your life. It is your life which is mine. If your life were not experienced as yours, in you and for you, the experience would cease to enrich my life in the way that it does. If I repeat and insist upon this double aspect of the experience to the point of tedium, that is because it is the most revealing sign of the nature of radical love. It leads to seeing into the very heart of love. In this experience I am neither projecting my life into the other and so at root loving myself in you, nor am I so introjecting your life into me as to lose hold on my own distinct and unique self-identity. In fact, when the loved one's life as the loved one's own, as your own, is experienced as mine I become both more keenly alive to my own distinct and unique self and more keenly and reverently alive to you, the other, in your distinct and unique otherness. For this is the very puzzling but clearly observable fact, that not only is participation in the beloved's life, as described, in direct ratio to the intensity and purity of radical love, but so also is the realization of the distinct and unique personal reality of both the loved and the lover.

It is this participation we have just described that requires some sort of identification of the lover with the beloved in order to explain it and that points to radical love as the act that constitutes the identification. If the beloved's life—your acts and suffering, your joys and sorrows, triumphs and failures—are to me as my own, then there must be a conscious affective identification with the beloved as a person. This is confirmed when we note that the increase or decrease of radical love in intensity and in purity gives rise to increased or decreased participation in the beloved's life. Once attention is thus focused by the logical implication of participation we then understand what was already confusedly in our lived-experience, namely, that radical love for the other is the ground of the experience and is itself an affective identification with the other at a deeper level than that of the other's thoughts or affections or activities or sufferings. It is an identification with the personal center of your reality, with your personal being, realized and revealed in all your thoughts and affections and actions. Such affective identification can also be thought of as a participation, but a participation in your very act of personal being as distinct from the actions and passions in which your being is realized in particular ways and which constitute your life. It is because affectively I am the other person—because I am you—that when I am aware of your action or suffering, your success or failure precisely as yours, they are as my own.

It is easy to find scattered in profusion through literature expressions which imply such affective identification. Sometimes it becomes explicit, as in the following striking passage from Emily Brontë's *Wuthering Heights*. Catherine is speaking of Heathcliff.

I cannot express it but surely you and everybody have a notion that is or should be an existence of yours beyond you. What were the use of my creation, if I were entirely contained here? My great miseries in this world have been Heathcliff's miseries, and I watched and felt each from the beginning: my great thought in living is himself. If all else perished and he remained, I should still continue to be; and if all else remained, and he were annihilated, the universe would turn into a mighty stranger: I should not seem a part of it. My love for Linton is like the foliage in the woods: time will change it, I'm well aware as winter changes the trees. My love for Heathcliff resembles the eternal rocks beneath; a source of little visible delight, but necessary. Nelly, I am Heathcliff! He's always, always in my mind: not as a pleasure, any more than I am always a pleasure to myself, but as my own being. So don't talk of our separation again (Brontë 1963, 73-74).

While certain scriptural expressions are to be understood as referring to a union even deeper than the affective identification we are considering, they include this and powerfully illustrate it. Thus, Jesus, when speaking about the last judgment, says of those who have been kind to whom they encounter: "I was hungry and you gave me to eat; I was thirsty and you gave me to drink; I was a stranger and you took me in…" (Matthew 25:35ff). And to Saul, who was persecuting the Christians, Jesus says on the road to Damascus, "I am Jesus, whom you are persecuting" (Acts of the Apostles 9:5). And Saul after his conversion into Paul exclaims: "For me to live is Christ" (Philippians 1:21). There is a surprising reversal of viewpoint in a passage from Augustine's *Confessions,* where he shows that not only is the beloved's life experienced as the lover's but the lover experiences the lover's own life as the beloved's. Augustine is speaking about the dearest friend of his youth and how he felt after that friend's death.

And since I was his other self, I wondered the more that I could go on living when he was dead. The half of my soul—well has someone said this of his friend. For I felt my soul and his to have been one soul in two bodies. And therefore I dreaded life because I did not want to live mutilated. And therefore perhaps I dreaded death, lest the one I greatly loved should die entirely (trans. of Augustine 1962, lib. iv, cap. 6, BA, XIII, 426).

If the experience of participation leads us to perceive the depths of union reached in radical love, the direct ratio between the intensity in radical love and realization of distinction between lover and loved sets the limit. And if we wish to state in condensed form a conclusion to which these two observations lead us, it is this: in radical love, the lover is the loved as other and is more fully oneself.

Some Unanswered Questions

How can this be? We can cast light on the paradoxical experience by saying that it reveals a person as relational. As a person I am by relation to other persons and am actualized in my conscious life by radical love for other persons. Therefore, the more I enter into union, i.e., affective identity, with other persons, the more I am myself. Valuable as this insight is, it does not provide any deeper insight into what a person does when loving. Granted that as a person I am actualized in my own unique self by the response of radical love that constitutes me as a gift given into the beloved so intimately as to be affectively identified with the other, the question remains: *how is* this done? What do I do when I love by which I constitute this union with the other person?

Perhaps we cannot answer this question. Perhaps we have now touched on the mystery and can only say that love is that act in response to another's personal actuality which constitutes the lover in the relation we have described. But let us at least be aware of the question and not think we have answered it. To call it a mystery instead of a problem is significant but leaves the question unanswered. We saw above how spatial modes of thinking can create false problems. It can also blind us to the real problems we have to face. That could be the case here. Spatially, one being is present to another in the sense of near to or in another or having another in it merely by position. The food in my mouth or in my stomach is in me by reason of a prior act of transferring it from the plate to my mouth or of swallowing it. Being there in me is the result of the act, and the act ceases when the result is attained. Cognitive and affective presence, which transcend space, are constituted by the acts of knowing and loving and are actual only so long as these acts endure. Now, we can note in reflection on our lived experience that the lover is by love affectively present to the loved one without yet understanding with any clarity *how* this is, without understanding what the act of love is that constitutes this presence—just as we can note that the knower is somehow present to the known without yet understanding how this happens, without understanding what knowledge is that it can constitute such presence. We are saying something about the act of radical love when we observe the fact that it is experienced as an *act of self-giving* and an act of accepting the loved one and know what these mean: We are saying something deeper yet when we observe the fact that it is experienced as an *act of affective identification* and give that some meaning. Can we go any further and see into this act deeply enough to understand *how* it constitutes the lover and loved as mutually present, how it constitutes the lover as a gift to the beloved and the beloved as accepted into the lover, how it constitutes even an affective identification?

There is another problem. For we want to understand not only how each one of these relationships is constituted by the act of radical love but also how all of these can be aspects of one and the same act. The resolution of this second problem seems to lie in the first. If we could describe what the act is in itself which constitutes such relations between lover and loved, we could, very likely, by that very fact see how it can be both giving and accepting, both a being in the beloved and having the beloved in the lover. As yet, we are not in a position to resolve these problems. Before pressing our investigation further, it will be well to state the second problem in more detail and show the genuine difficulties involved.

When discussing presence as mutual in-being, objections to the possibility of this based on spatial modes of thinking were said to be irrelevant. This allowed the fact of experience to stand without error or confusion. But it did not offer any understanding of the fact. What is the act of radical love that is not merely unitive in the sense of conducing to a mutual in-being as a result of the act but in the sense of actually constituting that union? What do I do when I love, by which in one and the same act I am in the loved one and the loved one in me?

Again, we saw that, while the giving that is a consequence of and a revelation of self-giving is observable and is easy to describe, this is not so for the self-giving. Therefore, we readily tend to be satisfied with explaining the self-giving only in terms of the easily understandable sort of giving. For ordinary practical purposes, this is necessary and satisfactory. For something of what self-giving is shows in the acts that are its consequences. But if we look for a description of the act in itself rather than in its consequences, what can we say? It is understandable that this question should be left without any definite answer or not even raised in discussions on love. Nothing we have uncovered so far enables us to do more than point out the reality of the self-giving that underlies the other forms of giving and is distinct from them. What the act of giving self is, how anyone can give one's very self to another—if this question can be answered at all, it cannot be answered without a deeper penetration of radical love than we have as yet made.

The same must be said about love as accepting the loved one. It is not difficult to say what is meant by accepting an object offered to me. Neither is it difficult to say what is meant by accepting another's thoughts, hopes, ways of acting, and so on. I can agree with your thoughts or find them interesting, I can concur in your hopes, I can approve of your ways of acting. But what do I do when I accept *you?* Is it that I approve of your being or am pleased that you are? This does seem to carry something of what happens in radical love. But it is hard to see how approving your being or being pleased with it expresses the flaming, powerful energy of intense love or how it constitutes a mutual presence of in-being or is really a giving self to the other. Neither does it explain why radical love necessarily has such consequences as tending to give the lover's possessions to the loved one or to share with the loved one the lover's wisdom, strength, humor, etc., or to resonate with the loved one's desires, fears, joys and sorrows.

Finally, there is the puzzling fact of both giving self and accepting the other as aspects of one act. *Prima facie,* accepting seems to be the correlative of giving from the side of the one to whom a gift is given. Nevertheless it is the lover, the giver of self, not the beloved, who is said to accept; love is said to be an acceptance of the beloved. If giving and accepting were merely accompaniments of one another, really distinct acts in a complex experience, or if one were a consequence of the other, there would be less to puzzle us here. But if one and the same act under different aspects is both giving self and accepting the other, then radical love is an act which in the very giving accepts and in the very accepting gives. What can that act be? Or to put it more strongly, we are looking for an act in which we give by accepting and accept by giving, in which giving is accepting and accepting is giving. This is a very odd thing to say. Nevertheless it is what we have to say about radical love unless we are to question the validity of experience on the basis of a conceptual opposition.

I have heard this difficulty explained by analogy with shaking hands. If I shake hands with you, it is said, I cannot give my hand to you for the act without accepting your hand in the very giving of mine. To a point this is indeed a helpful analogy, but only to a point. And that point is by no means at the depth we are searching. Let us suppose for the moment that there is an accurate parallel between the giving and accepting aspects of shaking hands and those of loving radically. We still have to ask what is the act of love which has these parallel aspects? The parallel suggests how it is possible to have these two aspects in some one act, but it says nothing about what the act is. I can describe the act of giving my hand and accepting yours in the handclasp. But what can I say about the act of love that is analogous to this? Further, even if we could describe the love would it parallel shaking hands? Shaking hands is a mutual act in which each of us gives our hand to the other and accepts the other's given to oneself. If you do not give your hand to me, I cannot accept or give. There is no handshake. Do you have to give yourself to me and accept me in a return of love in order to make possible my love for you, just as you have to give me your hand and accept mine to make a handshake possible? Does love also have to be mutual in order to be? There are some who think so (Guitton 1951, 80; Nédoncelle 1966, 19, 92, 138, 176; Johann 1955, 36-38). The reasons offered are far from convincing; but there is no need to settle the issue here. For, even if that opinion should be right, the problem we are discussing would remain: what is the act of love by which each of us at one and the same time gives self and accepts the other's gift of self?

7
RADICAL LOVE AS AFFIRMATION

To make a start toward answering the questions just raised, let us
return to that element in the total concrete experience of love that
was said to be the most revealing sign of the nature of radical love
and that led us to see radical love as an identification with the loved
one. I refer to the experience of my loved one's life as my own. If the
other's life is to me as mine precisely because it is yours and I love
you, then by love I am affectively related to you as I am affectively
related to myself. Now, at the root of all my self-regarding affections
I find an affective affirmation of self. This is not to be confused with
the self-affirmation which is my act of being, not even with this as it
is conscious. The two will be distinguished at length further on; for
now it is sufficient to say that the affective affirmation of myself that
roots all my affirmative self-regarding affections is a reflexive response
to my actuality, to my act of being. All my self-regarding desires,
hopes, joys, sorrows, fears, presuppose, and include a basic affirmative affective response to myself. This is what accounts for the fact
that I desire what will fulfil me, rejoice over my own well-being,
sorrow over my loss of well-being, hate and fear what threatens it. If
I had only a negative affective attitude towards self or were indifferent, none of these other self-regarding affections could be intelligible. Therefore to experience your joys and sorrows, fears, desires,
and so on as my own precisely because they are yours, means that
this basic affirmative response to myself has been, in this act of love,
transformed into an affective affirmation of you, so that affectively
you are to me as I am to myself. Note well that I do *not* affirm you *as
myself*, that is, as an extension or projection of myself, your personal
reality absorbed by mine or mine by yours. I affirm you *as I affirm
myself*.

The relation can be expressed another way from the side of the
loved one's self-affirmation, of your self-affirmation. If I am by love
so identified with you that I experience your affections as mine just
because they are yours, then by love I am affectively related to you *as
he is to himself*. At the root of your affective life, you affirms yourself,
and this affirmation grounds all your self-regarding affections. In the
act of radical love I affirm you as you affirms yourself, making you
the term of the basic affirmation by which I affirm myself. And so

my act of affirmation is one with your act of self-affirmation; in some sense, it is yours (even though you are not conscious of it) and it is mine.

To say that in radical love of the other I affirm you as I affirm myself at the root of my affective life or as you affirm yourself, does not mean that I always affirm you in the same full measure that I affirm myself or you affirm yourself. There are endless degrees of affirming self or the other, from the minimal to the highest. Ordinarily we find that affective self-affirmation supersedes affective affirmation of the other. But it does appear to happen on occasion that one affirms God or some human person more than one does oneself. When radical love is intense enough the lover's affirmation can be so completely given over to the beloved as to affirm the latter's being at the cost of the lover's own, not only at the cost of one's being in this world, but one's being simply. Some of us believe that persons are immortal and will never cease to be. One who believes this can so love that one would be willing to sacrifice one's total being, even for eternity as well as for time for the loved one if it were needed and possible. That such a subjunctive mode of affective affirmation can be genuine is confirmed by the fact that some who do not believe in life after death are still willing to die for their loved ones. This is not exactly the same since it would be harder to sacrifice an eternity of bliss than to sacrifice a few years of life in this world. But the latter shows a willingness to give all of life.

In a very true sense, but one which requires careful understanding, lovers do yield, surrender, their own acts of self-affirmation to the beloved to be an affirmation of the latter. The surrender of self as available for service, the surrender in sexual love, and so on, should not be confused with this far more basic act of giving self in the yielding of one's act of self-affirmation. The latter is the essential act of love; without it there is no love. The other modes of yielding or surrendering are expressions of it and not essential to love. This surrender in radical love is what involves some denial of self as the correlative of affirming the other. That is why many try to say what love is in negative terms: love, they say, is self-forgetfulness, a negation of self. And this is also what frightens many from trying to love others. There is a problem here with serious consequences. Do I have to make a choice between loving myself and loving others? Even if I want to love others instead of self, is it possible to escape self-love?' If it is possible, is it really desirable? Do we not find that those who fail to love themselves fail to love anyone else? Do they not in fact become more harmful to others than people who love themselves even unreasonably? All manner of serious questions can arise here once we set up an opposition between loving self and loving others; these questions have profound and extensive implications both morally and psychologically. (The reader who is concerned with the problem tentatively bracketed above, whether we can justifiably speak of self-love, will pardon the use of the term in the following few paragraphs. The present problem is so commonly discussed in terms of self-love that the point might be obscured by the use of some non-committal substitute for self-love.)

The practical implications of these questions for moral guidance and clinical psychology are not our concern now. But the answers to these questions also bear on the nature of love. The problems raised can be readily solved if we clearly distinguish two meanings of self and two corresponding meanings of self-love and self-denial. If by self is meant the egocentric self, the self who is only for self and not for others, the self who sees any giving to others as a loss to self, who sees all things ultimately as for self alone, this self gives rise to a self-ish self-love. The denial of this self and this self-love is really a cor-relative of radical love for others. One cannot love self in this way and still love others with radical love. The lover has to make a choice between self or the other. There is, however, a second meaning of self, which is that of the personal or interpersonal self. Self in this meaning is only actualized in loving others with a genuinely radical love, an affirmation of the other for the other's own sake. The denial of this self makes genuine radical love of the other impossible. For such self-denial is really the other side of an affirmation of the egoistic self. Conversely, to affirm self as a person is the other side of a denial of the egoistic self. I cannot cease to affirm my personal self (at least implicitly) without my love for the other ceasing; in the measure in which I fail to become or cease to be that personal self, in that measure my radical love for others fails and *vice versa.* Nor can I cease to love others for their own distinct, unique selves without my love for myself as a person ceasing also. In the measure that I put myself disguised as the other in place of the other, my ideals or needs in place of the other, or affirm the other as something merely useful or pleasurable to me, in that measure my love loses its character of radi-cal love for that person and becomes what we will take up later as implemental love springing out of a radical love for my selfish self. At their fullest, radical love of self as a person and the other as a person are correlatives.

A comparison might be made with knowledge. I cannot know an-other without obliquely knowing myself knowing the known; and I

cannot reflectively know myself as knower without obliquely knowing that by knowing which I am in act as knower. So also I cannot
love another with radical love without obliquely affirming myself
loving the other; and I cannot affirm myself as lover without obliquely loving the other by loving whom I am in act as lover. I am
actualized as knower and lover in the measure that I know and love.
Therefore I can know and love myself most fully in knowing and
loving others. The full solution to the problem that has been raised
can only be seen in an analysis of communion, where love comes to
its consummation. Anything like an adequate discussion of communion presupposes some clearly worked out understanding of what is
meant by love. One cannot discuss reciprocal love and the transfor-
mations of love that take place in that experience without knowing
first of all what is meant by love.

Returning our attention to love of others under the aspect of affirming them as the lover affirms oneself, let us try to deepen our
understanding of affirmation and see how affective affirmation of
radical love differs from any other form of affirmation. In part 1,
Ortega y Gasset's thought was used to illustrate a view in which the
dominant notion of love is affirmation (see ch. 3, above). Perhaps he
can put us on our way.

Ortega y Gasset on Affirmation

Love for Ortega is an affirmative psychic movement (a going out-to,
a migration). Yet, time and again, it is set off in opposition to desire,
which is also movement and also, presumably, affirmative (would he
wish to call desire a negative affection like hate or fear?). Desire, he
says, can be satisfied and dies when it is satisfied. In this he thinks to
contrast it with love that is eternally unsatisfied. But if this is the
only difference, then love would look like a certain sort of desire, one
that can never be satisfied and brought to rest. For to speak of love as
satisfied or unsatisfied puts it in a class of affects with appetite or
desire. What can an affective response be other than appetite or desire if it can be said to be unsatisfied or for that matter, satisfied? Still,
Ortega clearly does not want to think of love in this way. He has
another difference: desire is self-centered, drawing the object to self,
waiting passively for it to come to self; love on the contrary goes out
to its object. Leaving aside the conflict of elements in his description
of desire, other very disturbing questions arise. Does Ortega, then,
wish to deny the reality of unselfish desires, desires for the well-being
of a loved one? And does he want to deny the reality of self-love?
Whether he does or not, he has arrived at a position where he has to

make love for the other the source of self-centered desire—for he has told us a number of times that desire is a consequence of love.

Leaving aside all this confusion about love and desire, the very notion of affirmation is itself uncertainly expounded. Sometimes affirmation is described in a way that sounds like radical care, as when he says that love is intentional preservation or vivification, an actively favorable sentiment. Again what he says can suggest a relative love, which itself implies an absolute love without the latter being made explicit, as when he says that in love we exert ourselves in behalf of the loved one. Only once, and in one phrase, does his explanation of affirmation appear to go deeper and suggest the affection I have named radical love. That is where he speaks of the affirmation of love as "a participation in and enactment of" the loved one's right to exist. But this phrase is an *obiter dictum,* never repeated, to my knowledge, never explained, evocative of thoughts in the reader, but not subject to any certain interpretation.

While Ortega does flash off valuable insights and suggestions as he goes his brilliant way, the overall result is something of a multicolored blur. Grateful for whatever stimulation and suggestion he provides, we are still faced with the task of getting love as affirmation into focus so as to remove the blur and allow its clear light of intelligibility to enter our attention and understanding.

Affirmation by Love and Other Forms of Affirmation

Perhaps the best place to begin a study of affective affirmation is by looking at affirmation in a meaning with which we are more familiar. The most common and obvious meaning of affirmation is one that refers to an intellectual affirmation expressed in a statement. This may yield some meaning for affirmation that with necessary changes is applicable to affective affirmation also. To affirm intellectually is not only to be aware of persons (the context allows us to confine our discussion to affirmation of persons) nor only to understand them or entertain a thought about them; it is to assert with conviction the truth of what is thought or formulated in a proposition about them, I affirm that so-and-so is or that so-and-so is this-or-that. The one affirming not only lets the reality declare its intelligibility to one's mind; but one also, by an affirmative judgment, backs up that declaration, makes it firm against negation.

Such an intellectual affirmation is related to two other affirmations. First there is a prior affirmation by the ones about whom something is affirmed, their self-affirmation in their very act of being. Second, there is the affective affirmation by the one who makes the intellectual affirmation. The intellectual affirmation is prerequisite for the affective one, and the latter completes the partial affirmation of judgment. Let us look at the act of being and then at affective affirmation.

The place for each one of us to begin understanding the affirmation that is an act of being is our experience of our own being. My privileged experience of being from the inside is my conscious experience of being myself. Grounding all my activity, realizing itself in all my activity, present to my consciousness in all conscious acts but fading into unfathomable unconscious depths, is the primordial act that constitutes me as actual. It underlies all intellectual and affective affirmations. It is the energizing principle of all I do, the source of actuality for all the ways of my being, and for all my drives or tendencies to fuller realization of my being.

Whatever else can be said of this evident but mysterious act of being, for me to be, to exercise my act of being, is to declare myself in and to reality—i.e., in the root meaning of *de-clarare,* to shed light. To be is to shine intelligibly into the world, not as illuminating an already real self but as constituting myself by shining intelligibly into reality. It is also, therefore, to affirm myself, in the root sense of *ad-firmare,* to make firm. By my act of being I establish, found, myself firmly in the world for as long as I exercise being. By firmness I do not mean lastingness. The act of being makes self firm for a moment or forever. And there can be endless degrees of firmness; every act of being establishes the being with some degree of firmness. Nor is this affirmation something really different from declaration: it is by declaring myself that I am actual; declaring myself is affirming myself in the world. For our present purpose it is enough to focus on the act of being (and affective self-affirmation) as affirming self to the world; but we cannot ignore the fact that the act of being is not only an affirmation of self in isolation; it is an affirmation of myself in the world and, therefore, at least obliquely, an affirmation of the world. This latter affirmation is not, however, an affirmation which is constitutive of other beings as it is of myself. It is more like the affirmation of radical love, which we have yet to describe, an ontological love, we might say. Fuller treatment will become necessary when we speak of truthful love. Then we shall see the importance of noting that the affirmation by one's act of being is a way that it can only be realized, can only find full expression of itself, in the fully conscious and intense affirmation of God and of the created universe in its total concrete reality.

Affirmation here is declaration in a sense similar to and also differing from affirmation as a statement or judgment. It is like the latter a declaration which makes the declared firm against negation. But it is not an indicative declaration or affirmation *about* or *concerning* self, a declaration that points to what is independently of the pointing. It is, rather, a declaration and affirmation of self that is actually and actively *constitutive* of self in reality. In my act of being, I say me—not something to me or about me; and by saying me, I am. However, the self-declaration is not active in an efficient manner, as God's imperative and creative affirmation is; it is not a creative, effective imperative to self. The act of being is, as it were, an exclamatory affirmation of self, an actively constitutive exclamatory affirmation. By being I do not stand outside myself and say, "Be," or "Let self be." In order to do that I would have to be prior to my being. Nor do I merely affirm *that* I am: I have to be prior to affirming that I am. By being I exclaim myself; and in and by this exclaiming, I am myself in reality.

Although this primordial act of being is not a self-imperative, much less an actually efficient act reflexively, it is nevertheless dynamic, virtually self-preservative, self-creative, and self-communicative. To be so is an essential *property* of the act of being: no one can be constituted in being by a conatus to continue in being or to actualize potentialities or to give self; only one who is can tend to preserve self or to grow or give. Now, one who tends in these ways may actually fail to preserve oneself or to grow or to give because of opposing forces too powerful for oneself.

When this happens, we are not inactive, we are only ineffective. To fail to preserve our own or a loved one's life or integrity of being is ineffective, but we may be very active in our effort to do so. Even in a hopeless situation where nothing can be done at all, we will still feel an active urge to do something. Our act of being is still *virtually* effective; only let the required conditions obtain and we will be *actually* effective. The dynamic character of our self-affirmation in the act of being is, then, apparent in our tendencies or drives and in our sense of frustration when these drives are hindered from actualizing their goals. We saw that to confuse these drives with love blocks any insight into what radical love is. To confuse these drives with the act of being blocks any insight into the latter. When, however, the drives are kept distinct from and related to the act of being, they reveal its active and virtually effective character.

Affirmation of self and of the world by the act of being has both unconscious and conscious dimensions. The latter increases as we let the world and our own selves affirm themselves in our minds. Then, by judgment, we intellectually affirm them and by so affirming make possible the fuller conscious realization of our act of being by the affective affirmation of self and others in radical love.

In focusing attention on affective affirmation, we should have in mind an act of intense and transparently pure radical love; the act is seen and understood best in its fullest and purest instances. If not everything we see in such a love appears with clarity in every other instance, it will be because these others are defective instances of love.

If radical love is affirmation, it must in some sense make the beloved firm against negation. In what sense it does so will emerge by contrast with intellectual affirmation, with affective affirmations other than radical love, and with affirmation by the act of being. Intellectual affirmation was said to ratify a proposition that something is or is such: by it the one judging or affirming backs up the proposition against denial in thought. The proposition, indeed, is about reality, but the judgment is of itself neither actually nor intentionally effective of anything to or for the reality outside the realm of knowledge. It is true that an intellectual affirmation is the prerequisite condition for the possibility of love as conscious affective affirmation; but the latter assumes intellectual affirmation into itself and goes beyond it to a deeper union by a fuller affirmation. It is directed to the beloved's act of being and affirms the beloved against negation in the beloved's reality independent of the lover's thought or affection. That is why radical love modulates into the affirmation of care when the latter is aware of the beloved's needs and issues in joy in so far as the beloved is actual, whereas one who affirms intellectually may have no care at all, may even be hostile to the one being affirmed. The lover, by contrast, is no mere observer passively affirming that the other is, perhaps even coerced by the inescapable evidence that the other is, wishing the while it were not so. Such a one affirms and remains in the state of complete egocentricity. The one who loves another with radical love breaks through one's own egocentric gravity into the sphere of the beloved, affirming the latter with an active, virtually effective, affirmation, which in this respect resembles more the beloved's self-affirmation in the very act of being than it does any intellectual affirmation.

The loved one's act of being, however, is constitutive of the loved one's reality, whereas the lover's affective affirmation is response to a reality constituted by its own act of being. Even affective self-affirmation presupposes the actuality of self and responds to it reflexively. Holding that obvious difference clearly in mind, we can say that the response of radical affective affirmation does join the lover's act of being, realizing itself in affective affirmation, to the beloved's self-constitutive act of self-affirmation. The lover affectively identified with the beloved's act of being co-affirms, co-declares, the beloved.

What this means can be brought out by seeing what is revealed in the language of love at the peak experiences of love. At peak moments of love, lovers commonly express themselves in one of two ways in speech. They may say over and over, "I love you." And this they say not as narrating a fact, as an intellectual affirmation about themselves, but rather as an exclamation, not so much to communicate a fact to the loved one as simply to give expression to love under the natural impulse of the spirit to bodily expression. Thus they may exclaim it even at times when there is no one to hear them, neither the loved one nor any other. What is even more common and more significant is the exclamation of the beloved's name over and over, the proper name or some form of address such as: "O my son Absalom, O Absalom, my son! Would I had died instead of you, O Absalom, my son, my son!" (2 Kings 18:33). And Christians remember that the Holy Spirit who pours forth the charity of God in their hearts is the one who in them makes them cry "Abba, Father!" (Romans 5:5; 8:15; Galatians 4 :6). Readers of the New Testament will recall how Mary Magdalene's suddenly joyful love at hearing Christ's "Mary" could find no expression but "Rabboni!" (John 20:16). Or how it was with Thomas when his positivistic demands were met by Christ: his shamed but burning and believing love could find no word save "My Lord and my God" (John 20:28). And how many are those given to a life of prayer who finally come to the point where there is nothing to say but, "God!" or "Jesus!" or over and over the words of Thomas, "My Lord and my God!" George MacDonald once remarked somewhere that all prayer can be summed up in the words, "Oh God!" So also in romantic songs and poetry, the lover at the highest pitch of love finds that one word, the beloved's name, says all, as "Maria" (*West Side Story*) or "Roxanne" (*Cyrano de Bergerac*).

And the reader should not be misled because a Cyrano in the play talks lengthily about how his whole world and his whole love are expressed in the name or because John of the Cross writes poems and books about the experience of love for God. A poetic discourse is "emotion recollected in tranquility." Lovers will have Cyrano's experience of the beloved's name ringing as a bell in their hearts and vibrating through their blood until their being is singing the beloved in that name. But they will not compose poetic narrations of how it happens until the experience subsides and their attention can be focused on their experience instead of on the beloved, any more than will mystics in an ecstasy of love, singing God with all their being, compose theological treatises on prayer at that time. Loving discourse arises under the impact of love on the imagination, and the moments of discourse about love can be filled with love; but at the peak moment, lovers are not attentive to nor discoursing about their own affective responses to the beloved. They affirm the beloved and by affirming are the beloved. Lovers and beloveds wholly fills the moment without room for reflection or discourse. At that moment, the only expression of one's affective self is exclaiming one's beloved. So it is, whether we are talking of romantic love, or paternal, or filial, or nuptial, or religious love, whether we are talking about joyful love, or sorrowful love, or peaceful love. In these most intense moments of radical love, the whole energy of conscious being seems compressed into a word of the heart and that word is the beloved. The lover's whole life at that moment is an exclamation of the loved one. This exclamation of the heart finds vocal expression in exclaiming the beloved's name.

All this fits with, confirms, and perhaps lets us see more deeply into, the nature of love as affirmation by which the lover identifies with the loved one. For we have already shown that the act of being (here the beloved's being) is, as it were, an exclamatory affirmation by which a being declares self to the world and in so doing constitutes self in the world. Correspondingly, the act of radical love is an exclamatory affective affirmation by which the lover actively co-affirms the beloved along with the beloved's own act of being and, in a way, constitutes the self of the beloved as the lover's other self.

In fact, if we understand rightly what has been said, we can now see how lovers with their own acts of being affirm the beloved. For we have seen that we are constituted ourselves in reality by our acts of being, and that our love is (as are all our acts) ourselves in act, our acts of being actualized in the love. Grasping the continuity of the lover's act of being with the lover's radical love for the other, we can see that love is the lover's being in act affirming the beloved's act of being. In this act, according to the measure in which love is achieved, the beloved's self is accepted, the lover's self is given and the lover's love is co-being the beloved. It is not merely being-with in the sense of being simultaneously in the world, nor in the sense of being present to or in the beloved, but it is actively being the beloved *affectively*.

The Active Character of Affective Affirmation

The affirmative act of co-being constituted by radical love is manifested in its affirmatively active character. Just as the beloved's self-affirmation is always virtually effective of self-preservation, growth, and self-communication, so also the lover's co-affirmation has a transitively creative character. This creative character, however, must be qualified very carefully or we find ourselves carried away into enthusiastic claims about the lover's creativity of the loved one, claims utterly unfounded in experience. First of all, as shown above, radical love is a response to an existing personal subject who is valuable whether actually valued by anyone or not. No human love is absolutely creative of its object. One who is not loved may never come to value oneself correctly and affectively affirm oneself as one should if one is to fulfil oneself; but the reason why this failure is tragic is because one *is* valuable, lovable, in one's very act of personal being. If this were not so, it would not be so great a tragedy for someone to remain unloved and unloving.

In our responding to the other, our radical love can be but is not necessarily actually preservative of the beloved's life and creative of the beloved's growth, effective for fuller realization of the beloved's potentialities. When lovers are actually creative in these ways, they are so mediately and in dependence on many conditions. Human love offers no experiential evidence of being immediately effective of anything in the beloved: the effects intrinsic to the beloved are produced through mediation of the lover's desires, choices, and activities toward or in behalf of the beloved; and it is obvious how many conditions there are that can and do hinder the desired effects. Lovers' love itself can be effective without their desire and action just by being known and creatively responded to by the loved one. But again, how the beloved responds is conditioned by the lovers' psychological personalities, their moral character, their freedom, and by external circumstances.

Sometimes lovers cannot be creative because of the limitation of their effective powers. Sometimes, on the other hand, there is no need to be creative inasmuch as the loved one is already realized in fulness of being. Love in these situations is not less active nor even less creative in itself. It is still virtually creative so that if the beloved were in need and if the conditions under which the creative virtuality of love could be effectively actualized were present, the lover would be actually creative. Love is not to be understood merely in terms of what the lover can or cannot do, what the beloved needs or does not need. A love that does not issue in actions to fulfil the beloved's needs when these are beyond the lover's power, indicates nothing about the genuinity of the love. A mother does not love less because she cannot save her child's life. A bridegroom does not love less because he cannot actually gather up all the glory of the world and give it to his bride. A saint does not love less because she cannot transform the world into a burning and shining community of God centered love. Doing what they can do shows the sincerity of their desires, and the greatness of the desires shows the greatness and the active character of the radical care and love from which they spring. If the lover had greater directly effective power, love in the mode of care would activate it for the production of effects. The lack is in the lovers' other powers, their intelligence or learning or eloquence or physical strength or force of personality, and so on. As seen above, love is only mediately effective. The failure of actual effectiveness in no way necessarily indicates a lack of love nor argues against the creative character of loving affirmation as opposed to purely intellectual affirmation.

Similarly, a love is no less intense or virtually creative when it does not issue in effective activity because the beloved has no need or desire of what can be achieved by such activity. The mother who has successfully nursed her child through a mortally dangerous illness does not love less nor is her love less active virtually now that she rests with joy in her child's safety. If the situation should call for effective activity, her love would instantly turn to care and issue into desire and activity in so far as her power would allow. The difference is in the situation, not in the active character of her loving affirmation. So with the bride rejoicing in the joy of the bridegroom whom she was fulfilled. So with the saints rejoicing in the infinite life and joy of God. If, *per impossibile*, God should need them in order to stay God, they would do all they could and give their own being for that. Because there is no need, the love is not less nor less active virtually. It must be added in all realism, that it is impossible to be sure how sincere are our impossible desires until we are faced with the necessity of suffering and acting in order to realize at least the possible ones and so learn how creative our love is in those circumstances.

Truth and Falsity in Affective Affirmation

A difficulty arises here: if radical love as an affective affirmation has a virtually active character that shows in the lover's acts for the beloved when these are called for, how is it that love can give rise to destructive acts that negate the beloved's reality even as affective self-affirmation can lead to acts destructive of oneself? To answer that question it is necessary to take up true and false affective affirmation. This is of great importance not merely for resolving the above difficulty but for bringing to light something which almost all writing on love leaves in darkness, the inner differentiation of acts of love, their wealth or poverty of content, their constant fluctuations which are not only compatible with but required by their basic stability.

Affirmation is true or false, and when true is more or less truthful. All this is most readily observed in intellectual affirmation by judgment. Such affirmation can be at variance with reality; when it is so, it is untrue, an erroneous affirmation but still an affirmation. When a judgment is true, it may be more or less truthful. That is to say, it may affirm something about the reality of its subject, something deep or shallow, important or trivial, comprehensive or narrow. One judgmental affirmation is more nearly adequate to the reality about which the affirmation is made than another and this in endless degrees. Thus, I might affirm that St. Paul was a man, that he was a man of eloquence, that he was a Jew and a profoundly religious man. All are true, but there is an ascending scale of truthfulness, adequacy, in these affirmations. Radical love as an affective affirmation is also true or false, more or less truthful when it is true, more or less adequate to its object. The meaning of this statement can be clarified by clarifying the reality that is affectively affirmed in radical love and the accord or discord of the affective affirmation with this reality.

Before taking up these two topics, let it be clear that truth and falsity in this context are not being used as value words. This discussion is in no way a departure into the ethical realm. When I speak of truth and falsity of love in the context of this study, I am not speaking of what it ought to be in order to meet standards of morality or psychological health. It may, of course, turn out that the most completely truthful radical love coincides with morally and/or psychologically good love; but that question is of no concern here. Here I am not in the least concerned whether love is itself a value at all or what it has to be in order to be most valuable. I only want to show the meaning of talking about truth and falsity in *affective* affirmation and in so doing to bring out some points of essential importance in the reality of radical love. Even if a reader should think that truthful love, just as a truthful judgment, is not always good from the moral or clinical viewpoint, it would make no difference here. A successful embezzler might make financial judgments and practical assessment about the chances of deceiving others which are perfect of their kind and yet are taken up into a total human action that is morally evil. One could omit moral consideration and note the truth of the embezzler's judgment. Similarly we can for now leave open the possibility of having a truthful love that is not morally good and talk about what it means for love to be truthful. (I myself do not think it possible to have a concretely truthful love which is also morally evil. What that means I hope to show more fully and to establish in a following work on ethics.)

Keeping clear that this is description without valuation, we can now take up the first topic of the two mentioned above, i.e., the reality affirmed in radical love. Affective affirmation by radical love is a response to the total reality of the one responded to, the reality that is itself a call of the beloved's being to be affirmed. What is included in that total reality? It is the beloved's actuality as apprehended by the lover that is explicitly affirmed in radical love. Implicitly the potentiality and dynamism to more actuality are also affirmed, and these become explicit in care-love. Now, loved ones are actual primarily by their acts of being, which are their affirmations of themselves to and in the world of persons, things, and events. They do not exist except in the world, by relation to the rest of the universe. In this universe, their potentiality and dynamism find their meaning. So, their total reality involves endless relations with other realities. To affirm their reality fully is to affirm that reality as a being in the universe of ordered and interacting beings. Now, although human beings are in an intelligibly structured world, that world is temporal and changing and the loved one in it is constantly changing. So, it is only within a complex network of the natural and historical, of necessity and contingency, of stability and change, that we can accurately grasp the concrete actuality of the one to be affirmed, see the present meaning of the beloved's capacities and tendencies. We might bring out the point by going so far as to say that loving any person with fully truthful love is implicitly loving all reality truthfully; and loving any person falsely endangers at least to some degree, however slight, the truth of every other love. For each being is what it is by relationship with all the rest and finds its meaning only in the totality. Finally, we must add that neither the loved object nor the world can be understood adequately (or inadequately without danger of almost inevitable distortion) unless all is seen in relation to God, in whom all the universe finds its ultimate meaning.

This is what is meant by the full concrete reality of that with which an affective affirmation is in accord or discord. But what does it mean to say that affective affirmation accords with that reality or is in discord with it? Affective affirmation is conditioned by attention, perception, and judgment, not only as negative and limiting conditions but as positive conditions necessary for liberating the energy of love. But further, and this is of greatest importance, the response of radical love in human affectivity is not a formless, blind impulse released on condition of knowing the object but intrinsically unaffected by the form or structure of the object. Love is informed by the beloved as apprehended through the lover's perception, imagination, and judgment. It has qualitative differentiation and structure from the cognitive acts with which it interacts and interpenetrates in the total experience. All human love presupposes these acts and assumes into itself their differentiation and structure. Truth begins in the intellect, is given fuller actuality in love, and finds expression in desire, speech, and action. The adequacy of affective affirmation depends on, among other things, the adequacy of knowledge. And further, partly as a consequence of other factors, love is continually fluctuating. It can be as simple or as complex, as refined and delicately shaded, or as vague and confused, as stable or as flowingly changing, as our perceptions of, attention to, and judgments about the concrete reality of the person encountered. It can be as accurate or inaccurate as these acts, as wildly inaccurate as our projections, prejudices, and flights of undisciplined imagination. And therefore affective affirmations are intrinsically true or false, more or less adequately truthful, but always in dependence on cognitive acts. Lovers' beings are more fully actualized in truth when they judge and love truthfully than when they only judge truthfully. But the measure of the truth possible in the love is the truth of the knowledge.

In short, affective affirmation can be in accord or partially in discord with the concrete reality of the loved one. When it is in accord it can be more or less in accord. Even when it is false, the affective affirmation is still affirmation and is still love, a false love, a distorted love, but love—just as much as a false judgment is a judgment.

That love can be true or false is confirmed by a consideration of some consequences of love. Radical love, we saw, is always virtually active. It is a virtually active, affective, co-affirmation of the beloved in union with the latter's own act of being. Now under certain circumstances the active power of love gives rise to desire and other affections and so is actualized in the actions that flow from desire. Desire and action express the love. Sometimes these active consequences of love are creative of the beloved. Such active consequences give evidence of a love in accord with the concrete reality of the beloved. At other times, the active consequences of radical love are destructive, even though the lover sincerely cares for the beloved as the lover understands the beloved. The destructive consequences can in some instances be attributed to the failure of the beloved who twists the truly beneficent activity of the lover to the lover's own harm. In other instances, however, we are forced to admit that the harm comes from an unwise, false love that affirms the beloved at variance with the beloved's concrete reality. A partial disharmony in the lover's radical act of the affectivity shows up in the desire and in the acts that clash with the beloved's reality.

Even when love is true, we noted, it can be more or less truthful. This notion of love as more or less truthful even when fully true requires and deserves careful understanding. For the question arises: if radical love is a response to the beloved's total reality, how can there be degrees of adequacy to the object? It would seem that any radical love is fully adequate to the beloved, fully truthful, or it is not radical love—or else we have to revise the description of the object of love, omitting the word "total."

Understanding that affective affirmations have qualitative differentiation derived from knowledge provides the answer to this question. As a lover my awareness is of a totality known to include much that I am not perceptive of or not attentive to here and now. So, in some sense I am aware of what I am not perceiving or attending to explicitly. I am aware of "all that belongs to the beloved's reality but which I do not now perceive or attend to." Affective affirmation is of all this but without explication. Again, what I the lover do apprehend of the beloved explicitly can be apprehended in varying degrees of depth, fulness, and nuanced sensitivity. The quality of my radical love will also be characterized by corresponding depth, fulness, and nuanced affirmation of the beloved's unique individual reality as the beloved is at this moment of loving. To think of the response of love as though it were always the same intrinsically undifferentiated response, varying only in intensity and durability, is to treat love as a physical force or perhaps to fall into an unreal mysticism that thinks of the object of human love only in terms of the inconceptualizable and ineffable. There is, of course, the inconceptualizable and ineffable personal center, the inexhaustible center of acts and qualitative realizations. But that personal center is directly experienced as it is realized in and through the partial and flowing, conceptualizable and effable, revelations. What is known in these revelations very certainly makes the response of radical love to be constantly fluctuating intrinsically. Those who love truly surprise ever new and lovable qualities revelatory of the person loved, and so love grows in depth and fulness, in truthfulness.

By loving someone in depth I do not in this context mean what we usually mean by loving deeply. The latter means loving from the lover's most personal self, with sincerity, intensity, endurance, as opposed to loving in a shallow way, from the surface of the lover's being, with a fleeting, undependable love. To love in depth means to respond to the loved ones as seen in the revelations of their most inwardly personal selves. To affirm loved ones for and in themselves because I know that they are persons, without experiencing each one's unique personality as revealed in their deeds, expressions, and conversation is not as completely truthful an affirmation as is one that do respond to each one as so revealed. So also, to affectively affirm this unique person in a response informed by full, detailed, knowledge that catches the delicate shadings of each one's profoundest attitudes, moods, likes and dislikes, ideals, fears, hopes, capabilities, weaknesses, etc., is surely a more truthful affirmation than one which, while avoiding all false affirmation, accords with the beloved's reality only vaguely, with little understanding of each one as revealed in each's personal qualities.

The richly differentiated, constantly varying, quality of love is shown most obviously in its consequences: in shades of joy over the beloved's varying fulness of being, in different cares for different needs, in manifold desires for whatever will fill those needs and whatever will serve as a means to that fulfilment, in words and in silence, in the infinite subtleties of tone and gesture and smile and look, in endlessly different ways of acting and enduring, of giving and accepting. All the wonderful, even amazing kaleidoscopic flowing expressions of love that suffuse human life are a revelation of the vast complexity within the act of love itself and of its endless modulations as it responds to the ever flowing and complex reality of the beloved.

To stress the complexity and changeableness of love is not to deny its stability and simplicity. The persons loved stays themselves through all changes; they are always who they are even though they realize themselves in many different ways. There is at the core of each one's reality a simplicity and stability. An intellectual affirmation of that reality can be of each person as seen in a complex insight that unifies the multiplicity of elements. That insight and affirmation, if it is to be true, changes as reality changes. Nevertheless, the multiplicity at any moment is grasped in one simple act of insight; and, at the core of every succeeding insight, the person is seen, the person who in one way changes and in another does not. For it is the person who is different in each change but always that person. So also the radical love is always of each person, but always varied as each one varies.

If, then, we ask what would a radical love be that would not only be true but be also fully adequate in its truthfulness, the answer would have to be: a love as richly and delicately detailed in its structure as is the total reality of the beloved, as stable and as variable. And if each person's full reality implies the whole universe, the fully truthful love for that person would be as richly structured, as stable and variable as the universe. In other words, to love with truthfulness perfectly adequate to the one loved, requires a knowledge such as God has. A completely true affirmation is within human capability of judgment and love; a completely truthful one is not. Completely truthful love is a love that any human act of love will approach, more or less, as an ideal of love that is as fully affirmation of the beloved as love can be.

The other aspects of radical love will also be nearer or farther from the ideal in direct proportion with affirmation. That is, radical love will be as fully mutual presence, self-giving and acceptance, identification, as it is fully truthful affirmation. Insofar as affective affirmation is false, the lover is not present to the loved one or at the very least is not present consonantly. Falsity in affirmation produces a dissonance that in its effects resembles hatred. Given that affirmation is true, the more deeply and fully truthful it is, the deeper and fuller is the mutual presence of lover and loved in each other. Similarly with radical love as gift and acceptance. As we saw, the gift of self and acceptance of the loved one are two sides of the act of radical love in which the lover yields to the beloved the affirmative energy of the lover's act of being as it expresses itself in conscious affectivity; the beloved is affirmed by the lover as the lover's self-affirmation, with the very energy by which the lover affirms self. In a false affirmation, insofar as it is false, it is not the beloved in the beloved's own reality who is affirmed. In a true affirmation, the more fully and deeply truthful the affirmation, the more fully and deeply is the lover given to the beloved and the beloved accepted in the same act. Finally, and clearly in the light of what has been said of presence and of gift and acceptance, affective identification is prevented by false affirmation and is increased in proportion to the fulness and depth of true affirmation.

Affirmation the Root Aspect of Radical Love

With affective affirmation as a way of actively co-being the beloved, a way of joining acts of being through affectivity in the manner described, we seem to have arrived at the ultimate aspect of radical love. This is not to say that there is no more to know about radical love or no better ways of knowing than that of philosophical reflection and analysis. What is meant is that any philosophical reflection, although it may further enrich our knowledge of the various aspects of radical love, including the aspect of affirmation, will not uncover a more fundamental aspect than that of affective affirmation. For not only, as will be shown, does the irreducibility of radical love show up most clearly when we see it as affirmation, but the previously unanswered questions about the other aspects receive an answer when these are seen in conjunction with it. Let me elaborate this statement.

Before noting and describing affective affirmation, we saw that radical love is a response of the lover to the full reality of the loved one, explicitly and primarily to the latter's actuality. It is a response that liberates an energy within the lover and liberates us from the confinement of individual being. As a consequence of radical love we do not merely break out of our confines by being more aware of the world as spectators through knowledge. By love, we are able to experience the lives of those we love as in some way our own just because they are the lives of those we love. We are victorious over limitations, inheritors of kingdoms, of the beings and lives of those we love. And at the same time, by the response of radical love, we are captives, willing captives who gladly surrender to the loved one. Both the liberation and the captivity are constituted by union with the loved one, a union of presence. In that union of presence, the lover is in the loved as gift: our love is an act of being a gift. And the beloved is in the lover as accepted: the love is an act of acceptance. Strangely but certainly, love (unilateral love) constitutes mutual in-being; and strangely but certainly, the one act of love is giving and accepting. More than this, the act of being gift and of acceptance is such that the lover is the beloved affectively.

This brief summary of the principal aspects discerned in radical love prior to affective affirmation had a certain intelligible coherence but at each step left us with a question: *how* does the act of radical love constitute a liberating response, a union of presence, a self-giving, an identification? And *how* do we resolve at least the apparent conflict between some of these aspects? It was by discerning and descriptively analyzing love as affective affirmation that we came upon the insights into love that enable us to answer, insofar as we can answer, the questions raised about the preceding aspects.

/ Affective affirmation, like every conscious act of a human person, is a conscious realization of the actualizing energy of the subject's act of being, which act is an affirmation of self in the world. In radical love, the affective energy by which subjects affectively affirm their own self is centered on the loved one, who is affirmed as lovers affirm

themselves and as the beloveds affirm themselves. The being of the
lover in the act of love co-affirms the being of the beloved and constitutes a co-being. This co-affirmation lets us see into the aspect of
love as a liberating response: it is the very affirmatory energy of the
act of being realizing itself in affective affirmation. We also see better
what it means to say that the response of radical love is a liberation
from the limits of individual being. This began to be understood
better in each step of our description; union, consonant presence,
self-giving and acceptance, identification with the other. It is affective affirmation as co-being that gives the ultimate insight and clarifies all. In much the same way as liberation, the opposite aspect of
being captive grows in meaning at each step and reaches a climax in
affective affirmation. So also, without going into a detailed, point by
point account, we can say that insight into affective affirmation gives
the most ultimate understanding about all the other aspects of radical love, *how* love is each of these and *how it* can be all of them at
once. By yielding to the loved one the lover's act of being as it realizes
itself in affective affirmation, the lover performs an act of being-in,
of self-giving, of affective identification. At the same time and in the
same act the lover accepts the loved one into the lover's own self and
affectively is the loved one.

8

Radical Love As the Irreducible Root of the Total Concrete Experience of Love

If affective affirmation is the most fundamental aspect of radical love, then with it analysis of radical love can be ended. Have we therefore arrived at the end of the whole inquiry? We began with the unreflective, lived experience of love in its concrete fulness. Reflecting on this total concrete experience, we noted that it is a manifold of knowledge, freedom, and instinct, as well as of many affections. We set out to discover whether there is some element within this manifold that is the vivifying center by relation to which everything else in the experience (inasmuch as it is involved in the experience of love) can be said to belong to the experience. Without difficulty, all the elements save those of affectivity were eliminated from consideration. The purpose of this inquiry called for a reductive analysis of the affective part of the experience. For it was necessary to move with reflective attention from the more obvious and less fundamental parts of the conscious affective experience to the less obvious and more fundamental ones. The movement did not turn out to be reductive in the sense of reducing the experience to elements of less and less specifically human meaning; rather it turned out to be reductive in the sense of tracing the more obvious affections to more fundamental ones from which they derive their full human meaning.

This reductive analysis led to that affection we named radical love, allowing for the possibility that it might turn out to be something less than the ultimate root in the total experience of love. The question whether it is or is not radical seemed unanswerable prior to a descriptive analysis of the affection itself. At this point, therefore, we deferred any further reductive search for a more fundamental affection and focused attention on that affection tentatively named radical love, descriptively analyzing its various aspects as they appear in our conscious experience. This task has concluded with what appears to be the deepest aspect of radical love, affective affirmation of the beloved for and in the beloved's own self, in the beloved's very act of personal being.

Having completed a descriptive analysis of radical love, we are now in a position to pick up the question whether this affective act is truly deserving of the name we gave it. It is so only if it is itself irreducible to any other affection and is the root of all the other affective acts in the concrete experience of love. The question therefore has two parts: first, is what we have been calling radical love an irreducible affective response? second, is it the root of the other affective responses which are in the total experience of love and are themselves frequently called love?

Even during this discussion it will be necessary to go on using the name radical love. A reminder that the name should throughout be read as if in quotation marks or followed by a question mark will be less troublesome to both reader and writer than actually putting these devices into print. The only alternatives would be a constant irritating use of circumlocutions or else changing the name—which at this stage would certainly cause worse confusion.

The Irreducibility of Radical Love

First of all, then, is radical love reducible to any more fundamental affective act? A beginning can be made this way. Each of the affections we found in the dialectical survey and classification of opinions on love has appeared in the foregoing analysis, either as radical love under some aspect or as another affection which presupposes radical love. We find that when we consider any of the latter affections we can always ask why. Why do I desire? Why do I rejoice? Why do I "love" a means or a derivative, implemental end for someone? And we can always answer by naming a prior affection whether radical love or one intermediate between it and radical love. But in every instance we arrive finally at radical love. What if I ask why I love with radical love? Is there some more fundamental affection to point to? The analysis we have made has not turned our attention to any such affection. It may be, however, that we are missing something. It does not look as though we will find anything more ultimate in our affectivity to which radical love can be reduced. But does the description of radical love that has been achieved give evidence of an act such that it *cannot* be grounded in any other affection?

If there is evidence of radical love's irreducibility, it will be found in the most basic aspect of that love, affirmation, and in the most basic element of its object which gives it intrinsic differentiation from other affections. Radical love 1) affirms its object (i.e., persons), 2) for themselves, 3) in themselves, 4) directly and explicitly in their deepest actuality, in each one's act of personal being. What I shall try to show now is that each of these four factors progressively eliminates some form of reducibility at deeper and deeper levels, and that the final one eliminates the last *possibility* of reduction.

The ultimate irreducible affection could not be negative; every negative affection can be reduced to an affirmative one. For instance, I can experience no fear of harm unless I desire safety, no despair unless I desire what I despair of attaining. If we take hate as the radical negative affection, hate never arises except for what is opposed to what I love. If I loved nothing, I could hate nothing. As affirmative, then, radical love escapes the reducibility of negative affections.

Radical love might still be reduced to another affirmative affection. Now radical love is not only affirmative, it is affirmative of its objects (persons) for themselves, i.e., as radical ends. That excludes any reduction of radical love such as we saw is possible for desire or any affection which affirms its object for another. This latter sort of affirmation is derivative from and reducible to an affection toward that other. (This does not mean that in concrete experience we cannot love one and the same person with more than one kind of love. I can love persons for themselves and also love them as useful for others. For instance, if I have a friend who is a teacher or doctor, I can even love her in both ways at the same time when I affirm her as useful to others because I know that this is fulfilling to her to be so. And there is the situation where I love two others in communion with each other: I love each for each one's self and each for the other; and the very loving of each for the other, in this case, is loving each for each one's self, since each is realized as a person in being for the other as a person.)

The fact that radical love is an affirmation of loved ones for themselves, as radical ends, at first glance might seem to provide the evidence of radical love's unqualified irreducibility. To draw that conclusion would be altogether too hasty. Recall what we found in our experience of love, that we can love persons for themselves without loving them in themselves. This fact indicates that affirmation of persons for themselves is *necessary* for establishing an affection as irreducible but is not yet *sufficient* to establish that. So we must appeal also to that note of fully radical love which distinguishes it from what we named quasi-radical love. Fully radical love is an affirmation of loved ones not only for themselves but in themselves. That is to say, it is a response to them as lovable because of their own intrinsically lovable actuality, not merely because of a relation to someone other or others who are loved in themselves. Radical love as affirmation of

the loved ones for and in themselves excludes all possibility of reduction to another affirmative affection toward any other person.

There remains the possibility of reduction to another affirmative
affection toward the same person who is loved with radical love. As
long as this possibility remains we cannot be certain that radical love
is irreducible. We have already noted two other affections that have
as objects persons in and for themselves, the same persons who are
loved with radical love. These are radical care and joy in the primary
meaning. Analysis revealed care as a more complex mode of radical
love, therefore presupposing the latter and including it. It also revealed joy in its primary form as a consequence of radical love, a
necessary consequence but a consequence. Now, is it possible that
radical love should itself be a consequence of or a more complex
form of a simpler prior affection? The fact that radical love is an
affirmation of persons for and in themselves neither calls for nor
excludes this possibility. But that possibility is excluded by the fact
that radical love is directly and explicitly a simple affirmation of the
beloved persons in their deepest and simplest actuality, their very
acts of personal being by which they are in reality and by which anything else belonging to their total reality is real and lovable. No affirmation could possibly undercut this affirmation still be an affirmation
of these beloved persons in themselves.

Now, we can go back and answer the question we left unanswered.
If I am asked why I have any other affection in the total experience of
love, I can always reply, "because I love you with radical love." But
when I am asked why I love you with radical love, can I point to any
deeper affection in answer? We see now that this is not possible. My
reply can point only to the object of this love. *You* are why I love you.
If this is not the reason I love, the affection is not radical love. It is
you who call forth the affirmation of radical love, you in yourself, in
your own personal act of being in the world. It is you who are affirmed for yourself, as a radical end irreducible to any other, as a
value that is not for any other unless affirming you for another coincides with affirming you for yourself as a person.

A question could arise here: Do we not have to distinguish between unconditional and conditional radical love? What has been
said about irreducibility holds for unconditional radical love. Does it
hold for conditional? Is not the latter reducible to unconditional? I
think not. If it were, then the one who loves with a conditional radical love would have to be loving the same person more fundamentally with an unconditional radical love (an obvious absurdity) or
else that person's conditional radical love for one person would have

to be grounded in an unconditional radical love for another person (which is even more absurdly in conflict with the reality of radical love). So there are only two possible solutions to the difficulty raised; either it must be conceded that it was a mistake in the first place to hold the reality of a conditional love of persons for and in themselves or else the justification given for such love will now enable us to see that it too is an irreducible affection. I think the latter is the fact.

Conditional Loving with a conditional radical love, we saw, is not the same as loving persons inasmuch as they perform certain functions, even noble ones, and have qualities that enable them to do so. It is possible to love persons for and in themselves but to do so only on condition that they do act in certain ways and have certain qualities. In this latter way of loving, it is the persons themselves who are loved, not merely the qualities or acts; they are loved for and in themselves as persona, not merely as bearers of qualities. The modes of action and the qualities are not themselves what is loved. The persons realized and revealed in them are affirmed for and in themselves. The actions and qualities are the condition that must be posited if the response of love is to continue; the response is not to the condition but to the person on this condition. No doubt, this is illogical: if I love the person, then the conditions should not be placed. But logic is one thing and the facts of affective experience are another. Is it not true that unconditional radical love of one person logically implies unconditional radical love of God and of all created persons? But how many people's affective life follows such logic? How we *ought* to love is a matter of morality or (in a different meaning of "ought") clinical psychology. This investigation is only describing the facts that moral philosophy and practical psychology can use, not developing moral or psychological conclusions.

Whatever may be the case concerning conditional radical love, it seems clear enough now that at least unconditional radical love is irreducible. Even those who would not agree to the reality of a conditional radical love could agree to leave aside as a special question whether what we have said and will say about radical love as an irreducible source of other affections applies to conditional love or does not.

Resolution of Questions
about Self-Love and Pathological Egoism

This is a suitable place to recall the question that occurred but could not be answered when we were about to begin the description of radical love: is all love of other persons reducible to self-love, as the psychological egoists would have it? The most reasonable procedure at that time appeared to be that we leave open the possibility of an affirmative or a negative answer to the question and simply set about describing what is at least apparently love of the other and wait to learn whether it leads to the egoistic reduction or not. This question was then and is now complicated by the fact that there is a contrary position to be taken into account, namely, that there is no such thing as self-love, that the very notion is meaningless, even a self-contradiction. Whether this is so or not also had to wait on the result of our effort to describe the experience of radical love. Now, before answering the question whether all love of others reduces to self-love, we had better first of all answer the question whether it is intelligible to speak of self-love at all. The evidence brought to light in the preceding chapters enables us to answer both questions briefly and easily.

Is self-love an intelligible concept? We saw that radical love is basically an affective affirmation of the beloved as lovers affectively affirms themselves and as the beloveds affectively affirm themselves. In order to leave the question about self-love open, the term "self-affirmation" instead of "self-love" has been used up to this point. However, it must have been immediately obvious to the reader that if radical love for others is an affective affirmation of others as the lovers affirm themselves, then it is perfectly intelligible to say that affective self-affirmation is self-love. In fact it is for purposes of exposition the paradigmatic love. (This is not the same as to say that all love is necessarily rooted in self-love, but only that it is more obvious.)

Tillich, it will be recalled, says that we can speak of self-affirmation but not of self-love. Is he then speaking of self-love and only differing in words? Unfortunately, Tillich's position and the position attained in this study are not that easily reconciled. For love to Tillich is tendency, movement toward union of the separated. If he were to let self-affirmation be self-love, he would have to change his whole notion of love and agree that to love others than ourselves is also, most fundamentally, to affirm them; that only distinction, not separation nor estrangement, is necessary for the possibility of love; that love is not a tendency to union but is actually union, which under certain circumstances gives rise to tendency to greater union. This would mean letting go the central notions of his whole "ontology" of love.

If self-love as affective self-affirmation is an intelligible notion, then the question whether all love for others is reductively self-love is an intelligible question. And it is a question to which the answer has already been given by showing that radical love cannot be reduced to any other affective response toward some other object than the object of radical love nor to any deeper affective response toward the same object. In order to establish the position of psychological egoism it would be necessary to show that we never to any degree experience what has been described here as radical love for others.

It can be granted that most love is self-love. Let us even for the sake of the argument put the strongest case possible for psychological egoism and grant that almost all human love is selfish love, however subtly it may be so; that what arises as radical love for another imperceptibly and easily and usually slides off into selfish love or at least gets all mixed up with selfish love in the manifold of concrete affective experience and so becomes obscured by selfish love; that wherever there is a conflict of selfish love and radical love for another the former wins—let us for the sake of the argument make all these concessions. Nevertheless, if any slightest affection of radical love for another arises, however feeble and fleeting and mixed up with selfishness it might be, then psychological egoism is untenable.

What psychological egoism has to show is that no love of another, despite all appearances to the contrary, *can* be anything but an expression of self-love in ultimate analysis. The *prima facie* evidence is powerfully against psychological egoism; and the actual attempts to undermine the *prima face* evidence turn out to be not only failures but sometimes ridiculous failures. There is no need to repeat here Butler's classic reduction to absurdity of Hobbes' reduction of benevolent affections to selfishness. The least that can be said is that if the reduction Hobbes attempted can be done, nobody has yet done it, even speciously. Psychological egoism remains an assumption with enough bitter evidence in human life to make us emotionally ready to accept it when we feel cynical and discouraged about the world in general and, in those who have self-knowledge, about themselves above all. But a calm consideration of human experience reveals it as gross exaggeration.

The Root of Other Affections in the Total Experience

Can the quotation marks which the reader was asked to read around the name radical love or the question mark you were asked to put behind it now be removed? If the requirement for radical love were only irreducibility to any prior affection, you could. However, for an affection to be radical love it must not only be itself irreducible, it must also be the root of the other affections that are integral to the concrete experience of love. The reductive analysis made earlier is really sufficient for the purpose of establishing that this requirement is also fulfilled by the affection we have called radical love. However, in order to make the point clearer and at the same time to make evident the relation of the derivative affections to one another and to radical love, it will be worth while to reverse the movement of our thought and beginning with radical love show, by a progressive, synthetic procedure how these affections flow out of radical love and form one living unity with it and with one another. Ideally, what should be done now is to make a full examination of the relations between radical love and all the main elements in the total experience of love: the other affections, knowledge, instinct, freedom. Each of these is such a large and demanding subject that for the limited purpose of this book it is better to note them and be content with exhibiting radical love as the vital source of the other affections that appeared in the foregoing analysis and that are commonly spoken of as love.

Radical love, we discovered, in every instance necessarily issues in primary joy over the beloved's existence and is proportioned to the known degree with which the beloved realizes potentialities and enjoys the fulness of being. The object of this joy is the loved one as actual. It must be kept distinct from the secondary sort of joy which has an object other than the beloved but responded to by reason of its relation to the beloved, for instance, joy over some event that conduces to the beloved's well-being. Radical love can also issue in sorrow over the loved one's misery, over defective being. This, however, is not a necessary consequence of love nor is it mistaken for love by any eminent thinker. It is not necessary because the beloved may be full and firm in being or, at least, the lover may for the moment be unaware of or inattentive to the beloved's misery. Since radical love is always a conscious response to the beloved's actuality, there will always be some joy over the beloved's being. This affection alone is a necessary accompaniment of radical love in every instance.

When the object of radical love is perceived to be in need, radical love becomes care. Although radical love can and does arise without the form of care, the human condition is such that moments of simple radical love are less common than radical love as care and are fleeting. The reality of our constant human need insistently calls for the lover's care.

Joy is a terminal affection and does not of itself give rise to other affections, though it may *per accidens:* thus, the loss of an experienced joy can be the object of sorrow and the lost joy an object of desire. But joy in act does not of itself necessarily issue in desire or in sorrow. Care, on the contrary, of its very nature, *per se,* gives rise to an affirmation of whatever relative ends correspond to the needs of the one cared for, as also of the means to these ends. This is a relative affirmation of what is affirmed not for itself but for another.

Is this relative affirmation desire? Many would be ready to say so, and with reason. However, one fact causes hesitation: we found that there is also a joy that has as its object what is joyed in not for itself but for another, joy in a secondary meaning of the word as we spoke of it. So, affirmative affection toward something only for another and not for itself can be either joy or desire, desire for what is not yet attained and filling the need of one cared for or joy in what is actually filling the need of the loved one (or what we anticipate with confidence will fill that need). But the fact that we have these two affirmative affections toward the same object, which is a relative or implemental end, suggests that there is an affirmative response to this object that is the ground of both desire and relative joy and is not to be fully identified with either. Is this so?

There was no need to bring up this question when we were moving analytically toward the discovery of radical love: if there is such an affection, an analysis of it would undoubtedly lead us reductively to care even as desire and joy did. Now, however, when we are synthetically building up the main affective structure of the total experience of love, it will be a significant question. And we should take it up also because two authors of great stature, Augustine and Aquinas, assert its reality. Let us first of all ask whether there is reason at all to assert such an affection and then, if there is, whether it ought to be called love at all. For now let us speak of it tentatively as implemental love, keeping a mental question mark after it as we did for radical love until we either decide it is nonexistent and drop it out of consideration, or decide it is real and drop the question mark.

One reason for thinking that implemental love is a reality distinct from desire is the fact already noted, namely, that we affirm implemental ends and the means to these ends not only as objects tended to but also as attained and rejoiced in. If these objects are affirmatively responded to as qualified by two different relationships with the subject of the response (attained or unattained), then basic to both is a simple affirmation, unqualified by these relations, neither of which is necessary to the affirmation. The common way of speaking and thinking points to the reality of this same simple affective affirmation. Whether they should or not, people do speak of loving books and food, conversation and dancing, etc. And they speak this way not only about what they desire but also about what they are actually enjoying without desire (unless with desire for the continuation of what they are here and now enjoying). We love what is lacking and is wanted, but we do not cease to love it when we have it. We only cease desiring it. We love what we enjoy and we do not cease to love it when we are without it and are desiring it. We only cease to enjoy it.

The argument for the reality of implemental love is further strengthened by the fact that there is in our experience a continuity between joy and desire: desire when its object is attained does not so much appear to be replaced by joy as to be changed into joy; conversely, when the object is lost, joy seems to change into desire rather than be exchanged for it. A common affective basis is called for to explain this. Just as there is a radical love that grounds and explains both primary joy over the actuality of the loved one and radical care for the loved one in need, so also there seems to be an affirmation of a relative object (something for the loved one), an affirmation that grounds and explains other affections toward the relative object. The only two which are of direct concern here are desire and secondary or relative joy; for only these two in the total experience of love are thought to be love.

Once such considerations as these direct and focus our attention, we can see this common affection, which we have called implemental love, appear to us in reflection on experience. It does not appear by itself apart from desire or joy (or some other affection) toward the relative object. It is always in an experience of desire or joy. It can be taken for the constitutive ground of these other affections, so that it is these when it is qualified in a certain way by a certain adventitious relation with the object. Thus it is desire when the object is unattained or joy when the object is attained. This seems to be the way Augustine thought of it. On the other hand, it might be taken for a distinct affection which always gives rise to another such as desire or joy depending on the relation with the object. This seems to be the way Aquinas thought of it. Even in this latter way of seeing it, the implemental love forms one complex *affective* reality with the dependent affection. In either case we are justified in including within the affective structure of the total concrete experience of love as it commonly occurs the affection of implemental love.

The other question remains: given that there is in our experience a basic affective affirmation of objects which are relative ends or means to relative ends, does it deserve the name love? Is it not altogether an equivocation to call it by that name after the analysis made of radical love? Care and joy in its primary meaning at least have the same

object as radical love, those we affirm for and in themselves. But
 implemental love, so called, has a different object from radical love, a
derivative one not affirmed for and in itself. Is it merely confusing
things to call this affection love?

Some want to say that there is no love for relative objects. Love,
they say, is only for persons and only for persons as beings valued in
and for themselves. Others hold that things other than persons are
loved but to love them means to love them for themselves, in much
the same way as we love persons. Either opinion makes nonsense of
common usage according to which we love all kinds of things that
are not loved for themselves: food, drink, money, clothes, games, etc.
Since these opinions come into head-on clash with an almost universal manner of thinking and speaking, their proponents should offer
convincing reasons to support them if they are to merit serious consideration. When such reasons are not offered (as to my knowledge
they are not), then one can only think that the opinions are founded
on arbitrary definitions and spring from an understandable but un-
justifiable desire to simplify a complicated matter.

One might think that this is merely a war about words and it makes
no real difference regarding our understanding of the experience. This
could be true. If those who wish to limit the meaning of love to acts
with objects loved for themselves (or itself) would make clear the
reality and nature of what I am speaking of as derivative love, then
the only issue at the moment would be a rhetorical one, that is,
whether it is more advantageous for clarity of communication to use
one name, love, qualified in two ways or to use two altogether different names, love and something else. Even on rhetorical grounds, a
good case could be made for using the name implemental love. By
remaining with the word love, we continue to use a universal mode
of speech about a matter of universal importance and interest. By the
word implemental in opposition to radical we give precision to common speech. And finally we point up the close analogy of this derivative affection with the underived affection of radical love. Let us look
at that analogy.

The central note of radical love, we discovered, is affective affirmation of loved ones in their totality and for themselves. Now, implemental love is also an affective affirmation of its object—even though
not for itself but for another and not in its totality but only under
that aspect by which it is for the object of fundamental love. This is
not merely an equivocation. The house, the clothing, the music are
affirmed for someone to live in, to wear, to enjoy. But they are affirmed. The totally relative character of the affirmation is especially

clear when the being of the object is used up, destroyed, in the service of the ones loved for themselves, for example, food and drink. But it is clear also that these are in their relation to the others' health and pleasure truly affirmed. The one loving wills their reality under that aspect by which they are useful or pleasurable for another. Thus, while the common note of fundamental and implemental love is analogous, it is intrinsic to the implemental as well as to the radical love from which it derives.

The analogy with fundamental love can be carried a step further by pointing out that this derivative affirmation constitutes an affective union of the lover with the object of implemental love—again, only with the reality of the thing or activity loved insofar as and under the aspect by which it is an object of this sort of affirmation. Even as through fundamental love the lover's act of self-affirmation is brought into union with the loved one in the way explained, so also through implemental love it is brought into union with actions and things which are for the object of fundamental love, into a consonant union.

We can go further and say that by implemental love the one loving is in the object and in some sense identified with the object. This shows up in the experience of giving a gift to a loved one. Consider what is commonly seen as an act of gift-giving. Somehow the lover is in the gift and is one with the gift or it would have no meaning over and above its physical or biological reality. A rose given as a gift is immeasurably more than a rose in a garden. And the act of presenting it as a gift is immeasurably more than the same physical act performed by a florist for a customer. The reason is that lover give themselves in the gift; that is what makes it a gift. To say they give themselves in the gift is to say that their act of being, their self-affirmation, is somehow one with the act of being of that which they render a gift by their affirmation of it. But it is so only insofar as that object is a gift, is for the others who are loved for themselves. To accept a gift with love (and without love nothing is accepted as a gift) it to know this with a lived knowledge— though we do not understand by reflective analysis. A sign of this fact is our attitude toward the gift. We treat it with reverence, tenderness, or even at times with anger, which is like the reverence, tenderness, or anger shown to the person who gave the gift. It is true that other things than gifts are treated in a similar manner, e.g., photographs, books that have been used by a loved one, a manuscript written by the loved one, even though it is not written to the possessor. There is a similarity here inasmuch as in all these instances the personal act of being is thought to be in some way extended to these objects, rubbed off on them, as it were. And so they are treated in a way that indicates they are somehow taken up into the object of fundamental love. There is, however, something special about a gift. I may not have had the gift in possession for any length of time or used it. And even if I did, my union with the gift is something more than "rubbing off" on to it; I join myself to it in an active and conscious affirmation of it because it is for the loved one for whom I myself am. Now, is not everything provided for loved ones or every act done for them out of radical love really a gift? And these are all objects of implemental love. All that we said of the union, even identification, of the lover with the gift applies therefore to any object of implemental love. Does this not make very striking the analogy of this affection with radical love, justifying the use of love in both cases?

The foregoing considerations establish the reality of and illuminate the nature of implemental love as a consequence of radical love. It, in turn, is an immediate principle of desire and joy. How these two, desire and joy, differ from each other and how they fit into the affective structure of the total concrete experience of love has emerged in the course of describing implemental love as also in the earlier reductive analysis. Desire is not only a consequence of radical love but more immediately it is a consequence of implemental love. Desire is a conscious affective tendency toward *some thing* I affectively affirm by *implemental* love for you whom I affirm by *radical* love for *you*. To call desire (conscious affirmative tendency) love, and that without any qualification whatsoever, is to give the name to what is derivative from radical love and what is sometimes (very rarely) not even found in the full concrete experience of love. However fundamental desire is in human life as the source of activity, a more careful analysis of the experience of love than that made by Plato or Freud or Tillich shows how much in that experience is more fundamental than the tendency they call love. All that is most fundamental in affective experience is left unnoticed by them.

This point is so important and so commonly overlooked that one may hope to be excused for belaboring it. Even if we should bypass implemental love and even if we should grant that the human experience of love always involves at least the desire for union, the previous analysis shows that this desire is really a desire for fuller union springing from an already actual union constituted by a more radical affection. That this is so can be shown by asking why the lover desires union. Do I desire it for myself only or for the sake of the other also, for you? If for you also, as I do if my love is radical love for you, then I do not merely desire you as the term of the union that fulfils me; I have an affection toward you, the other for whom I desire the union with myself. This affection is more radical than desire in the total experience.

In short, no tendency affection is irreducible. And if one wishes to speak of desire as love, one can only do so in an extended meaning of the word. The fact that it arises in living unity with radical or implemental love gives some ground to justify such usage. For what has also shown up strikingly in the previous descriptions is that radical care and radical joy, implemental love, desire and derivative or implemental joy, all flow from, have their psychic life from, radical love, whether immediately or mediately. Not all arise in every experience of love but all that do arise in every experience from one complex whole with one life running through it, a life that springs out of fundamental or radical love.

Benevolence

A question can reasonably be raised before concluding our discussion of the affective structure of the total experience of love. Where does benevolence fit into this structure? After all, in the survey of notions of love, benevolence was said to be, along with desire, the most widely accepted notion of love. Yet, after saying so, it has not been mentioned, neither in the reductive analysis nor in this present synthesis of affections in the total experience of love. If this is an oversight, it could prove to be a serious one. If it is not, then how justify such a deliberate omission?

We can resolve the difficulty by analyzing benevolence. To my knowledge, among those who speak of love as benevolence, Aquinas provided the most discerning analysis. He points out that it involves a two-fold love: a primary love, which he calls love simply, toward the one for whom a good is willed; and a secondary love, which he calls love relatively, toward the good willed for the object of love simply. However, even his analysis is both imprecise and leaves questions unanswered. The definition accepted from Aristotle, willing good to someone, really expresses only the secondary love, love relatively. The love simply is not named in this formula, much less defined. It is merely implied. (Although Aquinas uses this definition for love more often than any other, he corrects himself in one text [2-2, q. 27. a. 2, obj. and reply to obj. 1]. He shows no sign of being disturbed at the thought of the large revision this one sentence might require in his writing on *amor* and *caritas*.)

This formula is a definition of relative love, of what has been called in this study "implemental love." For "willing good to someone" does not mention any act toward someone for whom a good is willed. Clearly the someone must first be "willed" (loved) if there is to be any willing of a good for someone. It is because I respond with love to people that I will the good for them. If I had no loving response to them directly, there would be no response to a good relative to them.

Even this is not really precise. For the implied response to people for whom I will a good may not be a response of love simply toward them. It is possible for me to will a good for people whom I do not love, whom I even hate. Thus, physicians can will a good for patients receiving treatment because it will bring fame or money to the physician; they may have only relative love for the ones they are treating, and may even hate them. Or people can will a benefit for those they hate in order to spite others whom they hate more. Willing good to someone may or may not spring from and express love of the beneficiaries for their own sakes. In ultimate analysis, there will always be some love simply (fundamental or radical love) at the root of benevolence, but it can be for the wellwisher's own self or a third party, as well as, for the beneficiary.

Finally, even when the fundamental love, love simply, is toward the one for whom a good is willed, willing a good to someone says nothing about what this love is. What is the love at the source of benevolence? To say that it is a love that gives rise to willing a good for someone does not tell us what it is in itself. And again what is the act of will toward the good for someone? It is neither desire nor joy but the principle of these. That does not tell us what it is in itself. How does it differ from joy or desire? And what is there in common between the love towards someone for whom the good is willed and the love toward that good which is for that person? What justifies calling both of them love? We have found no clear or coherent answers to these questions given by those who write on benevolence. The answers that can be offered coherently with the analysis of love already presented in this study are obvious. Love simply, love toward someone for whom a good is willed, is what has been named radical love and been described in detail. The "willing a good to someone" is what has been named implemental love and also described. That radical love is love most properly speaking and that implemental love is love analogously has just been shown.

Once benevolence has been analyzed in this way, the justification for ignoring it until now is evident. It adds nothing to our understanding of the affective structure of our concrete experience of love beyond radical love and care and implemental love. And, although the word itself serves for colloquial purposes, as a result of its being used to stand for love without qualification, it is altogether too ambiguous to serve our purposes. Therefore it has been better not to discuss it at all until this point.

Conclusion   *Formula*

Within the total concrete experience of love the ultimate *affective* root has been uncovered. Radical love has been shown to be itself irreducible to any other affection and to be the *root of all the other affections* that are integral to the experience of love and that are called love either in common speech or by theologians, philosophers, and psychologists. This affection is what we should call love without any qualification. However, the use of radical to set it apart from care-love or implemental love or desire-love (if one wishes to stretch the word) appeals as a safeguard against slipping back into confusion in speech and so perhaps in thought. And what we have discovered about radical love can be gathered up in some such formula as this: *radical love is a response in which the lover (I) affectively affirm the beloved (you) for yourself (as a radical end), in yourself (on account of your intrinsic lovable actuality), directly and explicitly in your personal act of being, implicitly in your total reality (by which affirmation my personal being is consonantly present to and in you and yours is present to and in me,) by which I affectively identify with your personal being, by which in some sense I am you affectively.*

9
THE CONSUMMATION OF RADICAL LOVE: COMMUNION

The goal of this book appears to be reached. That goal was to un-cover the irreducible root of the whole concrete experience of love, to describe this root and show its relation with the other major elements in the experience. Concluding at this point, however, would leave unexamined what happens to this root affection when radical love is returned and by a reciprocal interpenetration of loves constitutes the composite affective core of communion, that experience which is the consummation of radical love.

The aim of this treatment is not to give directives or cautions nor to celebrate the beauty of communion nor to urge its ethical or psychological value. The experience of communion to which I refer is usually discussed in these terms. The purpose here is both less exalted and more fundamental, namely, to bring out descriptively, with accuracy, something of the nature of this experience that is usually left unexamined in any detail or depth. It is impossible to do this without using expressions that connote values because they refer to what are generally considered to be moral and psychological values. The two principal terms of this sort are union and fulness of being. To eliminate these aspects of the experience would be to eliminate the experience.

The Meanings of Communion

The word communion can carry many meanings that are not to the point here. Let us try to make precise just what experience is pointed to by the word in this context. It is a participation; but it is certainly not just any sort of participation. It is an *experience* and, therefore, a conscious participation. It is an experience at the human level, one, therefore, involving intellectual knowledge and love. Strictly speaking, this is not accurate. Communion can involve a love falsified by reason of false insight and judgment; and a false insight and judgment is not knowledge. However, for ease of expression let us note this qualification and continue to talk of knowledge and love in communion, leaving it as understood that what is called knowledge can be to some degree false and so an intellectual act which is not really knowledge. Further, knowledge and love in the communion with which we are concerned are reciprocal, bilateral. Each person knows and loves the other simultaneously: the lover is loved and the loved is lover. In order to avoid ambiguity and at the same time to avoid the tiresome repetition of qualifiers, let it be understood from here on that whenever the word communion is used, unless explicitly stated otherwise, it refers to communion by reciprocal knowledge and love, a bilateral relation in which each of two persons knows and loves the other. (Thus not even every I-Thou relation is communion as the word is used here, unless one limits the I-Thou relation to a relation between persons and thinks that personal love always involves mutual love.)

The concrete experience of communion, of course, involves much more than intellectual knowledge and love. Multiple affections, the imagination, bodily reactions, and freedom, are all integral to full human communion. In order to give adequate attention to the core of the experience we have methodically to leave on the fringe of our attention all these other elements, even as we did in describing the experience of unilateral love.

And even at the core of communion, it is love, not knowledge nor the relation between knowledge and love, that holds the focus of attention. When studying love as affirmation, we saw how knowledge is a positive liberating condition for love and that it affects love intrinsically, mediating to love the differences within objects. In concrete experience, the relationship is much more complex. The lover's love in turn makes possible a knowledge that only the lover can have of the loved person; and, in the experience of communion, the other's love reveals the other and makes possible an even deeper knowledge and a qualitatively different love in the lover—even as the lover's love makes possible the other's knowledge and self-revealing love. If then, within the context of this study with its limited aim, attention is focused on love, and knowledge is attended to only as a positive condition for love, it is not an oversight but a methodical elimination of what would now be a distraction. The reason for attending to communion at all in this book is to discover what happens to radical love in this fullest experience of love and so to let the notes of such love as they appeared in the previous descriptive analysis of unilateral radical love stand out more intensely and clearly.

In doing this, we are concerned only with the single transient experience. Communion understood as reciprocal knowledge and love can refer to a way of life characterized by recurrent moments of such experience over an extended period of life together, the whole colored by these moments. On the other hand, it can refer to any one of those moments. It is communion in this latter sense that will be described. The other meaning brings up the vast subject of friendship which had best be left for a later study.

Even after we have confined the center of attention within the limits of reciprocal love, there are still multiple ways of loving that can be concurrent or rapidly alternating. Our previous analysis has brought to light three ways of loving: radical, quasi-radical, and implemental. (In order to avoid unnecessary complications and arguments, the distinction of conditional and unconditional love is omitted. If radical love can be conditional, so can communion; if it cannot, neither can communion.) Communion is of one sort or another by reason of the way in which two persons love reciprocally.

The reciprocal loves, at least the quasi-radical and implemental loves, can be founded in some common non-reciprocal love. When this is so, the more fundamental love does not itself constitute communion. Thus, suppose that you and I have a common radical love for a third person but love each other with a quasi-radical love in relation to this one. Then the communion between us is quasi-radical, not radical. There may or may not be radical communion between each of us and our common loved one, depending upon whether that third person returns the radical love. Or suppose we have a common implemental love: we both love dancing or philosophy or companionable drinking. If our loves are not reciprocal and so do not constitute communion of any sort. But they can be the ground of reciprocal implemental loves. We can love each other as dancing partners, as sharers in philosophical discussions, or as tavern companions. This reciprocal implemental love is what constitutes implemental communion.

The foregoing observations reveal how defective is the frequently used distinction between communion in which those who love "face each other" as, e.g., in romantic or married love, and communion in which they face in the direction of a common goal or ideal as, e.g., in "friendship" so-called. There can be no communion by reciprocal love (above all by reciprocal radical love, but even by implemental love also) without those who love facing each other in their love. (It is also true that human love does not endure well between those who only face each other and have no common goals or ideals. But that is a question of the conditions for growth and endurance of love and communion, not of their constitution.) If the situation is such that each loves the goal or ideal and knows of the other's love for it and is even comforted by that fact but does not love the other radically or at least implementally, they have a common love but they have no re-ciprocal love. Therefore there is no communion. All those who love one another face one another affectively. The character of the rela-tion is determined by the kind of love they have for one another, not by the kind of love they have for some third person or for some common finality, however exalted in itself or however deeply imbed-ded in the personalities of the lovers. Those who have in common and are aware of having in common the same goal to which they devote their whole lives may still have no love for each other or no more than an implemental reciprocal love, as for example, academic or political colleagues. On the other hand, even if the two have dif-ferent goals or ideals fundamental to their lives, so long as they love one another as persons with radical love, they are in radical com-munion. Thus a Christian and an atheist might be in communion, whereas two Christians or two atheists who do nor have a reciprocal fundamental love would not be.

Having discerned and clarified the three kinds of communion by reciprocal love, we can further limit the center of attention to com-munion by reciprocal radical love. For our purpose is to gain, if not a fuller description of radical love, at least a deeper understanding of the description already achieved, by seeing radical love in its most complete and intense moment. That moment is radical commun-ion.

Before leaving the other forms of communion aside and focusing exclusively on radical communion as the center, two final remarks about the way these several kinds of communion arise in concrete experience are called for. First of all, there are mixed types of com-munion. The question has probably occurred to the reader: what about those instances in which one person loves the other radically and the other loves the first implementally or quasi-radically? Such situations are certainly a part of our experience, and we certainly have to say that there is communion by reciprocal love in them. However, this offers no serious problem. We can simply say that in communion of the pure type, each loves the other in the way that oneself is loved. When they do not so love, we have a mixed type. The second remark called for in regard to the several forms of com-munion in the concrete is that communion can slide back and forth from one sort to the other so easily and rapidly as hardly to be no-ticed by those who do not question and examine their motivations. Love in the ordinary person glides, imperceptibly to ordinary atten-tion, from radical to implemental love and back again—i.e., love for one and the same person. We begin to love with a generous love for

the other and easily slide off into a selfish love, with the other as
object of implemental love. Sometimes our selfishness is taken off
guard and we find some spontaneous generosity has gotten us into a
situation that selfishness regrets. If love in the concrete oscillates in
this manner, communion will necessarily do the same and so take
varying pure or mixed forms.

Radical Communion

Our task now is to hold within the center of attention the fluctuating life of love in a moment of unmixed radical communion and
seize its reality as fully and as accurately as possible. Let it be a moment of radical communion at its deepest, when each knows and
loves the other directly experienced to some degree in the other's
unique personal reality. What is said of this sort of communion will
be paralleled in modified ways in lesser forms of communion. It is in
the fullest consummation of love that its nature can be most fully
revealed to us, and so we look there.

When we approach this consummation of love in communion,
the attitude that makes us tend to back away from analysis of love
will surely assert itself more strongly than ever. Are we not face to
face now at last with mystery? Who can penetrate the mystery of
communion? It can only be understood by living it. Such an attitude, it must be said, at least holds more awareness of the reality that
is here than the attitude of those who think to "explain" it all away by
psychological projection or sublimation of biological drives or the
attitude of those who think they have understood communion when
they have intoned a few vague evocative phrases. However, perhaps
this attitude mistakes the obscurity left by a failure to observe and to
think seriously about communion for a mystery which is real but lies
further on. Perhaps we can succeed to some extent in conceptualizing and formulating certain features of the experience that are beyond the superficial and banal. Even if it turns out that we cannot
and the effort flounders, the very floundering in the effort to understand what is going on in personal communion, to throw some light
on the profound union and fulness of lives bound together in its
exquisite interaction, will make us realize the reality and depth of
mystery better than we ever could without such an effort.

To begin with, we can note that in communion all that was said
above about the union established by unilateral love is doubled from
the side of the loved one, who now is lover as well as loved. And all
we said about being loved is doubled from the side of the lover who
now is loved as well as loving. I know and love you in and for your

unique self. You know and love me in the same way. My act is an act of union and for me an increase of conscious life. Your act is an act of union from your side and for you an increase of conscious life. My being loved by you is in some sense an expansion of my being into your conscious life. So also your being loved by me is in some sense an expansion of your being into my conscious life.

All this is so even if neither of us is aware of the other's love. But, in that case, the doubling and the union constituted by it does not enter the conscious life of either of us. Each of us actualizes in our own consciousness only one side of the reality of love, my own love or yours. Neither of us actualizes in consciousness the other's love or one's own being loved. (This last phrase is not merely redundant. Your love for me and my being loved by you are only two aspects of one reality seen from two sides, that is true. Nevertheless, the distinction of these two aspects is significant, as can be readily seen by noting what is missing when I do not know of your love for me. The joy I have over the expansion of my being by being loved and the joy I have over the fulness of your being in loving me are distinct joys.) What is missing is easily seen by noting what happens when we do come to know of each other's love. Because I love you, I already experience an increased fulness of life by union with you. Now when I discover that you love me, my consciousness is flooded with a new experience of fuller life in more complete union with you. I become aware of what already was: your love, your greater fulness of life in union with me, my expanded existence and doubled union with you in your love. What was reality before I became aware of it was conscious reality only in your life. Now it enters my conscious life also. And because I affirm you as I affirm myself, all that I now experience from your side enters my consciousness as my life, not only the expansion of my being by being loved, but also your increased fulness of life in loving me. I was already you affectively. Now your conscious life, which is mine by reason of my love, begins to enter my consciousness. The whole experience is paralleled from your side.

All this does not yet bring out as much as we can grasp of the interaction and interpenetration by knowledge and love in the union constituted by reciprocal radical affirmation. The union, we see, is doubled by reciprocal love. The doubled union of love enters each one's conscious life. But suppose one or both of us, while knowing that the other returns the love, does not yet know that the other is aware of being loved. Suppose I love you and I know that you love me. Suppose you know that I love you. But suppose I do not know that you know of my love and you do not know that I know of your love. Something of great importance in radical communion is still missing. The foregoing statement, no doubt, sounds very confusing and one might think we are merely playing with words or at least that the analysis is getting so exaggeratedly refined as to lose all real significance. The truth is we are now touching on what is perhaps the profoundest observable aspect of communion and the most significant one. And further, while it is hard to fix attention on this aspect and harder yet to formulate it in words even when it is caught sight of, once it is seen the reality itself is lucid. The following scheme may make the reality I am pointing to stand out more plainly:

A { 1. I love you.
    2. You love me.

B { 3. I know (2) and love you thus actualized toward me.
    4. You know (1) and love me thus actualized toward you.

C { 5. I know (4) and love you thus actualized toward me.
    6. You know (3) and love me thus actualized toward you.

We have already seen how B3 and B4 are necessary in order that A1 and A2 should be in the conscious life of both of us. What is the significance of C? C5 is necessary in order that B4 should enter into my Conscious life; C6 is necessary in order that B3 should enter your conscious life. And when this happens the reciprocal conscious acts of love so deeply interact and interpenetrate as in some sense to constitute one composite mutual act.

If we look at this union of reciprocal acts of love from the side of each as lover and from the side of each as loved the same truth flashes out at us. Looking first at the act from the side of each as responding to the other with love, we see not only that each is actualized by response to the other, but each is actualized by response to the other as actualized by response to oneself! Or, shifting the point of view from that of the lover to that of the beloved calling forth a response of love, not only does each beloved call the other into actuality as a lover, but each does so in virtue of the actuality called forth in each by the other! Let us loosen and expand these compressed statements so that the meaning can stand out more clearly.

Radical love, we have noted, arises as response to the whole reality of the loved one, including therefore potentiality and drive to actuation of potentiality. But it is primarily and explicitly a response to the loved one's actuality. In responding to the beloved's actuality, the lover's own energy of love is released and the lover is actualized as lover. We saw further that each response of love is intrinsically formed in a different way, has its unique differentiation by relation to the beloved as the lover apprehends the beloved. Thus in a very real sense the lover's love lives from the beloved and the lover is actuated as lover by the beloved. (Throughout this discussion, I will speak of love—and of the lovableness constituted by loving—as deriving from the loved one, taking for granted an understanding of what was said above about the act of love having its existential reality from the lover's own act of being, arising spontaneously from that act of being.) Further, it is in the lover's radical love for the other that the lovableness of the lover's own act of being is actualized here and now most fully, is revealed to the other, and so calls forth the other's love. If the lover's love is from the loved one, then the beloved's lovableness as actualized and revealed in that love and calling forth love from the other is from that other.

Now in communion two persons respond to each other in the way just described. So each is responding to the other as actualized and revealed in the other's response. My love for you is brought to life by you as you are actualized and revealed in your love for me. Your love for me, however, is brought to life by me as I am actualized and revealed in my love for you. Clearly then in communion what I do depends not only on your being lovable, but on your being in act as lover toward me. And your being in act as lover toward me depends on my being in act as lover toward you. Each of us is enabled to love the other in the way that each does in communion by the other's love for oneself. The acts are reciprocally actualizing and form one total mutual act.

At first glance the reciprocal dependence of knowledge and love in communion might seem to offer a difficulty about its origin. Does it not seem to require a sudden, reciprocal, love at first sight, in which knowledge and love in each begins at the same instant by reason of some pre-established harmony? If not, how can it begin at all? For I cannot know nor love you in the way described unless I am known and loved by you; and you cannot know nor love me in the way described unless you are already knowing and loving in a way that presupposes my knowing and loving. There seems to be a vicious circle here, each knowledge and love presupposing the other and therefore impossible unless they begin simultaneously. And such a simultaneous beginning seems quite outside our real experience of communion. If so, the foregoing description of radical communion as a mutual act must be relinquished or revised.

The point of the difficulty is valid. The conclusion is not valid. Communion as described can begin only in the simultaneity of radical loves, each depending on the other. But what seems such a great difficulty when raised in the abstract, vanishes when we look carefully at our concrete experience of the origin of communion. Only consider one or two normal experiences. I may love you though not yet with the same love that will arise when your love for me actualizes and reveals your lovableness to me in a new way. You can see my lovableness as realized and revealed in my love for you (the love preliminary to your reciprocation). This makes me more readily lovable to you and you can love me actualized in my love for you. This love you have for me, if known by me, makes it possible for me to love you now as actualized in this return of love. At that moment communion can begin. Or take a simpler case. Each of us may love the other without either knowing of the other's love. Then one day a situation arises in which each suddenly knows the other's love for oneself. At that moment communion can begin. In both of these instances, communion begins with simultaneous radical loves, simultaneously known to each other. But this does not mean that radical love cannot begin prior to communion and even prior to any mutuality of love. Prior love prepares for the moment at which communion begins, sometimes overwhelmingly, sometimes quietly. Without some radical love prior to communion, the latter would not likely ever happen unless there is such a thing as reciprocal love at first sight. If it is a reality, it is not a common reality and certainly not the ordinary way in which communion begins. Note that the question here is not one merely of love at first sight—that might happen very readily. What is in question is a reciprocal love at first sight, which happens from both sides at the same instant.

Lest some simulacrum of such communion as we are describing should be mistaken for it, one last observation is called for. It is a striking fact that this union of persons in a mutual act composed of their reciprocal loves is such that the more they are one in their loves the more they are distinct as persons to each other, not separate nor even separable, but distinct. As each one becomes the other affectively in a more burningly intense loving and being loved, the more each stands out to the other in the flaming distinction of each one's unique selfhood. Union and distinction turn out to be in direct instead of inverse proportion.

This surprising fact is something that our previous description of radical love and communion makes intelligible to us and that therefore confirms that analysis. In radical love the loved ones are affirmed for and in themselves as unique radical ends. This is so whether the lover responds to the loved one's unique value as experienced or only as something judged to be so without experiencing it; but we are now describing a communion in which each has experiential knowledge of the other's uniquely lovable personal self and responds with a love intrinsically in accord with that unique self. If radical communion is constituted by a reciprocal radical love, then it is impossible that a greater intensity of reciprocal love, which makes a more intense union, should in any way lessen the affirmation of the other in the other's own unique selfhood. On the contrary, the very nature of radical love necessitates that both become to the other more incomparable, distinct values to be cherished in and for themselves.

But perhaps there is the danger that affirmation of the unique other as it becomes more intense may mean that lovers lose something of their own sense of selfhood and merges with their beloveds. In treating of (unilateral) love as union, we have already seen that this cannot happen. It is made doubly impossible by the reciprocity of radical love in communion. For my affirmation is of you actualized and revealed in your unique affirmation of my unique self; and your affirmation is of me actualized and revealed in my unique affirmation of your unique self. How then can either of us identify by love with the other who is actualized by identifying with oneself, unless we both hold on to our own distinct and unique selves? I give myself to you who are actualized by giving yourself to me. Or rather, how can each of us love the other in the way we do in full-blown radical communion without each affirming each one's own distinct and unique self as affirmed by the other? We have already seen how truthful love of self and the other as persons escapes all opposition between the two loves; in fact, each one implies the other. In radical communion because of the reciprocal relationship (each love actualized by relation to the other love), not only does each love imply the other love, but each explicitly includes the other in its very intelligibility. Each love is the love it is by reason of the other love. I affirm you actualized and revealed to me in your act of affirming me. How can I affirm you in this way without affirming me as affirmed by you? The same holds from your side.

When we see that love of self blossoms from love of the other in radical communion, it is still necessary to insist that priority belongs to the love of the other. Otherwise all we have seen slides out of focus. We have been talking of how each one in radical communion is actualized by relation to the other's love for oneself, how each experiences fuller life by sharing the other's life. It is easy to lose firm hold on the essential insights previously achieved and fall into several misconceptions which often confuse discussion of love and communion. For we easily begin to assume that the reason for loving is the enrichment of the lover's life, self-fulfilment. Or we think that love in communion may to some extent go beyond self-seeking, but the very fact that we are so enriched by communion implies that our love is to some extent and necessarily an acquisitive, self-seeking love. And third, we can easily be led to think that if radical love is possible without reciprocation it must necessarily be a lesser love, a stunted love.

A word about each of these misconceptions. As soon as either of those in the act of radical communion loves the other *because* the other loves oneself and enriches oneself in any way or *because* one is enriched by one's own love for the other, radical communion is terminated. To love the other as a source of fulfilment is to make the other an object of implemental love, springing from care for self and ultimately from radical self-love. Radical communion may begin again as soon as each loves the other for and in the other's own self; but until then, there is no radical communion. When each does love the other for and in the other's own self, they are both more fulfilled than they are when loving for the sake of fulfilment. But being fulfilled does not make fulfilment the motive for loving. In radical love the motive is simply the other person to whom each responds as to a radical end. You love me because I am I, and I love you because you are you. The self-fulfilment of radical communion in the very nature of the case is the consequence of such love, but it is impossible as soon as self-fulfilment becomes the motive of love. Nevertheless, if that fulfilment is present only as a consequence of reciprocal love, then does not that fact point to the conclusion that radical love outside communion is a lesser love, an incomplete love?

To show that such a conclusion is also a misconception we have to note some other facts in our experience of love not explicitly attended to before, but implied by what we have observed and themselves observable. Whether or not you can be in this sort of communion with more than one person at the same time, at least it is clear that you can be in communion with different persons at different times or just be loving other persons without any return of love. It is also clear from experience that I can be aware of your loving others than myself and be moved by the beauty of your love for them—the beauty of your personal being actualized and revealed in your love. Further, your love is intrinsically differentiated from two sources. As a response to the loved one, it is differentiated by the loved one's reality which you apprehend. Each of those to whom you respond will call into conscious actualization some different facet of your personal self which no other can. Your love is also differentiated as your response. Your response to someone will not be just the same as mine; each is an expression of a unique personality responding to that one. By reason of the one to whom you are responding your unique act of being will express itself in a distinctive way. Now, someone else could easily call forth a more beautiful revelation of yourself in your love for that someone than I could. It is also possible that I could be aware of your greater, more beautiful love for that other one. Whether I am so or not usually depends on the measure in which I have conquered my egoism—though in a particular situation my egoism could be caught with its defenses down or even find its defenses shattered by the splendor of what I see. In that case, I respond to you actualized in love toward another with a greater love than I respond to you actualized in love toward me. The completeness of union with you (and the fulness of being) that would come into my life in radical communion by reciprocal love would be missing in this experience. But my unconsummated radical love would itself be a greater love in this case than it would be in communion with you. The love lives from you, not from the fulfilment you bring me. If you are actualized and revealed to me in a greater way by your love for another than for me, then my response of love to you so actualized (if I am capable of so responding) will be greater. (A theological qualification is in order. Once a someone believes as a Christian that every created person is a finite revelation of the infinite Word of the Eternal Father, then it follows that communion with the Word in the Holy Spirit can actualize created persons in all the ways it is possible for them to be actualized as the persons they are. But no created person can bring forth in a loved one what another person can.)

And once this is clear, I then see that even when the you I respond to in communion is the you it is by love for me, nevertheless, it is not because you love *me* that I respond with love in or out of communion. It is because of *you*. When I want to say why I love with a radical love, the last word is you. I love you because you are you. And I would be you by love without ceasing to be myself because I must be I in order that you may be you in the way that I alone can make you be you. If in so doing I become I in the way that only you can make me be, that is love's reward but not love's motive.

BOOK 2

PERSONAL FRIENDSHIP

THE EXPERIENCE

AND

THE IDEAL

Jules Toner

CONTENTS

DEDICATION

For the friend of half a lifetime
with whom above all I have experienced
and continue to experience ever more fully
the life-giving power of personal friendship.

INTRODUCTION

In a collection of recent philosophical writings on friendship, the editor remarks: "after a long eclipse, the years since about 1970 have seen a remarkable resurgence of philosophical interest in friendship" (Badhwar 1993, ix). Some signs of it can be seen also among theologians, psychologists, sociologists, and anthropologists.

This resurgence could hardly have been possible a half century ago. So much has the intellectual climate changed that it is hardly believable now, but less than fifty years ago anyone who wrote on love as a serious subject for learned discussion had to face the widespread attitude which Ian Suttie characterized as science's "flight from tenderness." It was to support each other in that adverse climate of thought and to promote research on love that in 1955 a group of eminent thinkers who saw the importance of such study founded, under the leadership of Pitirim Sorokin, the Research Society for Creative Altruism and in 1957 held their first "scientific conference on new knowledge of human values." The results of this conference were published in 1959 under the title, *New Knowledge in Human Values.* (Maslow 1959). The contributors constitute an array of outstanding thinkers in the United States at that time: Henry Margenau, Jacob Bronowski, Robert S. Hartman, Pitirim A. Sorokin, Ludwig Von Bertalanffy, Theodosius Dobzhansky, Gyorgy Kepes, Suzuki, Walter A. Weisskopf, Abraham Maslow, Gordon W. Allport, Erich Fromm, Dorothy Lee, Kurt Goldstein, Paul Tillich. (See also Toner 1964, 5-19, esp. 13-17.)

From this beginning, many eminent writers have contributed to the restoration of love as a subject of importance in many fields of knowledge. (Besides the members of the Research Society of Creative Altruism, there were other influential writers, e.g., Gabriel Marcel, John Macmurray, Teilhard de Chardin, Robert Johann, Ignace Lepp, Ian Suttie.) As a consequence of their work, the way has been opened for serious study and writing on friendship.

The Primary Focus of This Study

In writings on friendship, I find a parallel with what I earlier noted in writings on love: different kinds of love or friendship are noted; splendid things are written in praise of what is said to be the noblest kind; wise counsels are given on how to begin, preserve, and develop such love or friendship; moral issues about it are discussed. One could easily get the impression that what love and friendship are is assumed to be understood by all. But, as will be shown in chapter 1, notions of love among writers on it are many and diverse; and "friendship, far from being a common, ordinary, and simple relationship that we all understand…is an unplumbed mystery we believe we understand until we begin thinking about it" (Telfer 1970, vol. 71, 226). An outstanding exception to the ordinary vague, confused, and unsupported answers to the questions, what is love? and what is friendship? is the recent impressive volume by Edward Collins Vacek (1994). Unfortunately, my manuscript was completed before Vacek's admirable book came into my hands, and I have not been able to devote the time and labor it would require in order to work his thought into my manuscript in the way it deserves.

When friendship is attended to, the focus is usually on its relationship to moral or psychological development or (especially by feminists) to social and political issues. Attention is focused on the role of friendship in these areas. Understandably, the authors want to get on with their main interest, without delaying over the preliminary question, what is friendship? For the most part, when discussing friendship, a writer's answer to the question, what is friendship? is given in a few lines; any fuller understanding, if there is any, can be found only by gathering fragments that appear here and there in dealing with other questions about the experience. It is not easy to find serious and sustained attempts to answer that fundamental question and to justify the answer to it.

Yet, just as the answer to the question, what is love?, will influence all our thinking on what friendship is, so also the answer to the question, *what* is friendship?, will influence the answers to all other questions about it in philosophical anthropology, in ethics, in psychology, sociology, and political thought—in any study in which an understanding of it is important. (Although this essay is not theological, it might turn out to be of some value for Christian theological reflection on the Holy Trinity, on eschatology, on Christian agape and Christian friendship, on Christian Ethics.)

The first and most basic purpose of this book is to achieve a more or less full and coherent phenomenology, in the sense of descriptive analysis and synthesis, of the experience of personal friendship. It is not a book on the art of friendship, or on ethical or psychological problems that arise about living in friendship, or on the social and political importance and implications of friendship. It is an attempt to set the experience of personal friendship apart from the experience of any other kind of friendship, to uncover and examine its essential features, which largely escape our reflective awareness, to give a precise analysis of these and their interrelationships, and, by extrapolation from this description of experience to envision the ideal of personal friendship, which is beyond our observable experience but pointed to by what is in that experience.

The Order of Development

The core of personal friendship is mutual personal communion of love. Without accurate understanding of personal love, no satisfactory study of personal communion and friendship is possible. Achieving the necessary knowledge of personal love depends, I have found, on descriptive analysis and synthesis of the total concrete experience of love, within which the experience of personal love arises. It is, then, with the study of love (chapters 1-3) that this study of friendship must begin.

The results of this preliminary study make possible a sound typology of friendship, in which personal friendship can be distinguished from other types (chapter 4). Only then are we ready to develop a detailed description of the experience of personal friendship, showing its essential core and its properties and their relationships to each other (chapters 5-6). On the basis of that description, it is possible to project beyond our experience what the ideal of such friendship would be if it should ever be attained (chapter 7), to contrast personal friendship with mutual romantic love and to show the relationship of these two central experiences of human life (chapter 8).

Although I count the treatment of love in part I (chapters 1-3) to be necessary for an in-depth study of the experience of personal friendship, I am aware that some readers, perhaps, even among those who are keenly interested in such a study and willing to work at it will find part 1 not at all what they are looking for in a book on friendship. If such readers, instead of putting the book aside, would first look ahead to part 2, they might well find there what they are looking for and might also see the need for part I.

Some Stylistic Decisions

Unless alerted to a few of my decisions regarding style in this book, the reader might sometimes be perplexed or annoyed. The first of these decisions regards my use of the terms "lover" and "beloved" or "loved one." Although these terms usually have an erotic connotation, in this book they ordinarily do not. Unless the context clearly indicates otherwise, they simply mean "one who loves" and "the one who is loved," no matter what kind of love is being discussed.

A second decision concerns the use of pronouns which can become especially confusing both when trying to avoid sexist language and when referring to the one loved and the one loving. Instead of filling the text with such phrases as "he and she," "him and her," "his or hers," I have used the device found in much contemporary writing of simply alternating the feminine and masculine pronouns, using now one and now the other. When using pronouns in referring to the one loving and the loved one, if I use "he" for the lover and "she" for the beloved or the other way around, it is usually not because I am talking about heterosexual love; such usage in this study is ordinarily merely a device to avoid the confusion which can result from referring to both persons in a relationship as she and her or he and him.

There is one phrase which, despite the fact that it could be misread by some, I find difficult to avoid. That phrase is "the object of love." In much contemporary writing on personal relationships, the word "object" as applied to a person has a pejorative meaning: an object is thought to be merely a thing, something to be manipulated for one's own purposes. In my usage, the "object of love" is simply the referent of, the term of, the affective act of love, the one loved as distinct from the one loving. In this usage, "object" has no pejorative implication: the "objects" may be responded to as subjects, as persons worthy of respect and love in themselves for themselves.

Part 1

The Experience of
Personal Love and Communion

I

A PRELIMINARY PROBLEM:
DIVERSE NOTIONS OF LOVE

Preliminary to and fundamental to describing personal love and any of the modes of loving union that have personal love at their core, I must make clear what affective experience I am referring to by the term "love.

Trying to say what the experience of love is immediately runs into a daunting problem, semantic and phenomenological. The word love says Joseph Fletcher in his *Situation Ethics* (1966, 15), is a "swampy one, a semantic confusion," and one is tempted, he says, to delete it from Christian ethical discourse. (Ironically, James Gustafson, in his critical review of Fletcher's book, thinks that the word love runs through it "like a greased pig.") Gene Outka, in *Agape: An Ethical Analysis* (1972, 4), claims that the only thing certain authors have in common when they write on love is the employment of the same word. Michael V. Millor (1987, 23) concludes his review of Irving Singer's third volume of *The Nature of Love* with this discouraging suggestion: "Maybe the search for [the nature of] love is as close as we can get to [the nature of] love." Psychologists as well as philosophers and theologians join the chorus. C.G. Jung remarks that when discussing love we find ourselves talking about "a concept of absolutely unlimited extent and indefiniteness" (quoted in Hazo 1967, 5, n. 2). Theodor Reik says of the word love that "its diversity of meaning, its adaptability and its capability to quick change are astonishing" (Reik 1949, 9).

It is not surprising then, that some consider the question, what is love?, to be unanswerable; they deny the very possibility of finding any common factor in all acts and feelings given that name and, therefore, the possibility of any concept of love which can include them all. Love is said to be an "open concept."

Others, without explicitly denying the possibility of a general notion of love, ignore the need for it and write as though there were no such notion, or, if there is, as though it were of no importance for their purposes. They note and distinguish several kinds of love, but do not trouble themselves to ask what is common to all of them by reason of which every one of them is said to be love. C.S. Lewis, for example (1960, ch. 1), writes of four loves: eros, affection, friendship, and charity—each of which is a different mix of three more fundamental modes of love, need love, gift love, and appreciative love. What common meaning of love can be found in all these different kinds of love is a question he evidently sees for his purpose no need to ask.

Whatever may be the case with others who write on love, for my purpose this question is of fundamental and far reaching importance. But before attempting an answer, it will help in two ways to survey briefly and clarify the bewilderingly diverse notions of love to be found not merely in common usage but also in serious writing on love. An exhaustive survey is not needed, only one that is sufficient to suggest the wide variety of notions and to indicate the main groupings. In this study, such a survey will serve two purposes which can be understood better after the survey.

In this survey, let it be clear, I am interested only in concepts of love as a conscious human affective response. Throughout the history of thought, from the Greeks even to modern writers such as Teilhard de Chardin and Paul Tillich, there have been some who conceived of love not only as an affective act of human beings but as an ontological force in all being. Leaving aside without denying the validity of this notion of love I will focus only on the conscious human affective response. This narrowing of attention still leaves us with discouraging ambiguity.

Some Diverse Notions of Love

There are two most common notions of love in the history of thought on this subject. Many authors who differ in their understanding of love's origin and object and significance in human life all think of it as essentially some kind of affective drive or tendency toward union with someone or something that fulfils the lover. This is, for example, the opinion of Plato, Augustine, Freud, Teilhard de Chardin, and Tillich. The other most common notion of love in writing on this subject is benevolence, willing good to or taking responsibility for someone. It is found, for example, in the writings of Aristotle, Aquinas, Buber, and Fromm. (*Benevolentia* is clearly the predominant notion of love in the writings of Aquinas. However, he also thinks of love as *complacentia* a more fundamental affection than *benevolentia*. Thomas never fully developed his thought on *complacentia* or fully and clearly integrated it with his understanding of love as *benevolentia*, as willing the good of the loved one, whether of the lover's self in *amor concupiscentiae*, or of the other in *amor amicitiae* [not to be confused with *amicitia*]. The fullest, best known, and most respected treatment of *complacentia* is in Crowe 1959.)

It might not be in every one of these authors the only notion of love, but it is the principal one. Nédoncelle's (1966, 8) definition of love as "a will to promotion" seems to belong with benevolence. Closely related to Nédoncelle's definition is that of David Norton. Love, he says (1976, 291), is "aspiration to enhanced value" or the "will to the maximization of value," by which he means willing the actualization of the unique potential worth of the beloved, of his or her unique innate possibilities. Similar to this notion of love but more restricted in meaning is that proposed in the popular psychology of M. Scott Peck (1985, 81): "the will to extend one's self for the purpose of nurturing one's own or another's spiritual growth."

A concept of love which underlies both desire for union and benevolence is "affirmation." Josef Pieper (1974, ch. 2) employs this; so also does Ortega y Gasset—along with a number of other notions that are not all clearly aspects of affirmation or even compatible with each other (Ortega 1957,16-20).

Apart from the main ways of conceiving love, there are some rather singular ways. Thus Unamuno (1954, ch. 7) declares that love is pity (while Reik declares that love and pity for the same object are not even compatible.) Although almost all writers on human love see it as some kind of affective response to some kind of value in the loved one, Singer (1966, 9-16) does not agree. On the contrary, he says, love is a bestowal of value, that is, an imaginative projection of value onto the loved one, value which is not really in him or her.

Some want to talk about love as a combination or cluster of more than one response. Thus Dietrich von Hildebrand says in one passage (1966, 44-47) that love is a response to value for its own sake but, then, adds that it has two fundamental or essential characteristics, yearning toward union with the other person and yearning to make the other person happy. Rollo May in his definition of love (1953, 241) combines delight in the presence of the other person and affirmation of her value and development as much as the lover's own. Sometimes love is said to be a whole series of responses that others would see as consequences or accompaniments of love. Thus, love is said to be rejoicing over the existence of the loved one, longing for his presence, satisfaction over his well being, gratitude, loyalty, readiness to make sacrifices for him, and so on. (See H. Richard Niebuhr's beautiful statement, quoted in Outka 1972, 9-10.)

Differences among ways of conceiving love are often highlighted by what the authors say about self-love. Thus, for Macmurray (1961, 94, 158-59) and Tillich (1954, 6, 33-34) self-love is a self-contradictory concept: there is no such thing as self-love. Love, they think, can only be for others. At the opposite end of the spectrum, psychological egoists insist that all love is in ultimate analysis self-love. This, for example, is the view of Hobbes, Bentham, Mill, Spinoza, and Freud. Nygren sees eros as acquisitive self-love and altogether incompatible with altruistic love; whereas most others hold that self-love can be selfish or not selfish and that the latter is entirely compatible with altruistic love. In fact, some (e.g., Fromm and many clinical or social psychologists) think that well ordered self-love is a condition for being able to love others.

The Need for Descriptive Analysis

These illustrations of the diverse ways of defining love cannot be understood as merely diverse ways of seeing the same reality. Nevertheless, as I hope to show, they are related and can be integrated as elements in one complex concrete experience. Some of them, however, can appear in experience without others; and, even when they are integrated in experience they are still distinct from one another.

I said above that surveying the diverse notions of love serves two purposes here. The first is to show the need for a reflective study of the prereflective total concrete experience that people commonly refer to as love. Second, it serves to indicate what factors anyone attempting such a study should be alert to in the total experience. For, surely, when many intelligent thinkers point to different factors in our experience as being love, what each one points to will likely be at least a significant element in the unanalyzed total experience of love.

Any attempt to analyze and synthesize that complex total experience must not only take account of the many diverse notions of love but also help us to see why intelligent people give the name love to each of these manifold elements in human experience, how these elements are related in the total concrete experience, which ones are essential for any experience of love, which one of these essential elements can most properly be named love, and in what qualified sense each of the others can be so named. To simply assert without descriptive analysis in order to justify the assertion that this or that is love and that other things called love are "not really love" answers the question of what that particular author means by the word but leaves untouched all the above questions about the experience.

2

A Solution of the Problem: Descriptive Analysis of the Total Experience of Love

Concrete Experience of Love
If solving the problem described in the preceding chapter has its starting point in what I call the total concrete experience of love, we need to clarify that experience and show how it is to be studied.

The Total Concrete Experience of Love
By the total concrete experience of love I mean the complex experience which everyone or almost everyone would agree is to be called an experience of love, no matter that there are many opposing opinions on what particular factor or group of factors in the totality essentially constitutes love and justifies calling the whole unified experience by that name.

What goes on in the total experience will be more readily shown if we reflect briefly on how our conscious life in general includes distinct simultaneous experiences and temporally successive but intrinsically related experiences. For instance, I am walking along a busy street, hearing the noise of traffic, and enjoying the blue sky and warm sunshine. At the same time, I am thinking about a book I have been reading or remembering with love a dear friend. The experiences of walking, seeing the bright blue sky, feeling the sun's warmth, hearing the traffic, all readily coalesce in one larger experience. Except for simultaneous presence in my consciousness, these experiences might have nothing to do with thinking about a book or affectionately remembering my friend. However, my thoughts about the book and the noise of the traffic can be joined in one experience if the latter becomes a distraction to my thinking; for the two are now related in an experience of conscious tension. Again, it could be that the strolling on this beautiful day reminds me of the time my friend and I were together under like circumstances. Then the experience of strolling on this beautiful day and of remembering my friend can come together in one larger experience. The point of all this is

merely to call attention to what goes on in our conscious life, how
there are manifold components, some of which have no intrinsic relationship to each other and some of which are so related as to form
one unified experience.

So it is with the total concrete experience of love. This experience
includes cognitive acts—for example, sensations, imaginative images,
intellectual insights, judgments, concepts, sometimes projections or
idealizations. It includes also affective feelings of warmth and openness, of tranquility or disquiet, of union or loneliness, of sweetness
and delight or bitterness and sadness, and so on. It can involve affective acts of admiration, desire, hope, rejoicing, regretting, fear, gratitude, jealousy, benevolence. There can also be bodily reactions and
gestures, for example: increased heartbeat, sexual excitement, smiles,
tears, embraces, handshakes, kisses, acts of giving, and deeds of serving. Prior to reflective analysis and synthesis, the person having this
complex experience is aware only in a vague and confused way of all
the manifold elements in it, attention perhaps focused clearly on one
or another of them, while the others, even or especially the most
fundamental ones, are left on the fringe of attention. What elements
are most fundamental is a question I will try to answer.

A Method for Reflection on the Total Experience of Love

By a methodical reflection, we can successively bring all the principal
components into the center of attention, see their relationships to
each other, and be able to judge which ones are essential to any experience of love and which are contingent even though ordinarily
present. Then we can try to see among those that are essential to the
experience, which component or group of them is love more properly speaking and whether any other or others can be thought of as
love in an extended or derived or qualified sense. Finally, we might
be able to show in every one of the various affections named love that
which is common to them all and offers a basis for a universal concept of love.

To reach these goals it will help to have a series of questions in
mind. Among all the components commonly found in a total concrete experience of love, which are necessarily present if the experience is to be an experience of love? Which of those that are in fact
commonly present could be absent from an experience without it
ceasing to be an experience of love? Which of them can be present in
an experience without it being an experience of love? Among those
components that are not merely accompaniments but are necessarily

present if the experience is to be an experience of love, which element or combination of elements appears as the core or root, the unifying center which by itself can constitute an experience of love and by relation to which the other necessary factors are factors in the experience of love? Among the latter which ones are not themselves love but only conditions necessary for the experience of love or necessary consequences of it?

In *The Experience of Love* I have answered these questions and, in doing so, uncovered what I think is the essential structure of the total experience. While I would no doubt make some revisions and additions were I to rewrite that essay now, I have seen no reason to change the main lines of it. However, I do not think I can assume that readers of this book have already read and understood what is in the earlier one or will now take time out to do so. On the other hand, it is impossible to repeat here the search by which I arrived at my conclusions or even to fruitfully summarize it. All I can do now is to present those conclusions. In doing so, I shall follow an order which is the reverse of that by which in my earlier study I arrived at them. For the descriptive analysis in that book was carried out in a reductive order, going from the more obvious and less profound factors in the total experience to the less obvious and more profound ones, in which the former factors are rooted or at least on which they depend for their being elements in an experience of love. While that reductive order was more suitable for discovery, in the present account of the results, the reverse order will be more readily understandable.

In order to avoid distraction from the main conclusions, I will also assume the answers arrived at in that earlier essay to some preliminary questions: whether there is such a thing as self-love; whether, on the other hand, all love is ultimately self-love; whether one can love anything for itself other than a person. In the earlier essay, I have shown why I think we should assert the reality of self-love, the reality of loving others without reduction to self-love, and of loving for themselves objects other than persons.

The Essential Root or Core of the Total Experience:
Radical Love

In the total concrete experience of love there is one act which is the core of it, the unifying center. By relation to it and only by relation to it, all the other components—cognitive, affective and physical—belong to the experience. For reasons that will appear when the other components are described, this core element can aptly be called radical love. What is it? What does a person do when loving radically? To put it summarily, radical love is: 1. an affective act of affirming the loved one, 2. in herself for herself, 3. which act itself constitutes an actual union of the lover and beloved (rather than only tends toward such union). Each element in this definition needs explanation.

1. To say that radical love is an affective *act* is to exclude affective *feelings* as the core component of every experience of love. A feeling is not an act, but an affective state of being. In the total experience, radical love is at times suffused with powerful feelings of the kind we usually associate with love, feelings such as tenderness, warmth, sweetness, and so on, or, in some situations, feelings such as sadness or bitterness. Sometimes, while radical love endures firmly, these feelings are so tenuous as to seem entirely absent. Awareness of the distinction between the act and the feelings of love is necessary for understanding love in human life. For, identifying love with loving feelings leads to judging whether we love and how much we love by our inconstant and even capricious moods—with possibly destructive consequences. This confusion is abetted by the common careless usage which makes "feelings" a synonym for affections in general, without distinguishing affective acts and affective feelings.

Nothing of what has just been said should be understood as implying that feelings are insignificant in the total experience of love. Quite the contrary. The affective act of love without the appropriate feelings of love is not a full human response to the loved one. Fidelity in loving (in the *act* of loving) without these feelings in any notable degree is certainly admirable and necessary for living human life in our human condition. Periods of affective dryness even seem to be necessary for growth in mature, unselfish, love. Nevertheless, it must be said that such a way of loving is incomplete, needing to be filled out when and insofar as we can do so. While feelings of love are not essential for love, they are so for what I shall name *integral* love, the full response of human love.

The meaning of affective affirmation is a rich one, the richness of which will be drawn out when we describe the union of lover and loved constituted by the affirmation that is radical love. For now, it is enough to point to the obvious contrast between affirmative and negative affective acts, basically between love and hate. One who radically loves approves, endorses, intentionally confirms, the loved one's whole actuality insofar as it accords with his true self, along with his potentiality and dynamism toward fuller life.

Radical love is intentionally (not actually) creative of all that the loved one is and can become while remaining her true self. It will help to think of the way that a psychologically and morally healthy person affirms self; in a like way, the radical lover affirms the loved other. It will also help to recall and reflect on the experience of *being loved* with radical love. In that experience the loved one has a sense of being confirmed in existence, of being made more firmly and fully alive, more energetic in striving and stronger in facing the troubles and pains of life; of having increased inner peace and joy. This is so just because she is loved, not because the lover has wealth or power or wisdom or any other such gifts which enable him to do things for her. These may add to the experience, but they do not basically constitute it.

2. The foregoing description of radical love as affective affirmation is altogether inadequate, and it is subject to ambiguity or misunderstanding unless we add that the lover's affective affirmation is for the loved one *in herself for herself.* What this means can most readily be explained by contrast with affirming the loved one for another or for herself in another. When I affirm someone for another I affirm him or her as a fulfilling end for the other or as a means to some such end. Thus, I affirm you for myself or for a third person because you are an interesting conversationalist or good looking or charming and delightful to be with or because you are a skillful worker or an influential person or wealthy and open handed. The other for whom I will the fulfilling end is the one affirmed for herself. I can, however, affirm someone for herself *in another.* I do so when, for example, I affirm the wife and child of my dearest friend for themselves but precisely because they are related as they are to my friend. Then I am affirming my friend for himself in himself but his spouse and child for themselves in him. So also when I love my family and or associates for themselves but just because they are *my* family or *my* associates. This kind of love could be called quasi-radical love. The genuine radical love in these illustrations is for my friend and for myself.

The meaning of loving a person in herself can also be clarified by contrast with Singer's notion of love as a gratuitous bestowal of value. In this latter way of thinking about love, the lover attributes to the beloved a value which "exceeds anything in the object that may be thought to elicit it" (Singer 1966, 14). That persons who love others radically do sometimes (not always) also bestow value in this way seems evident; for example, the parent with his or her child, a romantic lover with his or her beloved. Such a way of loving (if indeed it is love) cannot be love for the other in herself. The truth is that gratuitous attribution of value where it does not exist in the loved one is not itself love, certainly not radical love, but only an accompaniment of, at most a consequence of radical affective affirmation of the lover's own self; or else it is an *untruthful* radical affective affirmation of the loved one (what that means will be explained shortly).

3. What is most significant in understanding radical affective affirmation has not yet been touched on: this affirmation is an act that itself constitutes a union of the lover and the loved one. Any concept of love as a drive toward union with the loved one, as a desire for such union, misses what is most important for understanding love in its radical meaning. As we shall see, desire for fuller union is usually found in the total experience of love and is love in some secondary sense; but it is not necessary to the experience and, when present, presupposes for its intelligibility radical love and radical care for someone, the lover's self or another. (Care is a modified form of radical love which will be treated a little further on.) Radical love is not a tendency toward union; it is an act that constitutes an affective union, a being-affection in contrast with a tendency-affection. How shall we describe this affective union?

The Facets of Union Constituted by Radical Love

The full richness of the union constituted by the act of radical love and directly experienced is not usually reflectively recognized by the person loving (much less by the loved one or the observer). Nevertheless, it is always in the experience and so can be brought to reflection and clarified by attending to its several facets as they appear in the experience. Doing so will also situate within the total experience several common but unsatisfactory ways of defining love. All the facets, it must be stressed, are just that, facets of the union constituted by the very act of radical love, neither distinct acts nor consequences of the one act of love.

The most obvious among these facets is that of mutual presence. Some knowledge (present apprehension or memory) of the person loved is a condition for the possibility of radical love. Now, this knowledge is itself a kind of presence to the one known and makes the known present to the knower. Radical love, as will be shown, assimilates this knowledge as its own form and is a fuller and more intimate presence than that by knowledge alone. That this is so can readily be seen in the difference between being aware of someone, when physically proximate to him, but without interest and, on the other hand, being lovingly aware of someone, whether physically proximate or many miles away. Being present to the beloved by his act of love, the lover, *by that very same act*, renders her present to himself and is in union with her, whether she knows it or not.

This way of thinking is not agreeable to those who think that while it is essentially characteristic of love to yearn for union, actual union takes place only when the love is returned. As I will try to show more and more clearly, in this chapter and in other parts of this essay, radical love constitutes a union of mutual presence even without mutual love, even when the beloved is not aware of being loved or being present to the lover. If the love is returned, the mutual presence is doubled: the one who before was present to the other only as a lover is now present also as beloved, and the one who before was present to the lover only as the beloved is now present also as the lover, with awareness of being so.

Even mutual presence of lover and beloved *to* each other does not adequately describe the presence constituted by radical love; such love constitutes, further, a mutual presence *in* each other, a mutual living in, dwelling in, even when the love is unilateral. How all this is so will become clearer in the next two facets of the union constituted by the act of radical love, giving self and affective identification.

In the act of radical love, the lover renders himself a gift to the loved one and in doing so, *in the very same act*, opens himself to and accepts the loved one into himself. Truly, as ways of expressing his love, giving signs of it, he makes gifts of his possessions of what he has that is extrinsic to himself. In whatever ways he can he also gives his intrinsic qualities to serve or give joy to his beloved, for example his intelligence, wit, courage charm, physical energy. But before all else and in all else he gives his very self, the subject of these qualities. In so doing, he accepts the other's self. For, while one can give all else from motives other than radical love for the one to whom they are given and without accepting the other's self, he cannot give himself without accepting the other's self in that very act of radical love. Giving self and accepting the other's self are not two acts but two sides of the same act, the act of radical love.

Though it obviously admits of degrees, so deep is this union of mutual presence, of self-giving and accepting, that it must also be spoken of as affective identification. This term "identification" is used here in a sense altogether different from two other ways in which it is used, particularly by psychologists. First it differs from the psychoanalytical meaning of an unconscious mechanism by which one tries to pattern himself after someone else, a parallel of imitation at the conscious level.

Second, it differs from another meaning in which identification is thought of as involving either an irrational subjection to or an irrational domination of another. This meaning has nothing to do with affective identification as I understand it in this context; for domination or irrational subjection excludes recognition of the other as a value in herself for herself and, consequently, excludes radical love.

Rather, as I understand it here, affective identification refers to an experience of affective union with the person loved for and in herself such that it results in the lover experiencing in some measure the loved one's life as the lover's own life in the loved other. The measure of affective identification in this sense can be great or slight, depending on the degree of love. The lover experiences the loved one's needs, successes and failures, joys and sorrows, pains and pleasures, fulfilments and frustrations, as his own in the loved one. The actual experience of the other's life as the lover's own in the beloved, however, is not itself the identification I am pointing out. It is made possible by and is a consequence and sign of the affective identification and reveals the nature of the latter (which is *constituted* by the act of radical love). By affective identification, the lover without losing his own distinctive self or diminishing the distinctiveness of the beloved's distinctive self, *is* the beloved affectively, and, *as a consequence*, experiences the beloved's life as his own in her. It is difficult to express this experience in words without being understood as talking about a self-centered, possessive love. If anything I say suggests such an understanding, my words are failing to express my intended meaning.

This most profound facet of union by radical love, so hard to express in words, will be developed at greater length in the treatment of personal friendship (chapter 8), where it takes on its main significance for the purpose of this essay.

All that has so far been said about the union constituted by the act of radical love is, I think, profoundly illuminated by ontological reflection, which shows that radical love is a medium through which the lover intentionally joins his own ontic self-affirmation, his very act of being, to his loved one's act of self-affirmation or act of being, where this ontological reflection is developed at some length). To understand this we must keep in mind that radical self-love is the expression in conscious life of a person's ontic self-affirmation. If this is so, then we can see that by radical love for another the lover in some measure turns the energy of his act of being toward the loved one, in some measure affirming her as he affirms himself and confirming her conscious affective act of self-affirmation.

Subtypes of Radical Love

In concrete experience, radical love never or hardly ever arises without some special affective tone or color by reason of other concrete relationships of the lover and the loved one and the feelings corresponding with these relationships. Radical love can be, for example, mother love, father love, filial love, sisterly or brotherly love, romantic love, spousal love, love for a heroic leader, for a loyal follower, for a comrade, and so on. There is no need now to develop this matter at length. Some development will be needed and given when explaining integral personal love (chapter 3), when describing personal friendship (chapter 5), and when contrasting and relating friendship with mutual romantic love (chapter 8).

Modified Radical Love and Implemental Love

In the foregoing pages, the two most common notions of love asserted in the history of thought on love, benevolence toward the beloved and desire for the beloved, have been excluded from the core of the total concrete experience of love. They are not even necessarily actually present in every total experience of love. Nevertheless they are always virtually present and, in fact, almost always actually present along with radical love; and, when actually present, they are more obvious than radical love in which they are rooted. That is why they are so readily and frequently named love without qualification.

Imagine a meeting after long separation of two persons who love each other intensely and tenderly. At the first moment, each one's response to the other can be and very likely will be purely radical love (as described above) combined with joy in the other's reality and their union—all finding expression in hugs and kisses, laughter, dancing, tears of joy. After the first moment has passed, each will become aware of the other's needs, and radical love will modulate into an affective affirmation of the other in and for herself precisely as in need. This response we can name radical care; with different shades of meaning it could be named concern for, taking responsibility for, benevolence toward, the loved one in need. Since the object of radical care is the one affectively affirmed in himself for himself, even though in need, care is only a modified form of radical love, not fully distinct from it.

Care, however, issues in another fully distinct conative affective act, an affective affirmation of something to be done or acquired to meet a need in the one radically cared for. What is needed and affectively affirmed can be seen and affirmed as an implemental end or as a means to such an end. An implemental end is a fulfilment rather than a means to a fulfilment, but it is not an end affirmed in itself for itself. It is affirmed for a radical end, that is, for an object of radical love and care. A means is, in turn, affirmed only in relationship to an implemental end; apart from the end to which it conduces, it has as such no value.

When, for instance, I care for someone in need of food or books, then I affectively affirm food or books in as much as these will fulfil the needs of the one cared for. When the act of caring is for the lover's own self and what she feels a need for is something that pleases her, she is commonly said to "love" it—whether it be attention and praise or tasty food or a certain type of music, and so on. There is sound reason for broadening this usage and giving the name "love" also to any affirmative affective response to whatever implements a need in any radically loved person, whether the lover's self or another. Some find difficulty with this usage, wanting to reserve the word love for a response to a person and speak of the affective response to other objects as "liking" or "desiring." These other objects, it is true, are distinct from the object of radical love and radical care and are affectively affirmed not for themselves but for the one radically cared for. It is also true that the affective affirmation of them is both fully distinct from and totally dependent on, the act of radical care love. Nevertheless, since, like radical love and care, it is an affective affirmation (albeit a relative one), to call it love seems appropriate as well as convenient, so long as it is suitably qualified. Since it derives from and in some sense completes the radical affirmation, affirming its object precisely in as much as it implements a need of the radically loved one, it is appropriate to name it "implemental love."

A more refined analysis than is needed here might require a distinction between implemental love and desire: desire is the form implemental love takes when its object is not yet attained. For our present purpose, however, such refinement is unnecessary, and we can use the two terms as synonyms. "Desire" will serve to stress the dynamic character of the act; "implemental love" will serve to stress its derivation from and dependence on radical care love. What must be avoided is letting the distinction between radical love (unmodified or modified) and implemental love or desire be lost; otherwise, precision in our understanding of the experience of love gained by descriptive analysis and synthesis will be lost, and we will slide back into the confusion from which we began.

Radical and Implemental Love for the Same Person

Although radical love is for the loved one in and for herself and implemental love is for its object only inasmuch as it is for another as an implemental end or as a means to that end, nevertheless, one can love the very same person in all these ways. Certainly, we do successively in different situations, love the same person in these different ways, now one way and now another. When we do so, are the ways of loving necessarily in conflict? Some writers, when contrasting love for a person as a person with love for him by reason of his roles, could give the impression that it is so. There is no reason to think this way unless the implemental love violates the dignity of the person as a radical value. Loving a person as one who fulfils the lover's need or even as a means to some fulfilment does not necessarily violate the dignity of the loved one as a person. Suppose I love someone implementally because she is delightful company for me or for someone else, an interesting conversationalist with a good sense of humor and a charming manner. Suppose I also love her as a means to some end for myself or for another, as one who is a capable collaborator in some project, a wise counselor, or an excellent teacher. None of these implemental or functional loves for this person necessarily conflicts with the love for her in herself and for herself. Rather, the implemental love may prepare for, lead toward, radical love.

Not only do we experience loving the same person in different ways successively but also simultaneously. Thus, when I am radically caring for you and implementally loving what will meet your need, I can also be caring for myself or for a third party with a consequent implemental love for you as fulfilling or useful to me or to the third party. This situation is a common situation for choice about which radical care for which person to give priority over the other. The two simultaneous loves in tension constitute an object for choice. In another kind of situation, the radical and implemental loves for one person are integrated into one total complex act. Thus, because I love someone for herself and because I understand that it is fulfilling for her to be loved as a fulfilling implemental end or as useful to me or others because of her capabilities—because I understand this, I choose also to love her in these implemental ways and let it be known to her that I do.

Some Concluding Remarks

The foregoing analysis of experience makes possible a universal concept of love as affective affirmation; for radical love, radical care love, and implemental love are all different forms of affective affirmation.

It seems reasonable to think that among the many descriptions and definitions of love, all of which have some correspondence with experience, that description of the experience of love deserves very serious consideration which offers an explanation of how the word love has been given so many diverse meanings both in ordinary language and in the writings of reputable philosophers, theologians, and psychologists; that shows how the principal meanings are related in a total concrete experience; and that also provides grounds for a universal concept of love, one that can include all basic forms revealed by descriptive analysis. For it enables us to see how love has come to be thought of as affirmation, openness, acceptance, self-giving, union, concern, benevolence, taking responsibility for, desiring, driving toward union, joy. It shows how some of these are always and necessarily, and most of them usually, involved in a total concrete experience of love, and how they are related to each other in that experience.

It shows which affective act can be named love in a radical or unqualified sense and which others can be so named in an implemental or qualified sense. It also shows what is the common note of all the basic affective acts in the total experience of love: Every one of them is an affective affirmation, radical or implemental.

The main conclusions of this analysis of the total concrete experience of love need to be kept in mind as we study the goals of human dynamism in the following chapters. Besides the essential structure of the total concrete experience, what has been said about the essentials of radical love, especially about the several facets of the union between lover and loved constituted by radical love and about affective feelings necessary for an integral, fully human, response of love— all these must be kept in mind in order to get the full force of what will be said about personal love, personal communion, and personal friendship. The description of what specifies each of these experiences without remembering what was uncovered within the experience of radical love which is involved in each of them, will leave them empty of their rich content.

Appendix to Chapter 2

A diagram of the structure of the concrete experience of love along with a glossary of terms used in the descriptive analysis of that experience might be helpful to the reader of the foregoing chapter. In fact, you might want to refer to this appendix while working through the analysis. These are given on the following pages (204-205).

Feelings

Affective Feelings:
sometimes dependent on cognition, sometimes v.v., when cognition is by affective connaturality

Corresponding affective feelings

Bodily Factors,
e.g., smiles, embraces, kisses, increased heartbeat, tears, words, gestures, movements in acts of service for the loved one, etc.

Acts

Cognitive Acts:
e.g., sensation imagination memory insight judgment

Affective Acts:
e.g., always dependent on cognition, and sometimes v.v., when the cognition is by affective connaturality

Radical love/ radical care

Implemental love

—of a fulfilling end for the one radically cared for
—of a means to that end

Structure of the Total Concrete Experience of Love

Glossary of Terms in the Descriptive Analysis of the Total Concrete Experience of Love

Act of Love: an affective affirmation of an object.

Radical Love: an act of affective affirmation of its object for itself in itself (i.e., as a radical end), the essential core of every total concrete experience of love; only by relation to it can anything else be an element in that experience.

Quasi radical love: an act of affective affirmation of its object for itself *in another* that is affirmed in itself for itself.

Personal love: radical love for a person when the lover knows that the loved one is a person (wide sense of the term) or has an implemental love. Total concrete experience of love.

3
PERSONAL LOVE AND COMMUNION: DESCRIPTIVE ANALYSIS AND SYNTHESIS

The preceding description of the union of persons by the act of radical love can leave no doubt about the centrality of such union in human life. If, however, we are to recognize and understand the fullest modes of union and life for persons, the preceding descriptive analysis of radical love is not enough. We need, further, to identify and describe what I will name *personal* radical love or simply personal love. The term "personal" is applied to many things and relationships and acts; as applied to love in the context of this essay, a very specialized meaning must be given to it.

First of all, by personal love I mean a form of radical love, of affective affirmation of the loved one in himself for himself. This limitation excludes love in the sense of desire for the lover's own fulfilment by union with the loved one. When love is identified with affective tendency or drive to fuller life by union, no love, not even personal love, can intelligibly be seen as a goal of dynamism, as a fulfilment— though some authors want to have it both ways. As has been shown, although a human being who loves another for herself in herself is by such love in union with the loved one, he will also desire fuller union. This desire, however, is implemental love, derivative from radical love for the lover himself or for the loved other. Inasmuch as it flows from radical love, it can be a component in a total experience of love which can be denominated personal if the radical love at its core is personal.

Not all radical love is personal as understood here. Some writers (Ortega 1957, 44-48; Lewis 1960, ch. 2-3; Scheler 1954, 155-56 and ch. 6) think we can and should love in themselves for themselves non-personal realities such as nature, works of art, science, beauty, wisdom. Also it is a fact that many people love beasts with radical love. Whether we can love in these ways without projecting personality onto such objects is a question we can leave aside. Even if it should be true that we do and should love non-personal realities with radical love, such love is not personal love in the sense used in this essay; the latter refers to love for another person.

Three Modes of Personal Love

Any affective affirmation by a person of another person in himself for himself could reasonably be called personal love in a loose or wide sense, but not in the narrower and richer specialized sense intended here. The basis for this distinction can be shown by recalling and developing what was seen above about the intrinsic differentiation of the act of love. Some kind of cognition, we saw, is necessary for any conscious act of affective affirmation: we can consciously love only what we apprehend. Since radical love is not a tendency or a movement toward its apprehended object, one act of radical love does not differ from another only extrinsically, by reason of the direction of a consequent tendency. Every act of radical affective affirmation is, rather, intrinsically formed by and differentiated from other such acts by the loved one who informs the lover's love through the mediation of the lover's knowledge. For that reason, it can be said that love is the loved one in the lover—and is so more profoundly than knowledge is the known in the knower. My love for Mary or Clare or Joseph or John is intrinsically as different from my love for each of the others as each of these persons and my knowledge of each is different from the others. So also, my love for one and the same person at various times can be intrinsically differentiated insofar as I apprehend him or her differently at these times.

Three modes of radical love correspond with three modes of apprehending the loved person as a person. In one mode I know only *that* the other is a person and perhaps know *that* she has some urgent need. I experience radical love and care for her as *a* person. In a second mode, I know experientially or by testimony of another that some person has certain amiable and admirable traits shown in his ways of acting; I know, for example, that he is wise, courageous, gentle, generous. Now I love him as a person who has these qualities. At another time I might be more aware of different traits, his kindness, wit, high intelligence, artistic gifts; and my love for this same person with these different qualities varies accordingly. In this second mode, I can love many persons but few in comparison with the first way.

Personal Love in the Fullest and Most Proper Sense

It is much more difficult to describe the third mode of personal knowledge and so also the third mode of personal love. For in this mode I apprehend the inconceptualizable, radically lovable personal self, unique and unrepeatable, revealed but never fully revealed in any of its acts or in any of the traits which constitute his or her personality in the psychological sense of that term. This knowledge can be relatively superficial (though always a deeper knowledge than in the first two modes) and fleeting in its effect; or it can be a profound experience that lastingly influences the way I remember and respond to this person.

Knowledge of others in the third mode is possible only by a non-discursive, non-conceptual, direct awareness—direct but, as experience shows, mediated. For we have no direct awareness of personal selves except as they shows themselves in and through their acts (including words and gestures) and their qualities, which appear in those acts. While personal selves reveals themselves in and through their acts and qualities, unique persons exceed any and all of their acts and actual qualities, possessing endless potentiality for and promise of new acts and qualities expressive of personal indefinable plenitude.

This mode of knowing another person mediates to the lover's response of love, as the intrinsic form of that love, the unique personal self of the loved one; and the love is, then, personal in the fullest and most proper sense.

It should be evident but needs to be stressed that knowledge and love of a human person in the third mode cannot occur apart from personal knowledge and love in the broad sense. For, as was said, the intuition of another person's unique self is possible to us only in and through her perceived acts and gestures and the traits or qualities expressed in these. Consequently, the total concrete response of personal love in the strict third sense will always include personal knowledge in a broad sense. The love, then, in this total experience will be informed not only by the loved one's apprehended personal self but also by her explicitly apprehended qualities and acts, potentialities and dynamism to actuality, by all that is as yet only implicitly apprehended as somehow part of the whole person, but all related to the personal self at the core of this personal being. In other words and more briefly personal love in the third mode is an affective affirmation informed through knowledge of the loved person in his or her total reality, primarily the unique personal self, but also and necessarily, in some way, by all else in her reality.

The intuition by which the beloved's personal self is apprehended is mysterious, never fully explainable. Some factors in it, however, can be noted. A necessary condition for the possibility of this experience is that the person who knows in this way must, at least at the moment, be free of self-centeredness, lovingly open toward the other with personal love in the wide sense. The one known must at the moment be open to others, at least in a general way (not necessarily to this person in particular), willing to reveal self and to be known. Given these conditions fulfilled, the intuition can happen. When it does, the reality of the personal self is revealed as we saw in and through the person's words, acts, and gestures. However, it is not revealed only or mainly in and through the meaning of the words spoken or the kind of acts performed or the kind of personality traits shown in them; it is revealed also and even more so by the indescribable way in which the words are spoken or the style in which the deeds are done. It can be the tone of voice in which the words are said, the fleeting compassionate smile or glance, the gracious gesture, the gloriously innocent laughter, the delicate tender touch which more than anything else carries the revelation. By reason of such an encounter one who would otherwise be to me *a* kind person, wise, gentle, brave, witty and so on, is now also an inexpressible lovable mystery. The more profound and certain and revealing the intuition, the more mysterious is the person to the loving knower.

Let it be emphatically clear *from here on that whenever I use the term "personal love" I am referring to the third mode of such love*, the fullest and most proper meaning we can give to the term, unless I explicitly indicate otherwise. Unless this use of the term is kept in mind, all that follows will easily be misunderstood. If others prefer to give a different meaning than I do to the term "personal love," there is no need to debate about words. What matters is whether the features in my description are accurately understood and whether they correspond with some real human affective experience, by whatever name or names others may refer to it.

Personal Love Is Integral

The preceding description of personal love in the most proper sense has left aside several features of such love which flow from its very nature. Without an awareness and understanding of these (along with all that was said above about radical love as constitutive of union between the lover and loved) the full richness of personal love will be missed. There are at least two such features: personal love is integral and intentionally truthful.

It was noted above that not every radical love is an integral response of love, that is, a response which includes some more or less intense feelings of love. It seems impossible for radical love that is personal in the fullest sense to arise without being an integral response; for, whether as a consequence of personal knowledge or as a condition for its possibility, feelings of love will be notably present in the experience. How could one by personal knowledge experience the wonderful mystery of another person and by personal love experience profound affective union with that person without experiencing joy, tenderness, warmth, sweetness, and, when the other's well being or suffering is known, sympathetic delight or compassion? Further, these affective feelings can have many different special tones or colorings by reason of many different relationships with the person loved (e.g., as parent, child, spouse, brother or sister, leader, follower, comrade and so on). Sometimes only one and sometimes several of these relationships and the corresponding special feeling tones enrich integral personal love for one and the same person.

Personal Love Is Intentionally Truthful

If as is often said or sung, "love makes the world go 'round," only truthfulness of love can keep the world spinning in its proper orbit and save it from smashing up. The term "truthful love" is not one in common usage. The term "true love" is, but it is also too ambiguous to be serviceable here. In various contexts it refers to sincere and honest rather than deceitful and hypocritical love, or to faithful rather than unfaithful love. It could also stand for the essential feature of personal love that I want to point out now. However, in order to avoid confusion, I will use the term "truthful love."

What is meant by this term? We saw that some cognitive apprehension of loved ones is a condition for the possibility of any conscious act of radical love and that the love receives the form of the loved ones as they are apprehended. A judgment, an intellectual affirmation that something is or is in a certain way, is truthful or untruthful by being in accord or discord with the reality of what is affirmed. So also, the affective affirmation that is the act of personal love and that is intrinsically formed by the loved one as apprehended by the lover in accord with or discord with the loved one's reality is truthful or untruthful. If truthful, it is more or less so, depending on more or less full and penetrating knowledge that informs the love.

The nature of truthful or untruthful radical love and its practical significance is clearly revealed in its modified form, radical care, that is, radical love for someone in need precisely as in need. When the radical care love is untruthful, the lover will be responding to the loved one as having needs she does not have or as not having needs she does have; and the lover's desires for what is seen as fulfilling or useful to her will also be untruthful, in discord with her real needs. He will not only fail to meet her real needs but may even harm her.

To use some blatantly obvious illustrations: care for a starving person as though her most urgent need were education, care for a person who is desperately in need of knowing she is loved as though her most urgent need were money, care for an adult as though she were a child or the other way around—these are a few blatantly obvious illustrations of the million ways of loving and caring untruthfully which can often be very subtle and difficult to discern.

It has been said that "anyone who genuinely loves knows what must be done." This statement can stand only if by genuine love is meant truthful love. For radical love and care can be genuine even when mistaken. So complex is the reality of persons, their actualities, their potentialities, need for and dynamisms toward further actualizations; so complex and changeable the structures of relationships in which they exist and develop; so limited our knowledge of all these factors in concrete life, that truthful care is a very difficult achievement even for one who loves sincerely. All we can say is that if one loves with sincere radical love, one will *efficaciously intend* to love truthfully and will, therefore, make the effort necessary to achieve truth about one's loved one.

What is involved in such an effort? First of all, the lover must try to become free of self-centered attention, interest, and attitude. He must try to become aware of and break free from unfounded assumptions about what the beloved is or should be and do. He must try to be flexible, ready to change his judgments and his affective affirmation to correspond with the changes in the beloved's complex and ever changing reality. Without such freedom the lover cannot see the loved one as she really is and love her for what she is in her real lovableness and despite her limits and faults. Even with this freedom, the lover still has to attend carefully and consider thoughtfully if he is to arrive at truthful love.

Insofar as a person, whether because of mental laziness or for some other cause, with or without clear reflective awareness of doing so, does not intend to love as truthfully as he can, is willing to risk loving the other untruthfully (which is to say willing to love a projection of his own mind rather than the reality of the other person), he fails of personal love. It is of no help, in fact it is false, to say that untruthful love is not really love, personal or otherwise. It is love—just as a false judgment is still a judgment and irrational fear and desire are still fear and desire. One who sincerely loves another person and tries to do all that is necessary in order to grow toward the ideal of fully truthful love, in short, one whose love is intentionally truthful— such a lover can be loving with genuine personal love even though, against his intention, he is in fact mistaken and in some way loving untruthfully. Actual perfectly truthful love is an ideal that is not necessary to reach in order to love personally. If it were, who of us could lay claim to personal love for anyone. It is enough for human love to be genuinely personal if it is intentionally truthful, enough and necessary.

Personal Communion: Its Essential Core

One who loves another with personal love tends toward personal communion with the loved one (see below, ch. 10). Personal communion involves much more than mutual personal love, but the latter is the first necessary step toward the communion to which the lover tends, as also its essential core when attained.

The term "personal communion" can be used for referring to lesser modes of union than the one I have in mind in the present context. The following description will, I hope, suffice to prevent ambiguity; it cannot of course, fully convey the richness of the experience. If no description of person and personal love can come near to fully expressing their riches as we experience them, much less can it do so with communion of personal love. What can be done, as was done for the description of love is to identify it clearly by drawing attention to its essential elements and their relationship, to distinguish it from any other experience, and to indicate something of the profound union it constitutes between persons.

Achieving even these limited aims is not easy. For, when we reflect to see what it includes, the attempt to say what is found seems exaggeratedly refined and altogether foreign to the warm and wonderful and apparently simple experience reflected on. So much is this so that one is inclined to just let it be a mystery too profound to be analyzed—and, ultimately it is such. Nevertheless, prior to settling for silence in the presence of mystery, there is much about the dynamic structure of the experience that can be brought to light and that has value for both theoretical and practical understanding of personal life. While the essential structure of loving personal communion revealed by descriptive analysis and synthesis is not explicitly known by those who have the experience, when it is explicitated, the experience itself can be enhanced and the persons in communion are better able to guard it from diminishment and to strengthen it.

Communion is in general any intimate, mutual, amiable communication of thoughts and affections. By personal communion or communion of personal love I refer to a very special kind of communion which is possible only between persons who love each other with personal love in its fullest and most proper meaning. While such mutual love does not itself constitute personal communion it is the core of that whole experience; by relation to it, all other essentials are elements of that experience.

Before attending to these other elements or features of personal communion, two brief observations may be appropriate. First, we have contrasted radical love with love understood as benevolence and as desire; and we have seen how these three affections are related in the total concrete experience of love. Conceiving love in general or principally as desire or even as benevolence makes understanding communion of personal love impossible. The latter is not at its core just a mutual desire for union nor a willing of some good to each other. It is, rather, an already actual affective union which is constituted by the mutual personal love.

The second observation is that such personal love will rarely appear in concrete experience without some non-personal love accompanying it, mixed with it. Those who love leaders with personal love also love them with implemental love as useful for the success of their cause. A romantic lover who loves the beloved with personal love also loves her with implemental love as the source of the lover's own emotional fulfilment. The non-personal love might or might not affect the purity of the personal love, might be fully integrated with it or be in conflict with it in the description which follows, attention will be focused on the personal love leaving aside the non-personal, without implying that the total concrete experience of communion is always purely personal.

Added Essential Features in Communion of Personal Love

Besides mutual personal love, there are other essentials of personal communion. Such communion comes to be only when those who love each other with personal love believe that their love is mutual and each is aware that the other so believes. I might know and love you personally and you know and love me the same way without either of us believing in being personally known and loved by the other. Plainly, in that case, there is as yet no communion of personal love. Further, even if each of us does believe in being known and loved by the other, I might not know that you are aware of my belief or you might not know that I am aware of your belief. Personal communion begins only when there is mutual personal love, mutual belief in each other's love, and awareness in each of the other's belief.

With this beginning arises a new knowledge of each other and a correspondingly new quality in the affective response. Now, the you that I know and respond to is not just the you that I was aware of when you first drew from me a response of personal love. I now know and love you as you are actualized and revealed to me in your love for me; and you now know and love me as I am actualized and revealed to you in my love for you. Perhaps the following device will help to understand what I am saying: I am now knowing and loving [you revealed to me in your loving (me revealed to you in my loving you)]; and you are knowing and loving [me revealed to you in my loving (you revealed to me in your loving me)]. If this description seems to be exaggeratedly intricate, I can only say that I have been tempted to think the same thing; but on reflection, I always ended up convinced that any effort to simplify the description deletes something essential for understanding the experience.

One Composite Act of One Composite Agent

Attending to how interdependent the mutual acts are in personal communion, how they interpenetrate inasmuch as each one's response to the other is taken into and affects the other's response, so that neither of them is possible except in their mutuality—attending to this complex interrelationship leads to an insight that reveals how marvelous is the union of the persons in this experience. The two acts of the two agents constitute one composite act of one composite agent. The moment of personal communion is a moment during which two persons, transiently and in at least some small measure, experience a beginning of one life lived by two without any loss at all of their distinctiveness. Rather, as experience shows and as the earlier descriptive analysis of love makes understandable, the distinctiveness of each person grows in direct proportion as the communion of personal love grows. On this preserved and increased distinctiveness of persons in communion depends the enrichment of life experienced by each in their union and, in truth, the very possibility of the communion.

A sign of how intimate is the union of the distinct persons in their composite act of communion can be found in the relationship of other-love and self-love in this experience. Although distinguishable, these two loves are in the experience of communion not only compatible but correlative and inseparable; as they arise within communion, each of them necessarily entails the other. For how can I love you as you are actualized in loving me without loving myself in the very act of loving you? Or how can you love me as I am actualized in loving you without loving yourself in the very act of loving me? Or the other way around, how can I love myself as I am actualized in loving you without loving you in that act and how can you love yourself as you are actualized in loving me without loving me in that act? What must be insisted on, however, is that in the communion of personal love, priority belongs to love of the other: self-love is subordinate to love of the other. In the moment of actual communion, I love you and love myself only and precisely as loved by you; while you love me and love yourself only and precisely as loved by me. As soon as priority is given to self-love by either person, the present act of communion ceases.

Conclusion

Keeping in mind the full preceding description of the cognitive and affective essentials found in communion of personal love and holding to the meaning given above to each of the key terms, what we have seen can be summed up in the following formula: Communion of personal love is the relationship constituted by mutual personal love, integral and intentionally truthful, when the persons in the relationship both believe in each other's love and are aware of each other's belief and are responding each to the other as the other is actualized and revealed in his or her love, the mutual responses so interdependent as to form one composite act of one composite agent.

Part 2
The Experience of
Personal Friendship

4
FRIENDSHIP: THE BASIC TYPES

Although unilateral personal love contributes to the fulness of human life, it is an incomplete experience until it is reciprocated. So also reciprocal love without personal communion and personal communion apart from personal friendship are incomplete experiences. Communion can attain its completion and its superlative mode only when it is communion between personal friends. Clarifying the meaning of this assertion and establishing its truthfulness requires that personal friendship be clearly distinguished from other kinds of friendship and that its essential features be brought to light. The first of these two projects will be undertaken in this chapter, the second one in the several following chapters.

Two Ways of Schematizing Types of Friendship
To accomplish the first project requires identifying and schematizing the basic types of friendship. There are, to my knowledge, only two successful explicit attempts to do this. If there are others, however good they may be, they do not seem to have notably influenced the literature on friendship. (Material for a different schema might, perhaps, be found in other writings, e.g., in Robert Brain's ethnological study, *Friends and Lovers* [1976]. To my knowledge, however, he has never presented an explicit typology.) Many of those who write on friendship do touch on the types of friendship, but most of these rely

basically on Aristotle's schema (NE bk. 8, ch. 2-3 [1155b-1156b]). His is the classic one, more widely known and more widely followed than any other. Some may differ from him in this or that detail but without radically revising the main lines of what he has given us. Because it is in its main lines easy to understand and is so generally known and commented on, a very brief statement of it will suffice. (Hunt acknowledges that Aristotle's model of friendship is "the prime philosophical referent for most theological treatments of friendship" [1991, 193; see also 93 and 96]. She finds his model inadequate for friendship between women and presents a new model [98-106]. It can be added that Aristotle's model is also the prime referent for philosophical treatments of friendship. This fact both points up the value of Aristotle's treatise and also the scarcity of original philosophical reflection on the nature of friendship during the centuries since he wrote.)

Aristotle sees three distinct bases for three distinct types of friendship: virtue, pleasure, and utility. That type which is friendship in the best and fullest sense is based on the virtue, the moral goodness, which each friend recognizes and admires in the other, for example, wisdom, honesty, courage, and so on. Such friendship provides both pleasure and usefulness, but it is not based on these. This type Aristotle calls "perfect friendship," not because it allows no room for degrees and growth but only because it is the perfect kind as opposed to the other two kinds. It is sometimes referred to as virtue-friendship. (John M. Cooper, in his highly regarded article, "Aristotle On the Forms of Friendship" [1977] prefers the term "character friendship." However, since character, even strong character, can be virtuous or vicious, virtue-friendship seems to be a more precise term.) The other two types are friendship in a lesser sense. That based on pleasure is said to be more like the perfect type than that based on utility, since it is based on some admirable and pleasant quality which each friend finds in the other, for example, wittiness, good looks, charming manner. In the third type, what founds the relationship is not what the friends find in each other's personalities but some value extrinsic to their persons, some gain which each derives through the other, their mutual utility, as for example, political influence, profitable business dealings, social status.

One rare attempt to produce an original schema without dependence on Aristotle, which seems to me eminently useful for the author's purpose as a social scientist, is that of John Reisman. He employs a different principle of division than that used by Aristotle and ends up with three main kinds of friendship, one of which, he thinks, includes Aristotle's three types.

His principle for distinguishing his three main types of friendship is "the balance of affection and loyalty" found in each of them. He sums up his discussion of these types in this way.

> We have been emphasizing that there are three kinds of friendship, not just one. A major distinction among them is the balance of affection and loyalty. When both parties give their love and loyalty to one another, the friendship is reciprocal. If one person gives love and loyalty to another who does not similarly return it, the friendship is receptive. If neither party feels loyalty or deep fondness for the other the friendship is associative (Reisman 1979, 26).

In Reisman's reciprocal friendship, the friends see each other as equals. Their mutual affection and loyalty makes possible a healthy frankness between them, their mutual honesty never experienced as cruel or threatening. This kind of friendship, Reisman says, has been and is regarded both by authorities on the subject and by people in general as the most desirable form of human association. Reciprocal friends, he observes, are commonly called "real" or "true," "ideal" or "perfect" friends, as though other friendships were false or less valuable (Reisman 1979, 19).

Reisman, for his part, suggests that the second type, receptive friendship, is "different, but no less meritorious." He gives famous historical examples which he sees as illustrating his view: David and Jonathan, Freud and his inner circle of friends, Jesus and his disciples (Reisman 1979, 22; at least the first and third of these illustrations show that Reisman's receptive and reciprocal types of friendship can and perhaps usually do fuse in any concrete instance. To imply that there was no clear and strong reciprocal love and loyalty between Jonathan and David or Jesus and his disciplines, even though a much greater love from the side of Jonathan and Jesus—to imply this is in conflict with the accounts in the Bible). Whether or not Reisman would agree that he and Brain are talking about the same thing, certainly a term used by the latter in his ethnological study would serve well as a descriptive synonym for Reisman's receptive friendship, namely "lopsided friendship." (Brain uses the term in referring to the friendly relationship between patrons and clients in a situation of conspicuous social and economic inequality [Brain 1976, ch. 5, esp. 111], crediting [269] Pitt-Rivers with originating the term and referring to the 1954 *Transactions of the New York Academy of Science* and the

International Encyclopedia of Social Sciences [1968]). For Reisman's second type of friendship is characterized by imbalance, inequality, by a superior-inferior relationship, as for instance when one friend is "loving and giving to the other, who feels gratitude, though little affection in return" (Reisman 1979, 21). One, for instance, teaches or bestows favors from a position of wealth and power while the other gives appreciation and loyalty in return. Sometimes the difference in status is so unequal that the receptive friend would be presumptuous to think of any other return to the giving friend. It could be argued, says Reisman, that the satisfaction or pleasure the giver finds in the very giving and in being appreciated is sufficient compensation (Reisman 1979, 21). He also points out, however, that where there is in fact a difference in status between reciprocal friends, the friends act to eliminate it, just as where there is in fact no difference in status to begin with, a receptive friendship tends in the very nature of such friendship to bring about a status differential.

Early in his book, Reisman remarks that while philosophers are mainly interested in what they see as the ideal form of friendship, his friendship of reciprocity, scientific studies are mostly concerned with what he names associative friendships, his third type (Reisman 1979, 28). Scientific study of the first type, he says, is very hard or impossible, while the latter is well suited for such study. The evidence seems to sustain his observation, and clearly his own book is primarily concerned with understanding and showing the value of associative friendship for social life.

A person in such a relationship, he says, is what is most commonly meant by the word "friend"; and this type of friendship is the one most commonly experienced. While reciprocal friendship is relatively rare, everyone has many associative friends: neighbors, classmates, members of a church congregation, fraternity or sorority members, office staff, teaching faculty, and so on. Although some of these relationships can develop into reciprocal or receptive friendship, for the most part they never involve any deep fondness or loyalty and people are content to leave them that way. They do not expect or seek anything more. It is enough that these relationships make life more pleasant and our work more effective.

Reisman notes what he calls two "variations on this theme of associative friendship." The first of these obtains among persons forced to be with one another and to interact because of their work, their roles, their social positions, their engagement in some common project. It is on these factors more than on personal qualities that the friendship is based (Reisman 1979, 63). The second variation or subtype of associative friendship is one that is established by preference and choice, a relationship that persons are not forced into by external circumstances. Those who enter into this kind of friendship do, of course, have reasons, sometimes compelling needs. These reasons, Reisman thinks, "can be reduced to Aristotle's three reasons: pleasure, utility, virtue" (Reisman 1979, 67).

My Need for a Different Schema

The value of Aristotle's schema has been proved and acknowledged over the centuries. Reisman's I have found enlightening and deserving of more attention than I am aware it has received. Nevertheless, neither of them can serve my purpose. For the precise function of schematizing types of friendship in this essay is to enable me to make what I have described and named personal friendship stand out clearly, free of any confusion with any other kind of friendship. Neither Aristotle's nor Reisman's schema can enable me to do that. Without detailing the points at which my schema will converge with and diverge from that of Aristotle or Reisman, it is enough to give my basic reason for devising and using it. (Brain [1976] gives a thought-provoking account of loves and friendships in other cultures than our own which questions some of our assumptions. But I have found there nothing which helps my effort to set personal love and friendship apart from other types or causes me to question the value of doing so in the way that I have.)

To me it seems unquestionable that whatever else is necessary for friendship, mutual love of one kind or another is the essential core and, therefore, that the most radical and significant distinction between types of friendship must be based on the distinct types of mutual love at their core.

It is true that each of Aristotle's bases calls for a love in a different sense, and his three bases could be easily transposed into three kinds of love. However, there are problems. First, among his bases of friendship, there is no basis for truly personal friendship in its fullest and most proper sense. Even in his "perfect friendship," love of each friend for the other is based on the virtuous qualities of the friends, their acquired moral dispositions, not on their enduring unique personal selves. Secondly, Aristotle's notion of love seems restricted to well wishing; what I have described as radical love does not even appear in his thought, much less what I call personal love. Finally it is at least questionable whether Aristotle's perfect friendship is not in ultimate analysis nobly self-centered. (I find that I am not alone in this opinion; see, for instance, Brain [1976, 216, n. 16] and McFague [1988, 161].)

As for Reisman's schema, he does not distinguish friendships fundamentally by kinds of mutual love but by the balance or imbalance of the love between the reciprocal and receptive friends or the degree of fondness between the friends which is found in each of his three types. The question of personal love as distinct from any other kind of love does not arise in his treatment.

Types of Friendship Corresponding with Types of Love

Since neither of the schemata presented by Aristotle and Reisman is suitable for my purpose, however valuable they may be otherwise, and since, as I said above, no distinction among types of friendship rests on what is most radical and significant unless it is based on differences among the several mutual loves at their cores—for these reasons, I find it necessary to draw up a typology of friendship that is based on the different, though related, types of love uncovered in the total concrete experience of love. Much more than mutual love is of course, necessary for friendship; I shall, in fact, spend several chapters describing the many essential factors in personal friendship. Nevertheless, the distinct kinds of mutual love are the fundamentally decisive factor for differentiating distinct kinds of friendship.

What descriptive analysis and synthesis of the total concrete experience of love has revealed allows for two fundamentally distinct cores of friendship, one in which the mutual love is implemental and another in which the mutual love is radical. In the first of these, each friend radically loves himself and implementally loves the other; it is the implemental love that is mutual. In the second core, each friend loves the other with radical love simply and, consequently, with radical care. His implemental love is, therefore, not for the friend but for what can fulfil the friend's need. Let us call the friendship with the first essential core implemental-love friendship and friendship with the second essential core radical-love friendship. It would be more convenient to simply name these fundamental types of friendship radical and implemental friendships. However, such terminology would be misleading; for radical friendship would not be a root of implemental friendship, as is the case with radical and implemental love. Implemental-love friendship is rooted in the radical love that each friend has for herself, not in their mutual radical love.

Each of these essential cores of friendship allows for two subordinate forms. Since implemental love can be for the friend as an implemental end, which fulfils the lover's need, or as a means to such an end, implemental-love friendships can be what in the Aristotelian tradition are named friendship of pleasure and useful friendship. (Cooper [1977] calls useful friendship "advantage friendship"; since the gain of pleasure can also be thought of as an advantage, the term "advantage friendship" seems to me better suited to serve as a synonym for what I term "implemental friendship" which is motivated either by usefulness or by pleasure.) When describing personal love, three modes or stages of personal knowing and loving another person were distinguished. The first of these cannot found a radical-love friendship. The second can, but one that is personal only in the wide sense of personal. The third was said to be personal in the fullest and most proper sense, that is, when the loved one is known in his or her unique, unrepeatable, inconceptualizable self. Radical love, then, is personal in the fullest and most proper sense when it is informed by such knowledge. Accordingly, only when the core of friendship is mutual love of this kind is the friendship personal in the sense that we are using it, the most proper and fullest sense. *It is this kind of friendship that will be meant by "personal friendship" in all that follows unless it is clear in context that some broader meaning is intended.* Since the term is used by others in referring to relationships other than the one I refer to by it (e.g., Reisman, 1976, ch. 7, "business friends"), it is critically important for understanding the rest of this book to keep this decision about the meaning of the term in mind.

To sum up, then, there are four basic types of friendship distinguished from each other by reason of four distinct essential cores, four kinds of mutual love: implemental-love by each friend for the other as useful or as pleasurable (implemental-love friendships), personal love by each friend for the other in the wide sense of personal or in the most proper sense (radical-love friendships). A brief comment on each of these types and their relationship will suffice before a detailed study of personal friendship.

Evaluation and Relation of the Four Types

Among all these types, the least worthy of being called friendship is that between those who love each other only as means for attaining their respective implemental ends. Sometimes the friends are useful to each other in pursuing a common purpose, for example, members of an athletic team, fellow citizens devoted to the civic common good, business partners. Sometimes they are useful to each other in like ways for each other's private purpose; such is often the case with politicians or with those who do business with each other. Sometimes the friends are useful to each other in correlative ways, for example, lawyers and clients, physicians and patients, leaders and followers. To say that friendship based on usefulness is less worthy of the name than the other types to be considered in no way implies that it is unimportant in human life. Without this kind of friendship, very much of what is valuable for human social, political, economic, artistic, scientific, and religious life would be lost.

More deserving of the name friendship is the mutual relationship in which each friend values the other as an implemental end because of his or her delightful and/or admirable qualities. The friends may have the same or different but complementary endearing qualities: thus both might be quick of wit, intelligent and eloquent (Falstaff and Prince Hal), or one might be so and the other not so, but still capable of appreciating a friend's great gifts (Johnson and Boswell). Further, these qualities on account of which the friends affectively affirm each other can be the basis for a more or less noble friendship. Thus, the admirable and delightful qualities the friends perceive in each other without concern for usefulness might be those just noted or qualities such as moral courage, gentleness, generosity, and wisdom. Criminals who are friends might be so on the basis of mutual qualities they see and value in each other, such as boldness, physical courage, ruthlessness and cleverness in criminal enterprises. Even this latter friendship, though not nobler, is in its *kind* more fully friendship than the type based only on mutual usefulness of the friends to each other in legitimate enterprises.

A yet better claim to the name of friendship can be made for that type in which the mutual love at its core is radical love but not personal in the fullest sense. The best claim belongs to that friendship in which the mutual love is personal love in the fullest sense, that is, personal friendship in the proper sense.

Let it be emphasized that each of these friendships in this ascending scale can include all that is most valuable in the preceding type. Thus, pleasurable implemental-love friendship can be useful, radical-love friendship can be pleasurable and useful, and personal friendship can be both pleasurable and useful and involve admiration for the friend's lovable qualities and love for her because of these. Only it must be equally emphasized that the value which prompts the mutual love in the preceding and lesser type on the scale is not what prompts the mutual love that is distinctive of the higher type.

There are of course mixed types, for example, when one friend loves the other with radical love and the latter loves the first with

implemental love. Similarly, just as there can be in concrete experience more than one kind of love for the same person (radical and
both kinds of implemental) alternating or combining, sometimes with
interior conflict, sometimes harmoniously, so also it is possible to
have more than one type of friendship with the same person. However, since our immediate concern is only to clearly set personal friendship apart from other types, there is no need at present to discuss all
these possible variations.

5
PERSONAL FRIENDSHIP:
ITS ESSENTIAL FEATURES

It is not easy to come upon serious and sustained attempts to penetrate the mystery of personal friendship in some measure by uncovering and describing essential features of personal friendship, showing their relationship, and envisioning the ideal toward which that
friendship of its nature tends. In this and several following chapters I
will make such an attempt.

The essentials of personal friendship to be identified and described
are obviously not all exclusively found in that relationship. This or
that essential or several of them together might be found in some
other affective relationships, including non-personal friendships, but
not all of them together. If all of these essential features are present in
any relationship it is a personal friendship. If any one of them is
missing, the relationship cannot be a personal friendship. Describing
these essentials will be done more easily and clearly if we have in
mind a friendship between two persons only. This limitation is not
meant to imply that a single personal friendship cannot involve more
than two persons. Whether there can be more and, if so, how will be
considered in chapter 13.

Lest what I am doing in this chapter appears to exhibit an unde-
clared male chauvinistic attitude, two things need to be said. First, I
have not ignored what feminists are writing on friendship between
women. However significant what they say for their purposes and
however important it is that we all hear it, I do not find it bears on
my purpose, which is to uncover what is essential and therefore common to all personal friendships whether the friends be women or
men or women and men. What seems to specify "female friendships"
as Janice Raymond (1986, 229) describes them is what she names
"Gyn/affection." This is an affection that "cannot flourish or be sustained without a passion for women (not necessarily a genitally sexual
passion) which stirs the imagination, memory, thought and/or feeling in some way," a passion that moves one to passionately work for
women and to actualize feminists' ideals. In a similar vein, Mary Hunt,
in a working definition of friendship says (1991, 29) it is a voluntary
human relationship between those who "intend one another's well

being and who intend that their love relationship is part of a justice-seeking community." If what these and other feminists include in their understanding of feminist friendship is essential to that particular kind of friendship, it is certainly not essential to all friendships. Second, I am aware that almost all of the illustrations I use in this book are drawn from accounts of personal friendships between men. This may be merely the result of my limited reading, and Janice Raymond (1986, 4-5) may be right in arguing against Virginia Woolf and others who acknowledge that written evidence for friendship between women is meager. The evidence that Raymond adduces helps but does not go far toward remedying an unfortunate situation—especially not if we are talking about personal friendship in the full and proper sense I am attempting to describe.

First Essential of Personal Friendship: Mutual Personal Love

If what has been said in the preceding chapter is true, there can be no doubt that the first and most fundamental among the essentials of personal friendship is mutual personal love. Given the actual spectrum of diverse notions of love among writers surveyed in chapter 2, we could expect to find a corresponding wide spectrum of understandings of the mutual love essential to personal friendship. What affective act I refer to by "personal love" has already been clarified—including personal knowledge (in the most proper sense) by each on of the other's unique personal self. Without going over this matter again, let me just add a comment or two. Since personal love is a special form of radical love, it will in the concrete usually modulate into radical care and give rise to implemental love, desire, for what the radically loved person needs as implemental ends or as means to these ends. Desire will motivate deeds. Recall that personal love, of its nature, will be integral love, that is, suffused with feelings of love such as warmth, sweetness, delight, joy, or in some circumstances, pity and compassion.

Second Essential of Personal Friendship: Mutually Congenial Personalities

But these feelings of love do not arise when I dislike the person whom I radically love. Consequently, to say that mutual love in personal friendship is integral implies that the friends not only love each other but, in some measure, like each other. For that measure to be adequate for personal friendship they must have congenial personalities.

Elizabeth Telfer writes incisively about the meaning of "liking," something that is hard to do and rarely done. For, as she says, "liking is a difficult phenomenon to analyze. Although it is a *reason* for seeking someone's company, it is not simply *equivalent* to enjoyment of his company as might at first seem." Rather, she says (1970/71, 226), it is

> roughly specifiable as "finding a person to one's taste," and depends partly on such things as his physical appearance, mannerisms, voice and speech, and style of life; partly on his traits of character, moral and other. The relative importance of these features as a basis for liking obviously depends on the liker.

(Part 1 of this article [223-230], gives an enlightening descriptive analysis of friendship; Telfer's use of key terms clashes with mine but her thought does not.)

What we react to, however, when we like someone is, according to Telfer, not a sum of attractive aspects, but "a whole personality as a unified thing," similar to our way of reacting to a painting or a sculpture. So it is often hard to say why we like a person (Telfer 1970/71, 226-27.)

This much seems clear: we can like a person without being personal friends, but we cannot be personal friends with persons we do not like. Two persons with common interests of the deepest kind, with common ideals, who respect and affectively affirm each other, who are benevolent toward each other, may yet have uncongenial personalities. As a consequence, they may be unable to really like each other, may get on each other's nerves and find it unpleasant to be together. Their chemistries, we say, do not mix well; they experience personality conflicts. This is not uncommon, even among psychologically and morally mature persons. Through no fault of either, personal friendship in the full and proper sense can be a present impossibility.

There are endless degrees of liking and disliking persons. The degree of liking someone depends basically on the degree in which the liker and the liked have congenial psychological personalities, have similar or complementary traits (temperamental, moral, religious), intellectual and emotional styles, tastes, ideals and enthusiasms. In concrete experience, of course, the degree of liking is further affected by other factors, by our ordinary mood swings and all the ordinary emotional clashes that can happen even between those who have congenial personalities. I do not know how to say what degree of congeniality and liking another is necessary for the possibility of personal friendship except in a vague way, a high degree.

Third Essential of Personal Friendship: Common Interest

Writers on friendship generally stress the necessity in any type of friendship of a common interest, known by the friends to be common. This factor is clearly necessary for personal friendship. It is most likely to be found between persons with congenial personality traits.

It can precede and lead to or follow upon mutual personal love. Discovery of a common interest opens the way to companionship, and companionship with a bond of common interest opens the way to mutual friendliness (an attitude which resembles that of friends to each other) and serves as a favorable matrix for growth into mutual personal love and friendship. But it might happen also that those who already love and like each other become friends only after they discover that they have a common interest. Whenever and however the persons become aware of their common interest it seems that no personal friendship can begin or continue without it.

The common interest may be anything from football or fishing to rearing a family or educating youth, to a shared vision of life's meaning based on religious beliefs, a shared quest for wisdom, or a common striving for freedom and justice—or a combination of such interests. The more precious the common value and/or the more intense the persons' concern with it, the more likelihood of it leading to and preserving friendship. A common interest in philately will not have the same unifying power as a common interest in rearing a family or spreading the Gospel. The interest can, however, change as the friends mature; or they may discover that they have for a long time actually had a deeper common interest without knowing that it was common. Thus, it may happen that a personal friendship that begins with a common interest in racing cars or rock stars or athletics may later on become a friendship with a common religious interest in the meaning of life.

Some say that the common interest has to be something inward and deeply important, a "common vision," seeing and caring about the same truth or the same significant project. This opinion is certainly not true in regard to friendships less than personal, and it seems to be an exaggeration in regard to personal friendship. It is certainly true that a common interest in what constitutes or touches on the deep meaning of personal life makes for a deeper and firmer personal friendship. Nevertheless, it must be said that, if there is mutual personal love between persons with congenial personality traits, even a common interest in something of lesser significance can serve for some sort of personal friendship. It can be a beginning, preparing the way to a more significant common interest. To insist on common interest in something inward and of profound significance seems to overlook what is more fundamental in friendship. Why cannot persons who love each other with personal love and care for each other's welfare, who like each other and enjoy being with each other, but have common interests which are relatively unimportant still be personal friends?

Necessary as it may be for a personal friendship, a common interest cannot be an element of personal friendship except in dependence on mutual integral personal love. It is well known that persons who are business partners, members of the same athletic team, colleagues in a search for truth, or dedicated to the same military, political, or religious cause, can collaborate successfully and yet not like each other and avoid a deep personal relationship. They may value and be satisfied with what Reisman calls an associative friendship. Even when they respect or admire each other and get along agreeably, and a desire for personal friendship is present, they may fail to achieve it. Ignatius Lepp, in his book on *The Ways of Friendship*, tells of his own experience which strikingly illustrates this fact. The author is intending to make a different point than I, but his experience also makes my present point.

> A few years ago I worked on the same project as a man close to me in age and cultural interest. I had high respect for both his intelligence and emotional qualities. We also found ourselves in perfect accord on ideological and spiritual matters. I have rarely so intensely desired to become anyone's friend; I confided my desire to him and from all evidence he had an identical desire. We made meritorious efforts to meet one another, endeavored to achieve as intimate a dialogue as possible and acted in all things like friends. It was all in vain; the emotional spark was not forthcoming. We had to resign ourselves to being good companions, "friends" in the broad sense of the term (Lepp 1964, 36).

Perhaps what Lepp calls friendship in the broad sense is what Letty Russell (1979, 199) writes about as "partnership," that is, "a relationship in which there is continuing commitment and common struggle in interaction with a wider community context" (also 34-36). This partnership is certainly not equivalent to nor does it always lead to personal friendship.

A more fortunate outcome is seen in the account by St. Gregory Nazianzen of his friendship with St. Basil. It illustrates clearly the essential role of common interest—with them a life of true wisdom—for the beginning and maturing of a truly personal friendship. After telling what led up to their friendship, Gregory continues:

> Such was the prelude to our friendship, the kindling of that flame that was to bind us together. In this way we began to feel affection for each other. When, in the course of time we acknowledged our friendship and recognized that our ambition was a life of true wisdom, we became everything to each other: we shared the same lodging, the same table, the same desires, the same goal. Our love for each other grew daily warmer and deeper.
>
> The same hope inspired us: the pursuit of learning. This is an ambition especially subject to envy. Yet between us there was no envy. On the contrary we made capital out of our rivalry. Our rivalry consisted not in seeking the first place for oneself but in yielding it to the other, for we each looked on the other's success as his own.
>
> We seemed to be two bodies with a single spirit. Though we can not believe those who claim that "everything is contained in everything," yet you must believe that in our case each of us was in the other and with the other (*Liturgy of the Hours*, I, 1285-87).

Fourth Essential of Personal Friendship: Communion of Personal Love

Mutual personal love between persons with congenial personalities and common interest does not necessarily lead to personal friendship; much less does it constitute friendship. A fourth factor is necessary, communion of personal love. Since this goal of human dynamism has already been described in chapter 3, there is no need to do more here than ask the reader to recall the earlier description and to add several comments which seem significant in the present context.

One observation is that it would be a serious mistake to think that personal communion of love can be experienced only in those moments when, in withdrawal from other activities of life, the two persons give full attention to each other. Communion of love can be experienced also obliquely, as it were, as persons go about their activities together with their attention focused more directly on what they are doing. Such communion is then more fully assimilated afterwards in memory of and reflection on the experience. Thus my friend and I might be engaged together in an effort to understand some event or some idea we have read about. We might be collaborating to produce a manuscript or be actively engaged in social or political action; we might be at a concert, a ball game, or a social gathering, and so on. Our attention is focused on what we or others are doing; but obliquely we are contemplating and loving each other as we are manifested in our ways of acting, of thinking, of emotionally responding to people and situations, in our smiles, gestures, ways of speaking, and so on. Through all, each is obliquely and lovingly aware of the other's presence and of the other's reciprocal awareness. Afterwards, each can remember all these manifestations of the other with admiration, concern, delight, regret, pleasure, pain—and through all, love. Even if these remembrances and responses are not communicated to each other, they are an extension and completion of the oblique communion of love during the activity together, more so when the thoughts and emotions are communicated.

Further, and this is the second observation, once friendship is firmly established, even when communication is rare or impossible for a long time, it is still possible to sustain some sort of real communion of love and real friendship by mutual remembrance and love with faith in each other's remembering and loving. A splendid illustration of this is the friendship that developed among a little band of men who came to know each other at the University of Paris in the sixteenth century, who afterwards labored and endured hardships together in the service of the Gospel, and finally formed the Society of Jesus (the Jesuits). The two most famous among them are Ignatius of Loyola and Francis Xavier. By the time Francis was sent as a missionary to the far east, his friendship with Ignatius and with the others in their group had grown deep and strong. Although at that time it took about two years to send a letter between Europe and India and get a response, Francis and the others were continually in each other's thoughts and love. Francis cut the signatures from their letters and carried them in a pouch over his heart. Communion and friendship survived and flourished even though the friends were worlds apart in space and their communication years apart in time.

There is touching evidence of this fact in Xavier's letters. In response to a letter from Ignatius, which reached him eleven years after their farewell, he wrote:

... God our Lord knows what a comfort it was to have news of the health and life of one so dear to me. Among many other holy words and consolations of your letter I read the concluding one, "Entirely yours, without power or possibility of ever forgetting you, Ignatio." I read them with tears, and with tears now write them, remembering the past and the great love which you always bore towards me and still bear... (quoted in Brodrick 1952, 459; Xavier had already died when Ignatius received the letter.).

While Ignatius had a place in Xavier's heart above all the others, his friendship with the other early companions was such as to last during their separation. To some of them in Rome, he wrote:

God knows how much more solace I would obtain from a sight of you than from writing this letter whose fate is so uncertain owing to the vast distance between here and Rome. Though our Lord has put us so far apart, yet, if I am not mistaken, the sundering miles cause no lessening of love, no forgetfulness, in those who love one another in Him and are reunited in charity. In my opinion, we see one another all the time, though we are no longer able to have the old companionable relations... You and all of our Society (of Jesus) are a continuing presence in my soul... (quoted in Brodrick 1952, 207).

Fifth Essential Feature of Personal Friendship: Sharing Lives

The account of Gregory Nazianzen of his friendship with Basil given above to illustrate the importance of common interest for the beginning and growth of personal friendship clearly points also to another essential which goes beyond having a common interest and experiencing communion of personal love. It is what I shall refer to as sharing lives. This essential feature could be thought of as a kind of communion, to be included in and discussed with what I have named communion of love under a general heading of personal communion. However, it seems better to speak of it under a distinct rubric, namely sharing lives.

Since this factor in personal friendship involves many matters of great significance for understanding the peak experience of friendship, matters which require extensive treatment, it seems better to take it up in a separate chapter rather than break the movement of this chapter and expand it beyond all reasonable limits. Readers who want to consider this feature of personal friendship right now can go immediately to the following chapter and then return to this point.

Sixth Essential Feature of Personal Friendship:
Mutual Commitment

Even with all the essential features of personal friendship already noted, something necessary to this friendship is still missing unless the friends are mutually committed to friendship. (A study of commitment in general and of commitment to personal friendship in particular, along with practical helps for living out a commitment, moral counsels on when commitments should or should not be kept—all this would take us far beyond what is necessary for and suitable for our present purpose. For an exceptionally wise and reasonably brief treatment of all these matters, see Farley 1988). This commitment involves both an efficacious voluntary intention of fidelity and a promise to fulfil that intention. Each of these components of commitment needs clarification.

By an efficacious intention I mean one that will issue in action for the sake of achieving what is intended when the opportunity is present, unless prevented by a force beyond the intending agent's control or by a withdrawal of the intention in some concrete situation. It might actually achieve its goal or it might not; if it does, it becomes an effective intention; but an intention can be efficacious without being effective.

In what way does each friend efficaciously intend to be faithful to the other? Since personal love is the most central or radical among all the essential elements in personal friendship, intending fidelity to such friendship is most fundamentally intending to persevere in personal love.

Persevering in genuine personal love means persevering in truthful love (see Farley [1988, ch. 4-5] for such a discussion). Insofar as personal love, in its proper sense, is radical love for persons in their deepest enduringly identical selves, faithful personal love will remain unchanged. Insofar as the total intrinsic form of the loved persons includes changeable features, faithful personal love for them will also be changeable in order to remain truthful. Insofar as this intrinsic form of radical love does not change with these changes in the loved one, it fails of fidelity.

The love to which friends intend fidelity is integral love. That is to say an act of love suffused with feelings of love. However, while the act of love is directly subject to our free choice, feelings are not. We are not able to have them whenever we choose to do so. Nevertheless, they are indirectly under the influence of volition and we can efficaciously intend, not only to persevere in the act of personal love when feelings dry up but also to do the best we can to keep feelings of love alive and, when they die down, to do what we can to bring them to life again so that the response of love may be as integral as we can reasonably make it. This is not the place to discuss how one can try to keep feelings of love alive or enliven them when they die down. It is enough here to note that, besides the act of personal love, feelings of love are also somehow included in the scope of commitment to fidelity in friendship.

Further since mutual personal love does not by itself constitute friendship, intending fidelity in love or even committing oneself to it is not yet intending or committing oneself to friendship. Since there are essentials of friendship other than personal love, the intention of fidelity in friendship is also an intention to be faithful in these. Thus, failure to be with, present to, the friend so far as is reasonably possible to do so; failure to communicate and listen; failure to share lives with a friend insofar as possible and fitting; failure to believe in and to trust the friend's commitment—these failures are all failures in the fidelity essential to personal friendship. Intending fidelity is an efficacious intending not to fail in these ways.

While intending is necessary to commitment, it does not by itself constitute the commitment essential to personal friendship. There is no commitment without a promise to fulfil that intention. Intending to be faithful does not itself commit me to fidelity any more than intending to do anything else, for example, to take a walk or to read the paper. Changing my intention, even when capricious, does not violate a commitment unless I have bound myself by a promise to fulfil that intention. The promise need not be explicitly expressed in words; it can be clearly implied without any declaration. By a promise each friend not only assures the other that he intends to be faithful; but also, as far as is possible for free and unpredictable beings in time, each friend, by the promise, determines his future in relation to the other. By the promise each renders himself a debtor of love, yielding to the other a lasting justifiable claim on her to fulfil her intention of fidelity (The seriousness of this promise is treated by May [1957, 159-70]; he notes how Dante sees Judas, Brutus, and Cassius at the innermost place of hell).

Seventh Essential Feature of Personal Friendship: Belief and Trust in Each Other's Commitment

Genuine mutual commitment (efficacious intention and promise of fidelity) is unavailing for the formation of personal friendship without a seventh essential. Firm belief by both friends in the other's commitment and firm trust that both will live up to their commitments, this twofold, response by each to the other constitutes the seventh essential of fully personal friendship. It is entirely possible for a person to intend unending fidelity to another without the other being aware that he or she does so and vice versa. One or both can even express an intention and promise of fidelity with one or both not believing that what is expressed by the other is honestly and sincerely meant. Again, each might believe that the other does truly intend to be faithful and does sincerely bind oneself by a promise and yet not really trust the other to live up to that promise; one or both might doubt that the other has a strong enough character to steadfastly carry out what is sincerely promised. In any of these situations no personal friendship in the full sense actually exists; it might exist in potentiality. If all the other essentials are actualized, the relationship could be called an incipient friendship, something that is already very precious.

When there are sufficient although fallible grounds to justify belief and trust in the other's commitment, then it is entirely reasonable to respond audaciously. Friendship, like all else that is most precious in human life, involves a risk; to wait for an infallibly sure thing is to infallibly miss out on a full life.

Eighth Essential Feature of Personal Friendship: The Virtue of Friendship

In this section, my understanding of virtue is based on Aristotle's NE I, 13–II, 6 (1102a–1107a) and on a fuller and much more enlightening development in Aquinas' ST, 1-2, qq. 55-58. In applying what they teach to the virtue of friendship as essential to the reality of personal friendship, I am on my own. Several facts readily observable in the beginning, the growth, the maturity of personal friendship point to a final essential are explained by it.

The first fact that points to and is explained by this eighth essential feature concerns its beginning. Usually, if not always, it takes a long time, with many experiences of loving communion and sharing of lives, in order to establish a genuine personal friendship. Prior to this achievement, such experiences are momentary events that resemble what goes on in friendship and may or may not finally lead to it.

The second fact concerns the growth of friendship already begun but only begun: as the friends faithfully live out their friendship they more and more do so effortlessly, graciously, consistently, and with delight.

A third fact concerns friendship that has grown deep and firm to the point where the responses of friends to each other have a high degree of the ease and grace, the consistency and delight spoken of in the second fact: such a friendship can endure and continue to grow even during long separations, when little or no physical presence is possible. The adage, "out of sight out of mind," which would have held earlier in the relationship, does not hold now. Rather, another adage now holds: "absence [as well as presence] makes the heart grow fonder." As we saw when commenting on the fourth essential feature of personal friendship and as we shall see more fully, friendship can reach the point where, together or apart, each one's life is so fully in relationship with the other that, even during separation, in memory and affection and hope the friends are in a sense always mutually present and always growing into deeper union. Their lives can be characterized as lives of friendship.

What the essential is that explains these three facts and how it comes to be in the friends can be illuminated by a comparison with other areas of human life. Consider how it is with an artist of any kind (a poet, painter, musician, teacher, athlete, plumber, carpenter, and so on). Persons become fully artists only after a long time of study, practice, making mistakes and correcting them, while developing the necessary knowledge and techniques. Gradually, they grow in capacity to perform artistic acts with relative ease, with consistent success, and with pleasure in doing so. In the measure that this growth has been achieved, persons are artists. They are then artists not only when actually performing artistic acts but also at all times, when living the rest of their lives. When eating, praying, playing, reading, even when sleeping, there is some enduring dimension of their being by reason of which they *are* artists. This is what accounts for the ability to perform artistic acts when the artist chooses to do so and to do so with relative ease and grace and with satisfaction. This is what inclines the artist to choose to do artistic acts. This enduring dimension in the artist includes innate talent and acquired lasting dispositions of mind, will, feelings, and body acquired by years of study and practice. These dispositions constitute the virtue of art, a second nature as it were, by which the artist is able to do connaturally what before would have been done with worrisome strain and with uncertainty of good results.

Similarly, theologians, philosophers, and scientists, who not only have God-given gifts of mind and heart but also have developed lasting dispositions enabling them to work effectively with *relative* ease and with pleasure in doing so—these persons have intellectual virtues. Similarly with persons in moral life: no one is a morally good or bad person by reason of this or that act or a number of them. What constitutes a morally good or evil person is character, and what constitutes character is moral virtue or vice, lasting dispositions for choice of morally good or evil acts by reason of which the agent chooses such acts readily, constantly, and with satisfaction in doing so.

Likewise, persons are personal friends not only by reason of this or that moment of personal communion or many scattered such moments or by reason of sharing lives. These are necessary on the way to becoming friends and for maintaining, expressing and growing in friendship; but by themselves these intermittent acts do not constitute the enduring reality of friendship. Only by some measure of the virtue, constituted by the firm and lasting dispositions resulting from repeated acts, persons are friends at all times and in all circumstances, even when not thinking of each other, in the same way that persons *are* dancers or musicians or theologians or philosophers or morally good persons even when not expressing these dimensions of their personalities in action. Only by the virtue of friendship can friends finally be bonded in a relationship that can persist through all stresses and strains or long separation, and that would have destroyed or diminished it at an earlier stage. The dispositions for fulfilment of the mutual commitment to each other are finally so firmly imprinted in them as ways of being that, in no matter what circumstances, their love for each other, their belief in and trust in each others' fidelity, their memory of each other, their desire for communion and sharing lives with each other are easily kept alive and are always a deep down source of strength and joy.

The question might be asked whether the virtue of friendship is an intellectual or artistic or a moral virtue or all of these or none of these. It does have a deep intellectual dimension. With good reason we talk about the art of friendship. The foregoing description of the virtue of friendship shows it to be a high moral value. However, there is no need in this context to answer the question just asked. It is enough to show what is referred to by "virtue of friendship" and the necessity of what is referred to in order to have personal friendship.

One factor which is usually set down as necessary for friendship I have omitted. That factor is equality between the persons. I have omitted any mention of it because if the essentials I have already mentioned are fulfilled, I can think of no kind of equality that would be of any added significance. Perhaps in some situations equality of some sort is *de facto* necessary in order to have these essentials realized. For in some cultures or in the case of some persons, notable inequality of social position, of natural gifts or education, and so on might prevent friendship, but certainly not in all instances. And, even where this does happen, the question must be asked: is this the result of some defective attitude, cultural or individual, rather than the lack of some element essential to personal friendship? All in all, the consideration of equality seems to have no place in a description of essentials of personal friendship. Those who love each other as personal friends will always find ways to lessen any inequality that does exist or to discount its significance for their union.

6
SHARING LIVES IN PERSONAL FRIENDSHIP

When stating the fifth essential feature of personal friendship, sharing lives, I pointed out the need for a separate chapter to give it adequate attention. More than anything else, descriptive analysis of this complex feature will reveal the union of minds and hearts that is possible for persons in personal friendship and the increased fulness of life constituted by such union.

Sharing lives in friendship comprises a number of factors, each after the first depending on and growing out of the preceding one. These are: being together in doing and enduring, mutual intimate self-revelation, the experience by each of the other as an other self, knowledge by each of the other's life from within, experience by both of them of the other's life as one's own in the other and one's own life as the other's in oneself.

Being Together

First, the desire to be always together and actually being together as much as may be are perhaps the most easily recognized signs of personal friendship. Personal friends want to see each other, to touch each other, to bask in each other's presence, and, as much as is possible and fitting, be together in what they do or in what happens to them: in work, in play, in conversation, in prayer, in striving for common goals, in success or failure, in pleasure or pain, in joy or sorrow. In a mature personal friendship, every personally significant experience I have apart from my friend is, by that very fact, in some measure incomplete; and whatever personally significant experience my friend has apart from me is to me in some way a deprivation—even when the circumstances of life make this deprivation inevitable and fitting and, therefore, in the concrete acceptable to me.

Ralph Waldo Emerson's attitude as expressed in his essay on friendship seems to be in conflict with what I have said. He seems to want to keep sharing between friends apart from everyday life, restricted to occasional sharing of great thoughts.

> I do then, with my friends as I do with my books, I would have them
> where I can find them but I seldom use them… I cannot afford to

speak much with my friends (Emerson 1904, II, 214-15; see also 209-11).

In this context Reisman's comments (1979, 44-45) on Emerson's understanding of friendship merit consideration.

One easily wonders whether Emerson in this essay is always talking of what I have called personal friendship or has sometimes slid into talking about an elitist form of implemental friendship, based on noble pleasure of mind. On the other hand, what he says does suggest in an exaggerated way a relevant truth which must qualify all that is said about friends being together. It is a fact that, given our psychic limitations, there are desirable limits to actual presence even of very good friends. We need physical and psychic space, times apart from each other, times of solitude. If these needs are ignored, being with even the dearest human person can become oppressive, smothering and limiting of growth.

That being said, it still remains that Augustine, when describing his youthful experience of friendship, is certainly more in accord than is Emerson with most human experience of personal friendship and with most writing on it. He tells how his group of friends wanted

> to talk together: to perform kindnesses for each other; to read charming discourses together; to make jokes or hold serious discussions; now and then to disagree without ill feeling, as one does with oneself, and to spice our usual unanimity with these very rare dissensions; to teach each other and learn from each other; to long with impatience for those not present at our gathering, to welcome with gladness those arriving; with such acts and feelings and manifestations of them by facial expressions, by voice, by looks, and a thousand gracious gestures, all springing from the hearts of those loving and loved, as with tinder to inflame our hearts and make one of many (*Confessions* bk. 4, ch. 8).

What has been said about the desire of personal friends to be together and share lives ever more fully can stand out sharply when contrasted with the attitude in a lesser relationship pithily expressed by a character in one of Elmore Leonard's novels:

> "We were friends when we saw each other," Jack said. "But if we didn't see each other, it didn't matter" (1987, 7).

Mutual Intimate Self-Revelation

It is not enough for those who are personal friends to be present to each other, to carry on activities and experience events together. Their love makes them tend to mutual revelation of and mutual knowledge of each other's inward lives. Desiring even fuller union, each wants to reveal to the other their significant or at least interesting experiences, their most intimate loves and hates, joys and sorrows, satisfactions and disappointments, fears and hopes, most secret thoughts about what is most inward and important in their loves; and each wants to know all that the other wants to reveal. It is this mutual intimate self-revelation that Aelred of Rievaulx in his little classic, *Spiritual Friendship*, considered one of the two principal factors in a "formula of friendship" (along with doing the friend's will). This thought he consciously derives from St. Ambrose and quotes with approval Ambrose's saying that "a friend hides nothing [from his friend]" (1977, 3, 83, and 130). At the peak of friendship, Aelred thought, there are no secrets hidden from each other; hearts are laid bare. That such communication is in our present human life prudently entered into only with a few, perhaps with only one, Aelred is fully aware. Perhaps, even with one, such sharing of life is in many friendships only an ideal which the friends desire and approach only in a very slight degree, in occasional small ways.

For the tendency to fuller and more intimate mutual self-revelation can overcome fear of embarrassment or misunderstanding only in proportion to mutually known growth of love and power of understanding with consequent trust. Only perfect love perfectly known casts out all fear. Prior to the requisite degree of personal maturity and mutual love, being known beyond a certain point by another can be dreadful and an obstacle to or destructive of friendship. "Marriage of true minds" between persons in the human condition can grow only with careful and intelligent tendance. The point is made dramatically by the extreme fictional case in a short story that has been justly called a "dazzling miniature." It is a story of two telepaths, a man and a woman, whose minds had touched while passing each other on trains going in opposite directions. After three years they found each other. Their "minds... leaped out and enfolded and became one"—with a sudden shocking aftermath. Neither could as yet bear being known as the other knew, "every last little wish and thought and buried uncleanness."

A boy and a girl went hand in hand, the thought hung cold under the sky, a single thought in two minds.—*get out, I hate your bloody guts.*— (Anderson 1969, 300-09).

Most or all of us can in our present existence endure being known without limits only by God. Fortunately, such complete telepaths as the characters in this story are nonexistent in our world. For us, without going beyond present appropriate limits (or holding far back from them), however great or slight these might be, mutual gracious self-revelation is a necessary constituent of sharing lives in friendship and also, when genuine friendship has begun, necessary for its growing deeper roots and flourishing. The more deeply friendship develops, the more the friends tend to communicate in these ways. On the other hand, without such communication there is the danger of the bonds of friendship weakening, danger of love and care becoming untruthful as the persons change over time without the intrinsic form of personal love and care changing correspondingly.

A difficult question arises: what about sorrow and pain? Do friends want to share these with each other? This question involves two questions. From the side of the one who receives the sharing, does he have a tendency as a friend to share the friend's suffering? From the side of the one communicating, does friendship imply a readiness to share one's own suffering with the friend? Let us take each of these questions in turn.

What is surprising and perhaps the surest sign of deep friendship is that each wants to share even the other's suffering, not just in order to support the other in her suffering (though certainly that also), not only to suffer for the other in order to protect or gain some good for the other (though that also) but, even if none of these goals is possible just to be in union with the friend as completely as possible, sharing the friend's life in every way, to have one life.

The second question is more difficult to answer. For even (or especially) friends tend to back away from sharing what would cause pain to the other and want to share only what would give joy to the other. Despite the greatness of his insights into friendship, Aristotle seems to have fallen short of the truth when he approves of this attitude (NE IX, 11 [1171b, 5-12]. The root of this error seems to be Aristotle's assumption that the comfort of sympathy is the only motive for sharing one's painful experience with a friend.) Much wiser, I think, about this matter was the person who wrote in the margin of a book I once read: "The one who keeps his sorrow from his friend wrongs him." For he deprives him of what belongs to him as a friend. Anyone who intensely loves a friend who suffers knows the truth of this; although, when he himself is the one who suffers, he may not see the truth as clearly. There are of course, exceptional circumstances which would make it wiser and more loving to keep one's own pain and sorrow to oneself, when, for instance, revealing it would harm the friend. In general, however, sharing these with one's friend seems to be what personal friendship calls for.

Friends As Other Selves to Each Other

It is commonly said that a friend is an other self. "An other self" appeals to me as preferable to "another self." Making this change may well seem too meticulous and of no use. To me, however, "an other self" seems to more strongly suggest the other's distinct otherness and less readily lend itself to any egoistic understanding of the phrase. If it does not seem so to the reader, at least it should cause no confusion. The expression without clarification is open to several interpretations which fall short of or conflicts with the meaning I intend here. To refer to a friend as an other self could be taken to mean merely that the other is also a self, a person who ought to be treated as such; used in this way, the term is "a merely abstract recognition of another's subjectivity" (Johann 1955, 34). Another meaning of saying that a friend is an other self is that based on the idea that similitude is the cause of love. This idea is developed at length by Aquinas (ST 1-2, q. 27, a.3; q. 28, a.1, ad 2 and *In libro de divinis nominibus*, VII, 9; Johann [1955, 21-27] gives a carefully nuanced interpretation of Aquinas' teaching on this point); and, Paul J. Wadell, after recalling Aquinas' thought on likeness and love, concludes that: "To be someone's friend, Aquinas knows, is to be 'another self' to them. To be so alike not just in tastes and interests, but in character, in goodness and virtue, that they come to look upon us as a reflection of themselves" (1989,137). Reisman writes (1979, 14) of "another I" as a mirror in which to see one's self. A third meaning of saying a friend is an other self is that in a notable degree I have concern for him, wish good for him, just as I do for myself (thus Aristotle, NE IX, 4; [1166a]).

The three preceding meanings all point to some truth about the relationship indicated by "other self." There is, however, another understanding of a friend as an other self that not only falls short of the deepest meaning of this phrase but is false and is coherent with a whole set of unfounded assumptions about love and friendship that denigrate the value of friendship in human life. Søren Kierkegaard is an eminent representative of this way of thinking. When contrasting friendship with Christian neighbor-love, he argues that friendship is by its very nature exclusive and selfish. To relate to a friend, he thinks, as an other self or an "other I" is a way of loving myself, is a form of selfish love. "The more closely the two I's cling together to form one I, the more this united self selfishly excludes all others" (Kierkegaard 1946, 47; see 37-50; for a detailed criticism of Kierkegaard's opinion on this matter, see Wadell 1989, 137-40).

Against this way of thinking, I have already shown that the mutual personal love at the core of personal friendship is not and cannot be selfish love. Other errors in Kierkegaard's thought on friendship could be shown, but presently, it is better to get on with my meaning of "an other self" in contrast with those meanings just given. The experience of a friend as an other self involves some affective identification with her or him, of the kind explained in my earlier descriptive analysis of radical love. Especially valuable here is the ontological analysis made of radical love. Such love is an act in which the lover joins his affective self-affirmation to the loved one's own affective self-affirmation, affirming her as she affirms herself. Further, affective self-affirmation is the expression in consciousness of the person's ontic self-affirmation, his or her act of being. Therefore, through his affective affirmation, the lover joins his very act of being to the loved one's, confirming it. In other words, he affirms her as she affirms herself and as he affirms himself, both ontically and affectively. She is then, for the time of this affective act, however brief it might be, in some measure, however slight it might be, an other self to the one loving.

In personal friendship, not only is the act of affective affirmation and, therefore, the union by actual affective identification stronger and more frequent than in other relationships; but it has, as shown above, become engraved in the lover's mind and heart as a virtue, more and more deeply as the friendship matures. Hence, my friend is to me an other self in an ever fuller way and enduringly, at every moment of my life. By reason of the virtue of friendship my relationship to my friend as an other self continually colors my conscious life and even endures somehow during times of unconsciousness. In these ways, my friend is to me much more an other self than is the self of someone personally loved very much but without personal friendship. To be my friend affectively is a way in which I as a friend exist. At every moment my friend is an other self to me, actually or virtually affirmed in herself for herself, confirmed in her act of being herself by my act of being myself.

In Brontë's *Wuthering Heights* there is a splendid expression of the experience I am talking about (quoted above, p. 121). It could, of course, be argued that the childhood relationship between Catherine and Heathcliff had become romantic love and even romantic infatuation. It could even be thought that neither of them was capable of mature personal friendship in the fullest sense. Granting all that, one could still use Catherine's words just as they stand to express what happens in deep and mature personal friendship.

Understanding that a friend is an other self in this way leads to understanding what I shall speak of as "mutual knowledge from within" and finally to understanding the deepest and most significant factor of sharing lives and personal friendship, the experience by each friend of his friend's life as his own in the other and of his own life as his friend's life in him.

Mutual Knowledge from within

Inasmuch as my friend is to me an other self, what I am aware of in her life I am aware of in a way that resembles the way that she is aware of it, from within rather than as a spectator looking on from outside. It is true that without being a friend, even without loving the other, a person who has keen insight and imagination can project himself into the other and imaginatively experience what goes on in her; but that experience is very different from what I am trying to describe. It is knowledge *from without* of what is within another's inner life. (A paranormal mode of knowing another's inner experience from without appears in science fiction; abundant illustrations can be found in Frank Herbert's famous Dune trilogy, occasionally in Isaac Asimov's *Second Foundation*. It is at the core of Poul Anderson's "Journey's End." The "kything" that runs through Suzanne L'Engle's stories seems to be more like what I am referring to as knowledge from within, but of a paranormal sort. So also the telepathy between the children in Howard Fast's "The First Men" [1974, 317-43].)

What Buber calls "inclusion" (1955) seems to be one very limited mode of what I am referring to as knowledge from within. Inclusion takes place when what Buber calls the active party in a correlative relationship experiences an event from the side of the other whom, he says, is only receptive. This can happen when a teacher is teaching a pupil, when a husband is making love with his wife, when a counselor is counseling a counselee. Buber's understanding of one party as active and the other as merely receptive in these correlative relationships and limiting the experience of inclusion to the active party seems to me unfounded and misleading. The experience I am describing can just as well be had by the one that Buber calls the receptive party in these events, provided he or she loves the so-called active party. It can extend also beyond correlative experiences, as in the experience Maslow relates of tasting strawberries in his daughter's mouth.

Experience of My Friend's Life As My Life in Her

Flowing from my friend being an other self to me, her life known from within, I also experience my friend's life as my life in her. In some measure, I live both lives. Deeper than all that has so far been said about sharing lives in friendship is this experience that I am talking about. Nothing is more important than this experience for understanding sharing of lives in personal friendship, nothing more profoundly revealing of the inmost nature of personal friendship.

In this experience, just inasmuch as my friend is to me my other self, known by me from within, what he does I in some sense do in him and what happens to him, what is done to him, is in some sense done to or happens to me in him. This experience is more than being pleased that something good and fulfilling is going on in my friend's life or being grieved because of something harmful going on. It is more than sympathy; it is more than empathy. Suppose I am saddened by a tragic event in my life, of which my friend is altogether unaware, and my friend, on the contrary, feels like jumping for joy over some happy event in his life. I may be unable to respond with any feelings like his in union with his; nevertheless, his feeling of joy is to me mine in him. It is no less mine than it is when I, too, feel like jumping for joy with him. Even now, while I am feeling sad, I have a joy in *his* heart.

What I want to bring out here may be easier to understand in terms of pains and pleasures instead of affective feelings. Suppose my friend has a splitting headache and I know of it. My own head is still in fine shape; I do not experience any headache in sympathy with my friend. Nevertheless, in the measure that she is to me an other self, her headache is to me mine just because it is hers. I have a headache in her head. Or the situation may be that my friend is enjoying the pleasure of good music or a delicious dinner, while I am sick and unable to enjoy either music or food. The other's pleasure is still to me my own just because it is hers. Her pleasure is mine without any feelings of sympathy or empathy. Deep down I am more content than I would be if she were ill and I were having these pleasures.

Contrasting the experience of a friend's life as mine in him with an experience which bears some deceptive resemblance to it but is really its antithesis can illuminate the former and prevent any confusion of it with the latter. To do this, consider two situations: first, a situation in which the other person experiences some fulfilling success and, second, a situation in which the other experiences some humiliating failure.

To illustrate the first situation, suppose I am a man whose hope for fame as an athlete or a politician or an artist has been frustrated, but my son or someone closely related to me is successful and acclaimed, the success and honor redounding on me. Suppose I experience and rejoice in the other's achievement and fame as a substitute for my own, as at least a partial escape from my own sense of failure and frustration. I am in some sense experiencing the other's success, honor, and joy as mine, but not from within the other loved in himself for himself. Whether I know it or not, the kind of love that is really at the source of my response to the other's success is a self-centered radical care love, which issues in desire for and delight in the other's achievement and honor as my vicarious fulfilment. My love for the other is merely implemental; and my desire for or satisfaction in his success and honor is desire for or satisfaction in a substitute fulfilment of my ideal self-image. The whole experience is self-centered through and through. The other is an other self merely in the sense of an extension of my egocentric self.

When, on the contrary, the other is to me truly an other self in personal friendship, loved in herself for herself, I desire or delight in her success from within her, as hers, for her own sake. By my love for her I identify with her. It is *her* success and honor, *not my* vicarious success that I desire or delight in. I have a joy in my loved one's heart—if my love is great enough, greater joy than I would have if I myself had achieved the success she has.

The second situation reveals even more surely how a friend experiences his friend's life as his own in her; this is the situation in which his friend endures failure and humiliation. He knows from within her what she is enduring. He does, of course, want to ease her pain; but insofar as he cannot, he experiences her failure and humiliation as his own in her, perhaps more deeply than he would if he himself had failed and been humiliated. When, however, the other is loved implementally, as a source of vicarious fulfilment, he now resents her as failing him, depriving him of vicarious success and honor. Thus, in the family, a child who does not fulfil a parent's expectations is made to feel she has failed and humiliated her parent and ought to be ashamed, is "not worthy of love." That is to say, she is not a fit object in which to find a substitute fulfilment of the parent's ideal self-image. Similarly, on the playing field, if the athletic hero makes a mistake or suffers a slump he is suddenly "a bum" to the fans and is angrily booed by them. Neither the parent nor the fan in these instances has any knowledge from within the other and much less any experience of what I mean by an experience of the other's life as his or her own in the other.

Completion of Sharing Lives

There is much more that has to go on in the complete experience of sharing lives in personal friendship. Given all that has already been said about personal friendship and in particular about one friend's experience of the other's life in the other, it will be enough to mention these additional elements without developing them. First, for a complete experience of sharing lives, the friend whose life I experience as mine in him has to have at least some vague unreflective and unexplicitated awareness or belief that he is to me an other self, his life in some measure known by me from within and experienced as my life in him. Second, he has to experience my life as his in me. Third, I have to have at least some vague, unreflective and unexplicitated belief that I am to him an other self, my life known in some measure by him from within and experienced as his life in me. Further, each friend has to maintain a conviction that the other is aware of his or her belief. Finally, both of us have to keep alive all these factors in our response to each other and our belief in each other's doing so until it all becomes part of the virtue of friendship, a stable complex disposition in both of our minds and hearts, which constitutes the way we exist at every moment in relation to each other and which makes the conscious actualizations of our life as friends easy, graceful, constant, and joyful.

As I said above, I am not asserting that for the complex experience of sharing lives a reflective and explicit awareness of all these factors in it is necessary. However, I am asserting, and asserting strongly, that without a reflective explicit awareness and conviction of all the main factors involved in sharing lives, the friendship will lack something of the intensity it would otherwise have and that the fulness of life and joy in friendship, to which personal dynamism tends, will be incomplete. One can go on living and unreflectively valuing the world and life in it and then, after some experience, for example, a close brush with death, come to a greatly heightened realization of the wonder of ordinary things, of the wonder of being alive in the world. So also, one can live unreflectively in friendship, valuing it and rejoicing in it but failing to be fully aware of the incredible richness of it until in one way or another the treasure is exposed in the light of reflection. This can happen (and my hope is that it will happen) as a consequence of having the treasure laid open by descriptive analysis such as we are doing here. It has happened to me while writing this book.

Conformation of Minds and Hearts

An inevitable consequence of sharing lives and a sign of it is the growing conformation of the friends' minds and hearts. Such a conformation is clearly unlike that imposed by any coercion or manipulation. It is the goal toward which friends' minds and hearts connaturally tend as a consequence of their mutual affective identification by personal love and sharing lives. Every person in the world, just by reason of being the unique persons we are, experiences the universe and human life in it from our own unique perspective. Further, each one of us sees it in terms of our own background and history. By sharing their conscious lives, each friend in some measure experiences life and the universe not only from his or her own perspective but also from the friend's unique perspective. Each friend, therefore, to some extent takes on the other's ways of perceiving, understanding, and affectively responding to the world they live in. They grow toward having one mind and one heart as much as may be without being unfaithful to the truth as they see it or to themselves. When they do not have one mind and heart in everything, they disagree with mutual understanding and respect, with openness to being influenced by each other, with earnest desire to see the truth together and to respond affectively in accord with the truth.

7
IDEAL OF MATURE PERSONAL FRIENDSHIP

When clarifying his own approach as a sociologist, Reisman observes that scientific studies of friendship are mostly concerned, as his study clearly is, with the type of friendship which he calls "associative"; whereas philosophers are mostly concerned with what is generally considered to be a higher type, "perfect friendship" (1979, 28). Whatever may be the accuracy of Reisman's observation, my main concern in this philosophical study is not only with what I see as the highest type of friendship but also with the ideal form of that type.

As with other living and growing things, in any personal friendship once begun, all the essentials are present in some degree, great or slight, at every stage of its development from very immature to very mature friendship. What makes a personal friendship more mature is mainly, along with a fuller reflective grasp of what has just been seen about sharing lives, the greater development of the virtue of friendship. It is by reason of this virtue that actual love, communion, and sharing lives arise graciously, constantly, and joyfully, and that mutual commitment and believing in each other's commitment is made firm. Since mutual personal love is the core of personal friendship, the developed lasting disposition in each friend for personal love of the other is the core virtue of personal friendship. Therefore, the maturation of such friendship is above all else a growth of the dispositions in the friends for loving each other with personal love. Study of the maturation of personal friendship must then give special attention to this central factor by relationship to which any other factor is involved in personal friendship as a condition for it or a help toward it or a consequence of it.

Ways of Maturing in Love

Some ways in which personal love can mature come readily to mind. It can become: 1. more truthful, 2. purer, 3. stronger, 4. more integral, 5. more generative. Let us look at each of these.

1. Recall briefly what was shown above in chapter 3. The meaning of truthful love readily emerged from the understanding of love as affective affirmation intrinsically formed by the loved one through the mediation of the lover's cognitive apprehension and affirmation

of the beloved. Recall that we love only what we apprehend and as we apprehend it and cognitively affirm it. Cognitive apprehension can be accurate or inaccurate; cognitive affirmation, judgment, can be truthful or untruthful. Since radical personal love, affective affirmation, is intrinsically formed by the loved one as apprehended and cognitively affirmed by the lover, it can also be in accord or discord with the one loved, be truthful or untruthful. The intention of the lover to affectively affirm the loved one as she really is makes the lover honest, sincere, but does not necessarily make the love itself truthful.

Further, even when love is truthful, free of discord with the reality of the loved one, it can still be more or less truthful, depending on how fully the lover knows the loved one. Now, the personal self of the loved one, we saw, always exceeds what can be grasped in conceptual knowledge of his fluctuating qualities, acts, and feelings. Further, even these qualities, acts, and feelings easily escape the lover's full awareness and understanding. Consequently, even when the lover avoids untruthful love, her love and care will never be equal to the loved one's full reality; it will always need to grow more truthful. Consequently, the dynamism of friends reaches toward ever increased fulness of life in ever increased union constituted by ever fuller truthfulness in their mutual love and, therefore, in the ever fuller knowledge of each other that is prerequisite for more truthful personal love.

2. The second way in which mutual love in personal friendship can become more mature is by growing in purity, that is, by becoming more free of any admixture of egoism. Clearly the act of personal love for the friend cannot itself be egoistic or even be tinged with egoism. Increased purity of love then refers to the total concrete experience of love, which, along with the personal love for the friend can include another self-centered radical love and care that issues in implemental love for the friend as fulfilling or useful to the one loving. We have already seen that these two loves can be compatible, but can also be in conflict when the self-love is egoistic and does not respect the dignity of the other person, in this case the friend. Think, for example of a married couple who have become truly personal friends. The woman who has personal love for her husband might still be inclined as a consequence of egoism to an unreasonable jealousy that causes him pain and cripples his healthy relationships with others. Or she might be inclined to tempt him to betray his own moral principles and/or risk the ruin of his reputation in order to become wealthy. A man who has a personal love for his wife might

also be inclined by his selfishness to use her merely for his satisfaction or to dominate her in ways that stunt her personal life.

Love in personal friendship becomes purer as it becomes less mixed with egoistic radical love and egoistic desire and beyond that, as it grows toward an ideal in which even harmless self-centered love is ultimately integrated into altruistic love for the friend. I may have implemental love that derives from selfish radical love and can harm my friend; I may also have implemental love for him as delightful to me or useful for me in ways that do not violate the loved one's personal dignity but are, nevertheless, largely self-centered. As my love grows purer I will more and more love my friend as delightful and useful to me, not only because of my healthy and truthful radical care for myself but because being so loved is fulfilling to, gives joy to, my friend, whom I love in and for himself.

3. Besides becoming more truthful and purer, personal love between friends also matures by becoming stronger, that is, more intense and firmer. We most readily think of more ardent or piercing or exciting *feelings* as rendering personal love more intense (though not necessarily firmer)—and they do to some extent. For intense feelings do complete love if the feelings are of a kind that accord with a truthful act of radical love and are of reasonable intensity in the concrete situation. More fundamental, however, and more significant than increased intensity of feelings is the increased intensity of the *act* of radical love.

A more intense love (the act or the feeling) is not necessarily firmer or the other way around; an intense love can be fragile, have little lasting power A firmer love is one that is more capable of fidelity, more powerfully resistant to any influence that tends to destroy or diminish it. The source of that adverse influence can be in the lover's self or in the loved one or outside them in some turn of events or some other person. The firmer the love, the more promptly and easily any of these hostile influences are withstood and overcome.

4. Even apart from their increased intensity, feelings of love (warmth, tenderness, sweetness) have an important role in mature love: they are necessary for an integral, a more completely human, love. Feelings of love are not always in direct proportion with the act of radical love. The latter can not only endure through periods when the feelings seem almost dead, but can also grow in truthfulness, purity, and strength during these times. On the other hand, it would be a grave mistake to belittle the value of feelings. Loving without them, however necessary at times for the maturation of personal love in human life, is not itself a perfection of love, not a goal of human dynamism.

The perfection of human love needs feelings, intense, deep, pervasive, and constant, to go with the act of personal love. Personal love can mature in truthfulness, purity, and strength without becoming more integral by increased feelings of love. Without the latter, however, the maturation is incomplete, the love is a less fully human love than it would be if it were more integral.

5. As the mutual love between personal friends grows more truthful, purer, stronger, and more integral, the friends become more and more keenly sensitive to each other's true needs and more generous in responding to them by deeds of love. As a consequence, their love grows more fruitful of these deeds and more generative of fully personal life in the friends. Growth of truly personal life in them will intensify their personal dynamism toward fulness of life in all persons and make them more generative of life in others.

Like Old Wine

The other essential factors in personal friendship relate in one way or another to the mutual personal love at its core; and the maturation of that love will involve as a condition for it or as a consequence of it the maturation of communion of love, of sharing of lives, of mutual commitment and trust in each other's commitment. More effortless, more lively, and more firm belief by each friend in the other's growth in all these ways, will allow their friendship to flourish and the joy of it to pervade their lives.

We sometimes speak metaphorically of "the wine of friendship" because like wine it warms and cheers the heart. A comparison of the stages by which friendship grows with the stages in winemaking might bring together what has been said about the maturation of friendship. The juices from different kinds of grapes account for different kinds of wine (chablis, burgundy, tokay, and so on); but before the juice of any kind of grapes can become new wine, a time of fermentation is necessary. Similarly, different types of mutual love account for different types of friendship. Only mutual personal love in the strict sense can become personal friendship, and it can do so ordinarily only over a prolonged time of fermentation, as it were. During this time the dispositions which will constitute the virtue of friendship begin and form what can be thought of as incipient friendship. Once the juice has, through the fermentation process, become wine, the new wine needs aging in order to reach its full flavor and bouquet; so also, new friendship, in which the virtue of friendship is present but still weak and shallow, needs a time of aging in order to mellow, to reach some full measure of maturity. That is reached when the virtue of friendship has become powerfully resistant to any destructive force and enables the friends to live their lives of friendship with notable ease, with grace and joy, with confidence and constancy, to enjoy its full flavor and fragrance which now pervades everything in their lives. "A new friend is like new wine. Let it grow old and you will drink it with pleasure" (Sirach 9:10).

The Ideal of Mature Friendship

Understanding of any process of growth as also wise tendance of it needs understanding of what the process is leading toward, what the living being in process is to become. Sometimes, we can this goal inscribed in that which is growing.

The ideal toward which the maturation of personal friendship tends is one life constituted by two lives so interpenetrated that each friend experiences the other's whole life as hers in the other and experiences the whole of her own life as the other's in her. (Even though the ideally mature friendship is not found actualized in human experience, that does not show that it is impossible. Even if it should be impossible, understanding it would still be of value for understanding personal dynamism.) Essential to this union of lives is the maintenance and even increase of each friend's uniqueness and distinction from the other; for this distinction without separation is necessary for the very possibility of union in personal friendship. What we have already shown of personal love and personal friendship makes that certain. By the very nature of the relationship, in personal friendship each friend tends both to live the whole life of the other in the other and to become fully his own unique self, and wants the other to do the same. Each tends to all this for the enrichment of the other.

By the virtue of friendship, we have seen, personal friends are preconsciously in union at every moment. This union, even in very mature friendships is explicitly realized in consciousness only at intermittent moments of communion and sharing lives, when in some measure, during a passing moment, they experience what it is to have one life without loss of, even with intensification of, each friend's distinctiveness as a person. As the friendship becomes more mature, however, the friends come to live much of their lives in the radiance of those glowing moments; that is to say those moments pervade and color, give tone to, much of what goes on in the rest of their lives.

When the personal friendship reaches exceptional maturity, each friend most of the time has, in some degree, at least a vague and unreflective sense of being who each is by union with the other. My friend and my sense of our union subtly and pervasively affect my ways of seeing persons and things and events and of responding to them. The joys and sorrows, successes and failures, hopes and fears of my friend experienced as mine in her give a tone to my life. My own joys and sorrows, successes and failures, hopes and fears have a special tone and color inasmuch as they are my friend's in me. All this is true also from the side of my friend in relation to me, and we are each sure that this is the way it is with the other.

The more frequent and more intense the moments at which friends experience the interpenetration of their lives and the more pervasively their whole lives are lived under the sway of these moments, the more the full flavor and fragrance of mature friendship pervades their lives. The firmer and more efficacious their mutual virtues of friendship become, the more they approach toward an ideal union so complete that, if attained, each friend's consciousness would at every moment involve the other as an other self with whom he has one life lived wholly by each and wholly by both together. In fact, were the ideal achieved, each friend could say to the other that this composite life is more totally mine just because it is yours and by love I am you; that this life is more totally yours just because it is mine and by your love you are me. Their whole conscious lives would be a life of friendship.

Did Montaigne have some intimation of such an ideal union when he said of what he called "extraordinary friendship": "In the friendship I speak of, our souls mingle and blend with each other so completely that they efface the seam that joined them and cannot find it again"? (Trans. in Schneider 1964, II, 160-61.)

I have been speaking of an ideally mature friendship only in respect of the degree of conscious union; such a friendship could still be far from ideal in other respects. The full ideal of a life of friendship calls for ever fuller development of the friends' personalities, intellectually, emotionally, aesthetically, morally, religiously, so that not only is their sharing of lives complete but what they have to share is as rich as may be now and ever more so as they continue to grow. It should be evident, then, that an unusually high degree of personal maturity is prerequisite to any notable, even though limited and imperfect approach toward the ideal of friendship. So high a degree of spiritual maturity is necessary, so great is the cost, and so many contingent events must converge, to make possible such growth to mature friendship that such friendship is understandably a rare occurrence. Those who experience it and reflect on it are filled with gratitude to God and to each other and marvel that it ever came to be. It is a rarity, a wonder, and a joy.

It can also be anguish in a world where friends may have to live in separation and where death can take one of them from the other. But this anguish also underlines what has been said above about the fulness of union that is possible in mature friendship. Two who have written most movingly of their personal experience of extraordinary union in friendship and of losing the friend by death are Augustine and Montaigne. Each has left us a record of his thoughts and feelings after the death of a friend with whom he had experienced sharing of lives so deep and wide and constant as to affect his whole conscious life. Their accounts illustrate and confirm what has been said: that a friend is an other self, that each friend's life is the other friend's life in him; that friends can so fully share lives that they have one life; that consequently living without the friend is to be only half alive to be half myself.

Looking back later in his life on the death of the dearest friend of his youth, Augustine wrote (*Confessions*, bk. 4, ch. 6):

> It was strange to me that other mortals could live since he had died whom I had loved as if he were not to die; and it was stranger yet that I should live since I was another he. Well did someone speak of his friend as half of his soul, for I deemed my soul and his soul to have been one soul in two bodies. Therefore, life was a horror to me, because I did not want to live as half a man. On the other hand, for that reason perhaps, I feared dying lest the one whom I loved so much should totally die.

Montaigne (1946, I, 259-60), speaking about his life after the death of Estienne de la Boetie, echoes Augustine's sentiments.

> ... for, in truth, if I compare all the rest of my life—although by God's mercy I have found it sweet and easy, and, save for the loss of such a friend, exempt from any poignant grief, full of contentment and tranquility of mind, having been satisfied with my natural and original advantages, without seeking others, —if, I say, I compare it all with the four years that it was given to me to enjoy the sweet companionship and society of that lofty soul, it is but smoke, it is but a dark and mournful night. Since the day I lost him... I do but drag out a languishing existence, and even the pleasures that offer themselves to me, instead of consoling me, redouble my regret for his loss... it seems to me now that I am only half a man... there is no act or thought of mine in which I do not miss him....

8

PERSONAL FRIENDSHIP AND MUTUAL ROMANTIC LOVE: CONTRAST AND RELATIONSHIP

This chapter could at first appear to be a digression from my main line of thought or merely an addendum to it. As will appear, however, it has three significant functions in this essay. The first is to counteract some diluted and vapid notions of friendship which show up in several false ways of contrasting it with the experience of being in love romantically and, in doing this, to emphasize some important aspects of personal friendship. The second function of this chapter is to call attention to and to clarify the relationship between personal friendship and being in love romantically by showing how the latter can lead to the former and how the two can be integrated so that each one is enriched by the other. The third function of this chapter is, in the light of what is said about the relationship between being in love and personal friendship, to show how being in love fits into the human transcendent dynamism toward ever fuller human personal life.

The Forms of Erotic Love

Before critically evaluating some commonly proposed contrasts between friendship and being in love, we need a brief description of what I am referring to as erotic love in general and then of what I am referring to as romantic erotic love in particular. By erotic love in general I mean a total concrete experience of love in which the lovers' acts of affective affirmation and their affective feelings of love have a sexual quality or tone, either in the narrow genital sense or in the broader, more pervasive, psycho-sexual sense.

Like every other total concrete experience of love, erotic love is rooted in an act of radical love (for the lover's self or for another) and almost always a modification of that act into radical care, with a consequent act of desire (implemental love). Radical love without qualification as erotic is simply an affective affirmation of someone (self or another) in herself for herself, her whole reality, including all that is involved in her sexuality, but not focused on the latter. It is focused on the loved one as a person, a radical value, and is not of itself erotic. When, however, it modulates into care for the radically loved one (self or the other) precisely as in need of sexual union (psychosexual or genital), it takes on a sexual orientation and quality; it becomes erotic. So also does the consequent desire (implemental love) for what will fill the need of the one cared for. Along with the acts of radical care and of desire, the total experience of erotic love includes, is suffused with, erotic feelings, feelings that also have a sexual orientation and tone. Depending on the form of radical care and the consequent desire in conformity with it, erotic love can take three distinct basic forms.

In one form the affective act of desire derives from an act of selfish radical care love, with a felt need for the other as a physical sex object; it is directed solely to satisfaction of the "lover's" appetite for physical sexual union.

In a second form, the erotic desire still derives from radical care for the lover's self with a felt need for union with the beloved, but not only in order to satisfy sexual lust. The desire is directed toward union with the beloved in his or her whole masculine or feminine reality, spiritual as well as physical, even predominantly spiritual sometimes. Such love is psychosexually erotic. It is nearer to personal love than the first form of erotic love is; but it is not yet personal, since the beloved is not affectively affirmed in herself for herself. The radical care at the source of desire is for the lover's own self in need; and the beloved is loved as an implemental value, as the lover's fulfilment.

In the third form of a total concrete experience of erotic love, the radical love at the core of the experience which modulates into radical care is personal, at least in the broad sense of the term, the sense in which every radical love for another person is personal. In it the lover's radical love is no longer for self; it is an affective affirmation of the beloved in and for herself or himself, focused on her or his whole reality as feminine or masculine, with a consequent desire for fuller sexual union (psychosexually and genitally) in whatever way is for the beloved's fulfilment.

Distinguishing these three forms of erotic love must not be taken as implying that each of these always appear in experience separately. Two or all of them can appear together in combination or in tension. The movements of the human heart are complex and perplexing. Some writings on love, whatever the writer might really think, seem to assume that our love for another is either self-centered or other-centered, one or the other only. As already shown, close attention to experience reveals something of central importance for understanding our experience of love, namely, that in our concrete experience of it we can and do love one and the same person in more than one distinct way. Thus, I can love you in and for yourself while also loving you as my fulfilment or even, in one of your roles as a means to some goal I intend. Sometimes I do this without any inner conflict, when my self-love is not selfish and what I desire is not opposed to your dignity as a radical value. The two loves are then distinct but not in conflict. Sometimes, on the other hand, we find ourselves successively or even at the same time spontaneously loving the same person in conflicting ways that put us under tension and require painful deliberation and choice of one or the other of the conflicting loves. All this holds for the total concrete experience of erotic love. With or without conflict, the second and third forms of erotic love are usually found together in erotic lovers, and not infrequently, all three forms (the first form in conflict with the second and/or third). The heroically noble lover alone or the most ignoble one loves others only with purely altruistic or only with purely selfish love.

Romantic Erotic Love

Not all the forms of erotic love noted above can be romantic, and those that can be are not always so. The first form can immediately be eliminated. It is in gross contrast with the usual meaning of romantic love and certainly with the meaning I want to give the term. The other two forms can be romantic but only when certain special features are present in some degree. I am not thinking of such features as idealization, unrestrained imagination, loss of touch with the real world, disregard for reasonableness, all of which are frequently associated with what is said to be romantic. These can, of course, be found in some experiences which are called romantic love; but not in all. They are certainly not in the romantic experience of being in love that I want to compare and contrast and relate with personal friendship. What I do include in the meaning of such love are features that are noted by poets, dramatists and story tellers, by philosophers, theologians, and psychologists, features that those who experience such romantic love readily recognize.

Of central importance among these features is a vision of the beloved's beauty and splendor, which calls forth from the lover a corresponding affective response. It is a vision that only the lovers see— and did not see before being in love, even though they may have known the beloved long before that. The beloved appears to the lover as suffused with a transcendent, indefinable glory. Surprising as the vision is, the lover can also experience "recognition," a sense that somehow the glory of the beloved has been known before. As a consequence of the vision, the lover's masculine or feminine sensibility is inebriated with amorous feelings, spiritual as well as sensuous, even predominantly spiritual. Preeminent among the feelings is that of reverence for the beloved, of being touched with awe. Especially when the love is known to be mutual, the romantic lover experiences a sense of completion, of an emptiness filled, and a glowing intensity of life. He feels as if his heart has sprouted wings and is soaring into realms of light and delight that he had never even dreamed of experiencing in his life. A singing comes to life in him, as if it were always latent in him waiting only for the vision of the beloved to bring it alive. Along with these feelings the lover experiences a spontaneous desire to be at the service of the beloved in little tender ways and in great and valorous exploits and sacrifices. Sometimes these desires turn out to be deceptive: self-centered, even selfish, merely velleities. But again sometimes they are genuine and effect a true transformation of the lover's character.

Diverse explanations of the romantic erotic experience are offered by authors who have diverse backgrounds, who come from diverse intellectual starting points and attend to different elements in the whole experience. Plato appeals to his myth of reminiscence: without the lover being aware of what is happening, the beauty of the beloved is a reminder of the Absolute Beauty contemplated in a previous existence. From that previous experience the present one takes on a power it would not otherwise have (see, e.g., *Phaedrus*, 250A-251B). Dante (1962) and Charles Williams in his thought based on Dante propose an interpretation which parallels Plato's in a Christian context: they believe that the lover experiences a moment of revelation, the uncreated glory of God manifested in the beauty of a created image (see Williams [1941] for a compact and a clear statement of his thought on romantic love; see also Shideler [1962, esp. 9-42]). Both these interpretations take account of a response that often seems to be out of proportion to the actuality of the beloved apart from the latter's relation to the divine. Dante and Williams, in their interpretations, acknowledge the gloriously lovable and admirable reality of the beloved as objective, even though not seen by persons other than the lover. On the other hand, some, as Freud and Freudians, tend to slight or deny the objective wonder and lovableness of the beloved in romantic erotic love; they appeal to sublimation and "overestimation" in order to explain the experience of such love. Singer (1966, 9-16) interprets the experience as a process of imaginatively endowing the beloved with graces he does not really have. Differing from and yet also resembling any of the foregoing interpretations is that which sees the beloved as an incarnation of the lover's unconscious ideal complement, for which the lover has always been seeking and with whom she hopes to find wholeness (Wylie 1958, 166).

The latter interpretation is developed by Jungians in terms of projecting the *anima* or *animus* onto the beloved. This can be done in two ways. In one way, *anima* or *animus* is projected onto the beloved as a false image so that the lover does not see the beloved's self as he or she really is, but as the lover wants him or her to be. When this happens, the projected *anima* or *animus* serves as a mask to hide the reality of the beloved from the lover. In a second way, the *animus* or *anima* serves as a lens through which the lover sees and is related with the beloved's true self (Haule 1990, 10, 16-18; Johnson 1983, 141-42, 193-97).

It seems reasonable to suggest that several or all of these interpretations can have some validity as partial explanations, sometimes more than one functioning together in different proportions in different persons experiences, sometimes one functioning in one instance and another in another. Whatever the truth of this matter may be, it is not necessary here to attempt to find it. For our purpose it is only important to note that all these interpretations of the romantic experience, of being in love, acknowledge the vision and its affective consequences as central and specifying features of the experience and needing explanation.

Romantic Falling in Love, Being in Love, and Infatuation

Beyond noting the special features of romantic love, it is also necessary for my purpose to distinguish romantic falling in love, romantic being in love, and romantic infatuation. All these distinct experiences are, in writing on romantic love, frequently and confusingly referred to by one or other of the three names, as if the experiences were all the same; or they are all lumped together under the general rubric of romantic love—as if there were no need to make any distinction. However, unless it is clear how what I refer to as being in love differs from the other two, everything that will be said by way of contrasting and relating it with personal friendship will be liable to serious misunderstanding.

The first of these, falling in love, has the features of romantic being in love but commonly, if not always, involves an emotional storm, a violent rapture, with consequent bewilderment. Dante speaks of a "stupor" when he first encountered Beatrice, and all who have fallen love can testify to the sense of being overwhelmed, thrown into confusion, joyful at being in the same world with such a heavenly creature as the beloved and yet pained by a sense of inadequacy and despair of ever being worthy of and ever winning his or her love. If genuine being in love follows on falling in love, it is more serene or at least less violent and disturbing, without being less profound or wholehearted. It even seems that one can come to be in love without going through the storms and stresses of falling in love.

Not only must falling in love be distinguished from being in love, but both must be emphatically distinguished from romantic infatuation. Falling in love, however disruptive of ordinary ways of thinking and loving and feeling, need not be irrational or lead to bizarre ways of thinking and acting—as does happen in romantic infatuation, which is a grotesque caricature of genuine being in love. In this experience, as Ortega y Gasset brilliantly analyzes it (Ortega 1957, 55-59; Ortega is describing what he names falling in love; it is, however, what I distinguish from falling in love and name infatuation), the lover's power of attention is so irresistibly and exaggeratedly fixed on the beloved as to leave little or no space in the lover's consciousness for other persons or considerations by relation to which the beloved and the lover's love could be seen in a rational perspective. As a consequence, the lover is disabled for thinking and acting with regard for reality. In this state, he can be destructive of the beloved, of self, and of others. For the infatuated lover, his "love" is a law to itself, tending to override all loyalties, commitments, and ethical norms for human actions. Romantic infatuation does not take over in every instance of falling in love. Those who fall in love are susceptible to it but can withstand the powerful drawing to let their feelings override reason and commitment. A beautiful and delicate study of victorious resistance is given cinematic treatment by David Lean in his *Brief Encounter*.

Those who are overcome by this "temporary imbecility" (Ortega's term) of romantic infatuation are favorite tragic or comic figures for dramatists and novelists. If Dante's *Vita Nuova* serves as a classic description of falling in love in a way which leads to a mode of being in love that brings to life what is noblest and most creative in the lover, by parallel the story of Phillip Carey's obsession with Mildred Rogers, in Somerset Maughm's novel, *Of Human Bondage*, can serve as an illustration of romantic infatuation. A classic symbol of romantic infatuation is the myth of Tristan and Iseult. If Denis de Rougemont's (1945, 27-32) interpretation of the myth is correct, then neither Tristan nor Iseult was really in love with the other but only loved the emotional experience of being romantically infatuated. If Robert Johnson's (1983, 79) fascinating Jungian interpretation of the myth is true, then Tristan is not loving the real Iseult the fair but only the projection of his unconscious *anima* and she in turn is not loving the real Tristan but only a projection of her unconscious *animus*.

When romantic being in love is not distinguished from the romantic infatuation symbolized in this myth, we find all romantic love condemned as a "fraud and crazy" (Brain 1976, 11), or said to be always like the relationship between Tristan and Iseult, an infatuation that leads to disloyalty, broken commitments, and misery (Johnson 1983, 96-103).

Friendship and Being in Love:
Some Common Contrasts and a Critical Evaluation of Them

Let it be clear, therefore, that in the following frequently heard contrasts between being in love and friendship, I am thinking of mutual romantic being in love, free of the aberrations found in romantic infatuation or even of the emotional storms of falling in love. It is love in this meaning that I think those who make the contrasts usually, not always, have in mind (though they rarely bother to be so precise); and it is contrast of friendship with this kind of erotic love that will be most fruitful for the study of friendship. The friendship I am contrasting and relating with romantic love is personal in the proper sense and involves mutual love which is integral, that is, suffused with feelings of love—though not necessarily with erotic ones.

1. One frequently employed way of contrasting personal friendship and mutual being in love is that of saying that romantic lovers face each other while friends face together in the same direction. This manner of speaking means that romantic lovers are united by their interest in each other and in their love, while personal friends are united rather by some common interest other than each other or their love. Such a generalization could perhaps be fully justified if the friendship spoken of were that based only on mutual usefulness. It cannot be justified even when the friendship is one in which the friends implementally love each other as reciprocal fulfilments. Least of all can it be justified when the friendship contrasted with being in love is personal friendship. By showing the error involved in this

contrast, light can be thrown on some facts about personal friendship that are sometimes obscured or falsified.

It is true that there is in this contrast enough correspondence with easily observed facts to recommend it at first hearing, before careful critical evaluation As was shown above, a community of interest in something other than the friends and their love for each other does seem to be an essential of friendship. For romantic lovers, on the contrary, at least when their love is intense, their consuming interest is in each other and their mutual love. They delight in detailing the wondrous qualities they find in or project on to each other, in telling of their love ("How many ways do I love you?"), and in giving signs and pledges of love.

However, when this much has been noted, it must still be said that the contrast is altogether oversimplified and exaggerated, that it fails to take account of many readily observable facts, and, as a consequence, leads to a shallow and even false impression of personal friendship. For the fact is that personal friends not only face in a common direction in as much as they have some community of interest but that they also, at a more profound level than their common interest, face each other. If they did not, there would be no personal friendship. (Most of those who have a common interest never become personal friends.) And friends do talk to each other or to others about their love and union. Only read, for example, the letters of St. Paul, chapters 4 and 9 of Augustine's *Confessions*, Aelred of Rievaulx's treatise *On Spiritual Friendship*, Montaigne's essay on friendship, Robert Brain's (1976) enlightening ethnological study of friendship in other cultures than ours. With friends, however, such talk does not have the almost obsessive and erotic character that it has with romantic lovers.

To assert that personal friends do face each other just as truly, even if not with the same preoccupation, as romantic lovers and often at a more profound level does not mean that they are usually thematically absorbed in each other and their love. Yet even this remark has to be qualified in two ways. First, friends can also be romantically in love (as we shall see). Second, leaving that first qualification aside for the moment, it is also true that on occasion one friend centers attention on the other, on her way of doing things, the charming qualities revealed as she talks and acts, the admirable character traits, the lovable unique personal self that shines through all.

Even when their attention is directly focused on some activity they are engaged in together, friends have a keen oblique attention to each other. There are clear and convincing indications of this in experience. One is that when doing some things together, for example, listening to music, contemplating the beauty of nature, entering into a social gathering, friends are by their presence to each other sensitized to the beauty of the music or of nature or other persons in a way they would not be if alone. A second indication is that during shared activities, even those that demand close attention to the activity, for example, working together at a difficult task that requires great concentration, playing competitive games—*during* these activities there is a special delight for the friends just because the activity is shared with each other. The same activity with some other person can in some ways be more interesting and enjoyable to me than it is with my friend; this is so when the other is more intelligent or witty or more capable in the activity we are carrying on than my friend is. But even in this situation, the activity lacks the special savor and joy it has when done with my friend just because it is done with him. This fact is unexplainable unless friends somehow face each other while facing in the same direction, attend to each other in their very attending to their shared activity, are aware of their common goals as held in common. A third indication that friends are in some special way facing each other when engaged in common activities is the fact that after their activity together, each frequently remembers not only what they were doing but what was revealed about the other's style and lovable qualities while they were doing it.

Finally, there is a fourth indication, more evident and more certain than any or all of the preceding indications. It is the fact that friendship *grows* during the friends' shared activities, whether those in which they seek enjoyment or those in which they work together for common goals.

> Old friends go to the concert together. As soon as the music begins, they are rapt and seemingly totally oblivious [each] to the other. But neither would consider for a moment going to the concert alone. Underneath the silent raptness, their friendship continues to grow quietly—a conclusion proven by a new depth of sharing as they return home amid slow, mulling conversation. Not rarely three friends hike the mountain trails for six to eight hours with only an occasional word and an almost silent midday lunch. Yet the enjoyment of each other is intense and, underneath the quiet calm intimacy grows. It would seem that the beauty of music and nature mysteriously sensitizes each person to the other instead of distracting each from the other (Hassel 1982, 40).

Although it is not part of my central concern here, it is worth no-
ticing that the questionable contrast under consideration, without
some qualifications fails also to do justice to romantic being in love.
For, as Charles Williams and others point out (and the experience of
romantic lovers confirms), when such love is at its best, in and through
their very facing each other, the lovers face beyond themselves to
God and to other persons. Each is an opening for the other to the
source of all beauty and lovableness and love and to all who participate in God's beauty and love.

2. A second way employed by some of contrasting the love between personal friends and romantic lovers is to say that personal
friends face not each other but the good each wishes for the other
(von Hildebrand 1966). This contrast comes closer than the first to
the truth that personal friends do very much face each other but in a
different way than romantic lovers do. Nevertheless, it is also defective. Leaving aside for the moment the question whether romantic
erotic lovers do not, *just by reason of their love*, also wish good to each
other, it must be said that this second contrast ignores the necessary
presuppositions of each friend's desire for the other's good. In the
earlier analysis of the total concrete experience of love we saw that
desire necessarily presupposes radical care, that radical care is radical
love for someone precisely as in need of some good. Therefore, wishing good to another for the other's own sake presupposes radical love
for the other and radical care. Now, every personal love in its most
proper and full sense is radical love informed, through an intuition,
by the loved one's unique self. In such love, especially, the lover is
surely facing the loved one. Certainly, then, personal friends above
all others are, in their mutual personal love, facing each other at a
deep and intimate dimension of their affective life. Clearly, the second way of contrasting personal friendship and mutual romantic love
rests on a failure to see what goes on in the total concrete experience
of personal love.

3. A third misleading contrast between personal friendship and
being in love asserts that the difference lies in the intensity of love in
the latter and the mildness of it in the former. Depending on one's
experience, observation, and reading or on the meaning given to the
word "intense," this contrast might at first hearing seem to be either
plainly true or plainly facile and false.

The first thing to be said in response to this third contrast is that
any generalization about the intensity of romantic love in any of its
forms is groundless. It overlooks the fact in experience that romantic
love can be very mild as well as overwhelmingly intense and any de-

gree in between. To think that such love is always very intense fails to take account of all its shades, from a fierce blaze to a soft, barely perceptible glow. This way of thinking identifies romantic love with the grand passion. It leaves aside the many mild but often beautiful and delicately fulfilling psychosexual responses that suffuse the relationships between the sexes in daily life.

Equally groundless is any generalization to the effect that personal love between friends lacks intensity or, at least, that it is always less intense than romantic love. Such a way of thinking would seem to rest on a confusion of serene even though intense feelings of love with mild ones.

The point can be made by recalling a few accounts of friendship that have classic status because they ring true to human experience and aspiration. (Much further significant historical data on the question whether friendship is lacking fire and intensity of love can be found in McGuire 1988). True, many of the tender expressions which occur in the correspondence McGuire presents are epistolary forms (fuller than but parallel with our "dear so and so"). However, much is also sincere although it does not sort comfortably with our current manners (Fiske 1970). Think of the friendship between Jonathan and David in the old Testament (I Samuel 18-20; II Samuel, 9). "Jonathan loved David as his own soul." For David he risked death at his father's hand and willingly ceded to David the kingship which was to be his by succession. "My brother Jonathan," cried David, when lamenting over Jonathan's death, "your love was wonderful, surpassing the love of women." Think also of the friendship portrayed between the aviator and the little boy in Antoine de Saint-Exupéry's *The Little Prince* or of Montaigne's friendship with Estienne de la Boetie. Of their friendship Montaigne wrote: "It had neither one ground, nor two, nor a thousand. It was I know not what quintessence of them all which absorbed my soul and plunged it into his, which seized upon his and made it lose itself in mine" (1946, 253). Recall Augustine's description, quoted above, of how he and his friends wanted to be with one another and share life and by so doing "to *set our souls ablaze* and to make one of many" (my italics). Recall also, and more importantly, his account of his youthful friendship with one young man in particular. It was in Tagaste at the time when Augustine first began to teach there. "My soul could not be without him." A year of that friendship before his friend's death was, Augustine said, "delightful to me above all other delights in that life of mine." When his friend died, Augustine's world was shattered. "I was miserable and had lost my joy" (*Confessions*, bk. 4, ch. 5).

I am not implying that all love between personal friends is as intense and as tender as it is in these illustrations or that it is always as intense as the love between romantic lovers. That would be obviously untrue. All I am saying is that both kinds of love can be very mild or very intense or any degree in between, that love in personal friendship is not to be contrasted with romantic love by reason of its being less intense. If we contrast these two kinds of love when they are equally intense, we find that the point of contrast is qualitative, that their very intensity or strength is qualitatively different. The feelings in personal friendship do not as such have the psychosexual tone that characterizes the feelings of romantic lovers. Further, intense feelings of those who are in love are usually like turbulent whitewater rapids; while intense feelings of love between personal friends are usually more like a deep river, quiet but steadfast and irresistibly powerful.

4. Finally, a fourth contrast focuses on greater or lesser union: erotic love, romantic or otherwise, is said to effect a fuller union than love in friendship. It is true that erotic love tends toward a more complete physical union, and this must be what is being thought of by those who make this contrast. Of itself, however, that physical union is transient; and, while it is actual, does not itself constitute more complete personal union than friendship does. Sometimes it fails of personal union altogether. Romantic love expressed in genital union might or might not lead to increased personal love and communion or be an expression of these; but genital union does not itself constitute these, least of all in the full and proper sense of personal love and communion. Those who are in love desire to be or feel themselves to be already two souls in one body. In a parallel way, personal friends feel themselves to be two bodies with one soul. The latter is hardly a less deep and complete mode of union than the former.

Even at those times when romantic love is more intensely emotional than the love between friends, the union effected can be less profound and lasting, can even be relatively superficial. What experience seems to show is that any romantic love which does not finally lead to personal friendship usually does not long endure. Hoping, perhaps, that he could be proved wrong, William Butler Yeats wrote (1962, 145):

> Earth in beauty dressed
> Awaits returning spring.
> All true love must die,
> Alter at the best

Into some lesser thing.
Prove that I lie.

If "true love" is understood to include the love in personal friendship, then human experience proves over and over again that he "lies."
If, however, "true love" is limited to romantic love, as seems to be
Yeats' intent, even then it can be proved that he lies; for romantic
love can and frequently does alter into or is integrated into a better
and more lasting thing, into personal friendship. On the other hand,
a strong case could be made that every love which begins as romantic
either dies or "alters into some lesser thing," unless it alters into or is
somehow integrated with personal friendship. So true is this that it
can also be said that to romantically commit oneself to lifelong love
for another is implicitly, whether the lover knows it or not, to commit one's self to finally achieving personal friendship.

Integration of Being in Love with Personal Friendship
The preceding criticism of some unfounded contrasts between friendship and mutual romantic erotic love clears the way for seeing how
these two modes of love can be related in experience. While it is not
believable that true personal friendships between a man and a woman
did not happen in earlier ages, it is true that friendship of this kind
between them was not taken into account by writers in ancient Greek
or Roman cultures and that the place of women in those cultures did
not favor the formation of such friendships. Women were not thought
to be capable of friendship in its fullest sense. Strange as this attitude
seems to us now, it generally flourished more or less until very recent
times. In our day and in our culture, it is otiose to raise the question
whether women are capable of personal friendship in its fullest sense
with each other or whether personal friendship between women and
men is possible. (Rosemary Radar [1983] makes a historical study of
a remarkable divergence from the normal pattern during the third to
the fifth century. On the present way of thinking, see Lepp 1964,
75-76; von Hildebrand 1966, 67-71; Meilaender 1993, 9-14. Some
studies on friendship in the United States during the last two de-
cades find evidence which indicates that friendship between women
are generally more intimate and more mutually supportive than those
between men; see Bernards and O'Neill 1989, 147-61, 207-17).

So also is it to ask the question whether it is possible for those who
are in love to also be or become fully personal friends with each other.
An illustration of a more recent and more truthful attitude on these

issues appears in one of Robertson Davies' novels (1983), 304-05; my italics).

> 'I think the world of you, Maria. So let's stop this foolishness and talk to the point. Will you marry me?' 'Why should I marry you?' 'That would take a long time to answer, but I'll give you the best reason: because I think we have become very good friends, and could go on to be splendid friends, and would very likely be wonderful friends forever.' 'Friends?' 'What's wrong with being friends?' 'When people talk about marriage, they generally use stronger words than that.' 'Do they? I don't know. I've never asked anyone to marry me before.' 'You mean you've never been in love?' 'Certainly I've been in love. More times than I can count. I've had two or three affairs with girls I loved. But I knew very well that they weren't friends.' 'You put friendship above love?' 'Doesn't everybody? No, that's a foolish question; of course they don't. They talk about love to people with whom they are infatuated, and sometimes involved to the point of devotion. I've nothing against love. Most enjoyable. But I'm talking to you about marriage.' 'Marriage. But don't you love me?' 'Of course I love you, fathead, but I'm serious about marriage, and *marriage with anyone whom I do not think the most splendid friend I've ever had doesn't interest me.* Love and sex are very fine but they won't last. Friendship—the kind of friendship I am talking about—is charity and loving-kindness more than it's sex and it lasts as long as life. What's more, it grows, and sex dwindles: it has to. So—will you marry me and be friends? We'll have love and we'll have sex, but we won't build on those alone. You don't have to answer now. But I wish you'd think very seriously about it, because if you say no—' 'You'll go to Africa and shoot lions.' 'No; I'll think you've made a terrible mistake.' 'You think well of yourself, don't you?' 'Yes, and I think well of you— better of you than anybody.'

(On spousal friendship, see Shanley's study [1993, 267-84, esp. 278-84] of John Stuart Mill's thought on such friendship as crucially important for the liberation of women from a form of slavery.)

The question worth discussing and pertinent to this present discussion is how personal friendship and romantic love between the same two persons not only comfortably combine (as the character in Davies' novel seems to be saying) but in some way interpenetrate and affect each other. This question can best be answered within a wider consideration of many love relationships which affect personal friendship and are affected by it.

   The core of personal friendship, we saw, is mutual personal love. Such love in the concrete assumes various affective tones or colors by reason of various other relationships between the friends. They may, for example, be related as father and son, as father and daughter, as mother and son, mother and daughter, sisters, brothers, sister and brother, teacher and disciple, leader and follower, and so on. Each of these relationships can specify a subtype of personal friendship in which the friendship is enriched by some special affective tone or coloring. That relationship which gives a special quality to a personal friendship is itself in turn transformed by the friendship and reaches its own maturity and beauty in friendship.

   What I am getting at I once found in a western story (the author and title of the story slip my memory now). One of the characters, an American Indian, was explaining to a white friend the word used in his tribe for the relationship between friends who had a blood relationship by birth or by a ceremony of mingling blood after saving each other's lives. They were called "brother-friends" to express a bond deeper and stronger than that of brothers only by blood or than that of friends who had no bond by blood. (For an interesting anthropological account of "Friends in Blood," see Brain 1976, 75-96.)

   Each relationship of brotherhood or of friendship was enhanced by a fusion with the other. It seems to me that in a parallel way such terms as sister-friend, father-friend, and so on, can serve to express a wide range of personal friendships, each of which has a peculiar affective quality.

   What holds for all these subtypes of friendship holds also for the one that is of special interest in the present context, that is, a personal friendship in the fullest and most proper sense between a woman and a man who are romantically in love and whose erotic love each for the other is of the third form described above. Recall that the first and second forms are self-centered. In the third form, the lover's radical love and care is not for himself or herself but for the beloved in his or her whole masculine or feminine personal reality.

   Neither a personal friendship nor a mutual personal romantic love in the fullest sense of personal ever happens easily, as it does in lesser forms of friendship or romantic love. It is achieved only by the persevering magnanimous endeavor of those who are dedicated to achieving such union. It is not surprising, then, that the integration of both these modes of loving union in a relationship of lover-friends is especially difficult to sustain, is rarely achieved in a high degree, and hardly ever without years of striving, of failing and forgiving, while refusing to give up. Continuing in the third form of erotic love while living in the closeness of personal friendship, persevering in personal friendship while living with intense erotic feelings and desires, this requires self-discipline beyond the capacity of any but very mature persons. The tension to be endured is often painful even for such persons.

If, despite the difficulty, such integration is achieved, in the measure that it is achieved, the total relationship brings to the lover-friends a greater fulness of life than either of the relationships could bring apart from the other. On the one hand, the personal friendship can save the romantic lovers from infatuation. It helps to put their erotic love in the third form of such love and to hold it there, keeping it from sliding into one of the self-centered forms. It gives constancy, holding the total combined relationship firm through all vicissitudes and keeping it alive through all seasons of emotional dryness. It enables the lovers to reach fuller *personal* intimacy, enabling them to share lives free from the impeding fear of embarrassment. In all these ways, personal lover-friends grow toward the fully mature beauty and joy of being in love. On the other hand, being in love brings the lover-friends to a more penetrating vision of each other's unique hidden glory, to a fuller personal knowledge of the kind we saw informs and makes possible personal love in its fullest and most proper sense. It also enhances the whole complex relationship of friends-in-love with special delightful, joyful, life-giving feelings and realization of union. In these ways their mutual romantic love helps personal friends-in-love grow toward the fully mature splendor and joy of being friends.

Being in Love and Human Transcendent Dynamism
Anticipating what will be shown in the following chapters, we can now see how the foregoing line of thought about the relationship between personal friendship and romantic love reveals also how the latter fits into the human dynamism toward ever fuller personal life. It is a step toward capacity to love with personal love, it leads the lovers toward personal friendship or enriches it; it gives special quality to the personal friendship of lover-friends, and reaches its own maturity in such friendship. For all these reasons, the experience of being in love clearly has a significant place in human dynamism to personal love and in the dynamism of personal love to personal communion and sharing of lives in friendship. (Donnelly [1984] gives a scholarly and spirited account of the role of sexual love and "sexual-spiritual friendships" in human growth toward human wholeness and Christian holiness.)

What of romantic infatuation? Although it does of itself tend to be exclusive, confining, drawing the subject away from life with persons other than the beloved, nevertheless, a good case can be made for thinking that it also has a role to play in human dynamism toward personal love, communion, and friendship. Romantic infatuation, Tyrell claims (1994, 13), can play "a vital role in fostering both human intimacy and intimacy with the Lord," if only we understand and wisely guide its force. Norton (1976, 269) shows what he sees to be its radical contribution to the dynamism toward personal love. In his understanding, "romantic love" is the equivalent of or at least includes what I have been speaking of as romantic infatuation. Friendship, he says, requires more developed capacities than does romantic love: some romantic lovers are incapable of friendship, whereas the capacity for friendship inevitably includes capacity for romantic love. He therefore assigns to friendship a relatively greater value than to romantic love. Nevertheless, he adds, one of the most important requisites for personal maturity is conferred by romantic love, namely, the capacity for "intense and sustained attention to a single object." Even though he concedes that "romantic love" (i.e., infatuation in his thought) is irrationally obsessive and delusive, a sort of madness, Norton sees it as also bringing to the lover a precious attainment, one that must otherwise await years of cultivation. Without it the undisciplined and restlessly roaming attention focuses only in a passing way on one indistinct presence after another. But, by reason of romantic love, the lover's attention to the beloved penetrates the refractory surfaces and perceives what is hidden from the non-lover, "the precious essence of his beloved" (Norton, 1976, 296-98).

Put briefly, although romantic love, including even infatuation, tends of itself to be exclusive of other loves *of the same kind*, it can in some ways contribute to attaining the goals of human transcendent dynamism. For romantic experience, even romantic infatuation, can be a way into personal love or into deeper and fuller personal love and, consequently, a step toward further goals of personal dynamism. Indeed, as we have seen, romantic being in love can become integrated with personal friendship so as to constitute a union of lover friends, a romantic personal friendship.

9
TRANSCENDENT HUMAN DYNAMISM

Ineradicable in the human heart and inescapable in our conscious life is an undefined urge or yearning, toward the fulness of life, whatever that might be, or rather toward that (something or someone) by union with which the fulness of life can be realized. This urge is the ultimate root of every experience of fulfilment or frustration, of triumph or tragedy in our lives. So deep within and so all-pervasive of our conscious life as to ordinarily escape clear reflective attention, it usually remains at once concealed in and vaguely revealed in every human desire. At rare moments of most persons' lives, however, it surges at least momentarily into the center of awareness, as at a moment of great tragedy that touches deeply one's own life, at a moment of encountering heroic love, at a moment of hearing or reading great poetry, of listening to great music, at a momentary experience of the holy. In a few persons, this yearning can become the more or less continual explicit center of their lives, understood by them as an "urgent longing" for God.

This urge or drive has been noted by philosophers, theologians, and psychologists and seen as something critically important to understand if we are to understand human persons and human life. To name some of the more famous who come to mind: Socrates, Plato, Aristotle, Plotinus, Augustine, Aquinas, Anselm, Bernard, Spinoza, Freud, Tillich, Marcel, Macmurray, Teilhard de Chardin. In the writings of these thinkers, this profound driving force in human life has been given different descriptions and interpretations, each one shaped by the author's explicit or implicit metaphysics, concept of human nature, and the questions he had in mind when considering it. It has also been given various names: eros (Plato, Freud, Tillich), natural desire (Aristotle and Aquinas), conatus (Spinoza), exigence to transcendence (Marcel).

These terms have taken on special meanings as they are used within the framework of thought of the respective thinkers who use them. In order to avoid identifying my interpretation of this drive with any of those already familiar to the reader (with which, of course, there is inevitable overlapping), I need a term that can include what is basic to the meaning of those other terms while remaining free to include or exclude the special meaning given these others in the context of thought in which they are used and also free to take on any special meaning which this study may lead to. Thus I could use the name eros were it not that this term is sometimes understood in ways directly in conflict with my interpretation, especially when eros is understood as exclusively self-centered, egoistic. I need a term which can be understood as inclusive of both ego-centered and other-centered drives. Likewise, my understanding of the affective experience I am pointing to bears similarity to and differs from what Aristotle and Aquinas call "natural desire," as also what Marcel designates as "exigence for transcendence." Using any of these terms which already have a set meaning or set meanings and strong connotations in the thoughts of those who have employed them in their writings could easily cause misunderstanding of my meaning. To avoid occasions for such misunderstanding, I shall use the term transcendent human dynamism.

Human Dynamism in General

By a human dynamism I mean a drive or tendency from within a human being toward an act and the object of that act by which some potentiality is actualized. The act toward which a dynamism is directed can be an immanent act (for example, thinking or loving) or it can be a transitive act (for example, communicating by touch or gesture or words, producing a work by artistic acts). The drive may of course be toward an act of appealing for and receiving the influence of an act by a second agent, for instance, a desire to be noticed, to be loved, to be assisted. The act of the second agent is the object of the first agent's act toward which his dynamism is directed.

Human dynamism is first known to us in its conscious expression. It appears in conscious experience as the affective act of desire to fulfil some felt need. This desire accounts for the consequent effort to achieve the desired fulfilment and for the feeling of satisfaction when the effort succeeds or of frustration when it fails. All this conscious activity reveals an innate preconscious dynamism. For, unless there is some preconscious urge from within, the agent could not feel need and desire arising from felt need or satisfaction from fulfilment of desire or frustration from failure of fulfilment.

A Threefold Innate Human Dynamism

To superficial observation there is only a confusing manifold of human dynamisms. These have been classified and put in some hierarchy by ethicians and psychologists. Maslow (1954, ch. 5), for example, in his well known classification, lists five basic kinds of needs: physiological needs, safety needs, belongingness and love needs, esteem needs, self-actuation needs. There are dynamisms to fulfil all these needs or any other needs that anyone might want to add. For my purpose all human needs and dynamisms to act can be more simply and helpfully reduced to three innate general ones, of which all others are specifications. The reality of these three dynamism and very much of what I shall briefly say about them is common knowledge. Nevertheless, the justification for recalling them as helpful background for the main development of this essay will, I think, appear as the descriptive analysis of personal dynamism is carried through.

The first of these is a dynamism to acts which preserve the agent's existence and/or any element of his already actual well-being. We have, for example, drives to eat and drink, to flee from or attack what threatens our well-being or our life. The second of the three general dynamisms is toward what either constitutes some new actualization of the agent's potentiality or some means to such actualization. We have, for example, tendencies to look, to listen, to touch, to wonder and reason in order to know and understand ourselves and the world we live in. We have tendencies to act for practical purposes and to contemplate the beauty of nature or art. The first and second innate dynamisms involve needs that imply deficiency, needs in the agent for what she lacks. Not every need, however, implies deficiency; there is a kind of need that is rooted in, originates from fulness of actuality, from superabounding being pressing for expression in acts which communicate something of that fulness to others, by which the agent is fruitful, generative. This drive to give, to generate, is the third general innate dynamism. It finds conscious expression in the tendencies we experience to beget and educate children, to care for the weak and the needy, to teach, to heal, to inspire, to create works of art, to establish social and political institutions that promote fuller and more secure ways of living.

There is a positive and a negative side of these dynamisms. The positive side, it is important to understand, is primary. The negative is secondary, presupposing as it does the positive side for its possibility and intelligibility, having its meaning by relation to the positive. It is only when some force obstructs the attainment of one or another of the positive goals or threatens the positive goal already attained that the negative side of the dynamism shows up in a tendency to avoid or to attack and destroy what is obstructive or threatening. This negative dynamism appears in such ordinary acts as jumping out of the way of an oncoming car or swatting a mosquito, in more sensational and terrible ways such as defensive warfare and exodus from war zones.

Negative dynamism is then a consequence of, flows out of, the positive dynamism under certain circumstances. It is in ultimate analysis directed in one way or another to the goals of the positive dynamism. There is no irreducible negative human dynamism. What occasions misunderstanding here is that the positive goals of some individuals or groups can become irrationally distorted and narrowed by egoism and, consequently, wildly and blindly in opposition with the goals of others (and with their own best interests), with resulting violent conflict. As a consequence, the negative aspects of their dynamism appear as if independent of the positive. We can, then, be led (as Freud was [1958, 70-75]) to posit an irreducible aggressive-destructive instinct. Belief in an irreducible negative instinct or negative innate dynamism cannot be sustained by descriptive analysis of experience: no negative tendency can be adduced which cannot be shown to be rooted in a positive tendency to preserve or enhance or communicate what the agent sees as some desirable element of human life.

Whether with positive or negative side predominant in consciousness, all of these dynamisms are functioning throughout our lives. However, one or another is more likely to be active under certain circumstances. Thus, when security is threatened in circumstances of physical danger, of biological illness, of psychological threat to the meaning of life, the ordinary person is less likely to be concerned about his or her development or the communication of life to others (unless, perhaps, when these somehow bear on his own preservation). On the other hand, one whose dynamism to growth in a certain way is aroused, may imperil his health or life and neglect his responsibility to other persons. When one is intent on giving to others what she has or is, she might withdraw from activities that are directly for the sake of her own benefit and might even tend to sacrifice her well-being or her life—as did, for example, Mother Teresa, Dorothy Day, Oscar Romero, Mahatma Gandhi, Damien of Molokai.

Likewise, we find that one or another of these dynamisms usually dominates at a certain stage of human development and that they usually do so in a certain order. The first task in life is to make self physically and psychologically secure in existence, and the energies of the child (or psychologically underdeveloped physical adult) are first of all predominantly concentrated on this goal. Secure in existence to some extent, a person tends to unfold and fulfil his potentiality. The more that these potentialities are actualized, the more does the dynamism to communicate one's being come into prominence.

Threefold Dynamism and Conscious Motivation

It does seem at first glance that the dynamism to self-preservation and to fulfilment of self are inescapably self-interested and that the dynamism to share with others what one is and has is purely altruistic. Reflection on experience, however, shows that such a conclusion would be badly mistaken. Thus, desire for sexual union can be solely for the sake of one's own pleasure or for the sake of the loved one's fulfilment or for the sake of generating new life; or it can be for all of these, one or the other primary. Again, a person can tend to preserve her own life along with the developments she has already attained and to grow toward greater fulfilments not only for her own sake but also and even principally for the sake of others whom she loves with unselfish love. For example, her innate dynamism for growth may be assumed into and find conscious expression in the desire to become educated in order to help others for their own sake. She may want to grow in union with God so as to bring God's light and peace into the lives of others for the glory of God in them. On the other hand in a parallel but contrary way, she might not only desire to live and grow but also to communicate the richness of her mind and heart mainly or exclusively for her own aggrandizement. Even the most egocentric philosopher, scientist or artist experiences the dynamism to communicate a work to the world; but her primary or even sole conscious motive can be not her care for the world but rather her desire for fame and fortune or for her own sense of achievement and self-importance, regardless of what others think of her.

Such common experiences show that of themselves the three dynamisms are neither egocentric nor altruistic. In conscious life they become one or the other by reason of the agent's egocentric or altruistic radical love from which conscious dynamism derives. Desire arising from altruistic radical love will be altruistic also; desire arising from self-centered radical love will be self-centered.

What I have been saying about dynamism and its motivation by self-centered or altruistic radical love, as also about how self-centered and altruistic radical loves and their consequent desires can be integrated in experience, will, I hope, become clearer and more convincing in the following chapters on human dynamism to personal love, communion and friendship.

Reduction to One Radical Dynamism

Although the three dynamism are distinct and, as I have already noted, one or another of them predominates at certain stages of human development or under certain circumstances, they all seem to imply each other and to be distinct aspects of a single radical dynamism. The goal of the first dynamism is presupposed by and is for the sake of the goal of the second dynamism; while the self actualization toward which the second dynamism is directed is in some ways necessary for the preservation of self and of others to which the first dynamism is directed. For it is necessary to us as changeable beings in a dangerous world to grow, to develop, in order to preserve our own or others' existence against destructive forces not only from without but also from within, from the internal tendency to disintegrate when we cease to develop. The goal of the second dynamism also makes possible the greater communication of life toward which the third dynamism is directed; one cannot give what one does not have. The second dynamism is then for the sake of the first and the third. The latter, the dynamism to communicate life to others, includes and goes beyond the second dynamism toward self-fulfilment: for communicating to others the actualization of one's being is implicitly and obliquely dynamism toward fulfilment of the agent himself; communicating life to others enriches the giver. All three dynamisms are aspects of one dynamism to fulness of life in self and others.

Since all the goals of this three-fold dynamism are attained by union with other realities, their unity might be put another way: all three are aspects of one dynamism toward union—or, more precisely put, toward fulness of life in self and others through union achieved by action and passion. This large and, if true, significant assertion needs to be explored and justified and will be throughout the rest of this book.

Endlessly Transcendent Human Dynamism

One of the most radically significant aspects of the threefold innate human dynamism is its transcendent character. Without an accurate understanding of what I mean by calling the dynamism transcendent, very much of what is said in the following chapters could lose its meaning. What, then, do I signify by calling human dynamism transcendent?

Innate human dynamism is an ascending gravitation from the depths of the psyche which reveals itself in human desiring and striving for the more and the better in all the manifold dimensions of human life: desiring and striving for better ways of providing food, building, manufacturing, transportation, communication, and so on; desiring and striving for ever deeper and wider scientific, philosophical, and theological understanding of the universe, especially of human beings in it; desiring and striving to create ever greater or more delightfully various works of art, whether poetry, stories, music, painting, cinema; desiring and striving to develop more just and humane social and political structures. More, always more, better, always better. There is in the human psyche an inescapable and insatiable desire for the more, the better, so that the human person can be "content with nothing which is wanting in what he considers preferable" (Bernard of Clairvaux 1951, 303).

What has so far been said of human dynamism to ever fuller life is interesting and valuable but as yet reveals nothing of great significance about personal life in particular. One aspect, however, of this dynamism which has not yet been noted does dramatically direct us to what is most intimate and glorious in personal life. Above all and central to all expressions of human dynamism, is the unquenchable and illimitable innate yearning of every person toward personal union, toward communion of love and sharing of life with other persons. This yearning, the expression of an innate preconscious dynamism, accounts also for why we hunger for stories, why we read novels, go to movies, read and empathize with lyric poetry that expresses another person's deep emotional experience. We want in some way to be other persons without ceasing to be ourselves. Each of us wants to live other persons' lives without ceasing to live our own. In the rest of this book I hope to show that this is so and to show that union with all persons and union of all persons with each other is the goal of every person's dynamism. Even beyond the confines of creation, human dynamism reaches toward personal union with God, toward somehow living God's life with God without ceasing to be ourselves.

Whatever seems possible or impossible to us, is there any definite limit which can be assigned to human dynamism toward ever fuller life? Is it not rather true that human dynamism reaches indefinitely toward ever deeper and wider and more intense, ever more perfect and more glorious, life in union with all reality? Is it not endlessly transcendent, driving us to take the glorious risk of letting go whatever we now are or have in order to reach out toward living all of life in which all that was let go of is found again but transformed? Did Unamuno see the truth about human transcendent dynamism when he wrote (1954,138):

And if it is grievous to be doomed one day to cease to be, perhaps it would be more grievous still to go on being always oneself, and no more than one's self, without being able to be at the same time everything else, without being able to be all.

Surely Unamuno was seeing deeply into human transcendent dynamism, but would have seen even more deeply or at least would have expressed his insight more fully if he had noted that the innate yearning in each person is not only toward one's own being all without ceasing to be oneself but also toward every person (including the subject of the dynamism) being all without ceasing to be oneself. (The opposite erroneous extreme is to delete from the goal of human dynamism the fulfilment of the self who has the dynamism, as is done, for example, by Macmurray 1961,159). "Implicit in the smallest impulse to self-actualization is the will to the actualization of unique worth by every person" (Norton 1976, 309)—and, it must be added, for the sake of every other person. That human dynamism in each person does drive toward such universal sharing in all life by every person will, I hope, emerge more and more clearly and convincingly as we establish and describe the successive goals toward which the dynamism tends.

10
DYNAMISM TO PERSONAL LOVE, COMMUNION, AND FRIENDSHIP

Dynamism to be Loved and to Love with Personal Love

The innate dynamism to personal union unfolds itself in conscious life by stages. The first stage is experience of a dynamism to be loved in and for oneself. That human beings do have a conscious dynamism, an inescapable deeply felt need and desire, to be loved with personal love is clear to ordinary observation. When so loved we experience it as the fulfilment of a need and feel more fully alive. But if ordinary observation should fail to take in this fact, clinical psychology has given overwhelming evidence of it, finding a psychological root of many, perhaps even most, emotional sicknesses in the frustration of that dynamism and showing the power of being so loved for healthy personality development and for healing unhealthy development. It even seems to be a truth of human experience that without awareness of being loved personally, we are unable to recognize our own value as persons and to value ourselves accordingly.

Considerable healthy intellectual, emotional, and moral development must take place before a person can become aware of other persons in their unique selves as values in themselves for themselves and become capable of personal love for them. Only after such development can the innate human dynamism to love others with personal love begin to function in the person's conscious life.

A difficulty immediately occurs about the intrinsic possibility of a dynamism to such love. If a conscious dynamism, as was said in chapter 1, is a desire arising from a felt need, which felt need presupposes an innate preconscious dynamism toward ever fuller life, then to speak of a conscious dynamism to love other persons with personal love seems to involve us in a contradiction. For it seems to imply that we tend to love others for their own sake in order to fulfil our own need for fuller life. The problem can be resolved by recalling two things. First, our innate transcendent dynamism is of itself neither egoistic nor altruistic; our desires which express that dynamism in conscious life are egoistic or altruistic by reason of the egoistic or altruistic radical love from which they derive. Second, the felt need from which desire to love others personally arises is not a need based on deficiency. Rather, it is based on a certain fulness of life in one who is capable of personal love, a fulness pressing to diffuse itself, to bring about fuller life in others for their own sake.

Signs of the reality of a dynamism to personal love appear both in those who do attain it and in those who do not. Even though our conscious motive in personal love is not our own fulfilment, when we love in this way there is usually a sense of being more alive, of doing what we exist to do, of becoming what we are meant to be and of joy in doing so. This sense of fulfilment is the consequence of personal love, not its motive. Of itself personal love has this consequence unless hindered by adverse circumstances. Sometimes the lover experiences the joy of self-realization as a person even when the love leads to or is accompanied by sorrow and pain. Recall the famous line in *A Tale of Two Cities*, Sydney Carton at the guillotine, after a life of drunkenness and disappointment in romantic love, expresses joyful fulfilment in his act of sacrificial personal love: "It is a far, far better thing I do than I have ever done." Near the end of Aldous Huxley's *Brave New World*, there is a momentary, deeply moving, scene of tragic farewell between the Savage and Helmholz and Bernard, the only three people in the "civilized" world who could still respond as persons: "There was a silence. In spite of their sadness—because of it even; for their sadness was the symptom of their love for one another—the three young men were happy."

Even those whose personal love is mediocre or less than mediocre respond with spontaneous admiration to heroic personal love seen in people they know or read of in history or fiction. They experience such love vicariously with a feeling of exaltation, and a desire, even if only a velleity, to actually love in this way and to do the deeds of such love. All these experiences point to an innate dynamism to personal love without which they are unexplainable.

On the other hand, in a contrary way, those who have no experience at all of personal love or who fall away from it altogether also give evidence of the innate dynamism. Those adults who love other persons only with acquisitive or functional love, as implemental ends to fulfil their own needs or as mere means to such ends, live shallow lives, are stunted as persons. Without personal love they may have intense pleasures but never deep joy. The satisfactions of less than personal union can momentarily dull the sense of emptiness and seem to heal the sense of loneliness, but never lastingly. Inevitably, such persons ultimately experience profound emptiness, loneliness, and dissatisfaction; for their innate need of union by personal love is unfulfilled, and they experience a vague sense of frustration, the source of which they may or may not recognize.

That without the union constituted by being loved and loving with personal love all else in human life has little lasting savor or little depth of meaning—this is a truth attested to by poets, novelists, preachers, psychologists, theologians, and philosophers. They are appealing to something in us all, of which we all have a profound even if obscure intimation. They evoke from the center of our being a piercing realization of our innate and ineradicable need and longing for, dynamism toward, union by personal love. "The suffering of being unable to love," this is what hell is, Dostoevski tells us through Zossima in *The Brothers Karamazov* If he is right and if Sartre's judgment that love is impossible were true, then Sartre should not say that "hell is other people" but that every one of us lives with our inescapable hell within a self that is forever frustrated of fulfilling its dynamism to be loved by other people and to love them with personal love.

The Dynamism of Personal Love to a Return of Such Love

In the measure that loving with personal love is realized, human dynamism channeled through personal love reaches toward ever fuller life in ever deeper and fuller modes of personal union, each of which presupposes personal love and includes it as its essential core. Human dynamism so affected by personal love is what I mean by the dynamism of personal love.

This term, dynamism of personal love, must not be understood to imply that personal love is itself a tendency. As has been stressed and will be stressed time and again in this essay, no radical love is an actually dynamic affection, that is, a desire or drive. It is, however, virtually dynamic inasmuch as dynamic affections derive from it.

Just as, when describing the experience of personal love, it was helpful to bear in mind clear and intense experiences of such love, so also now, when describing the dynamism of personal love and its goals of personal union, it will help if the reader has in mind clear and intense experiences of these, your own or others, real or fictitious. What is essential to personal love and to the goals of the dynamism of personal love can first be seen more readily in these more intense experiences and can afterwards be noted even in less intense ones where the essentials are not as readily seen.

Personal love, like every radical love, issues in radical care when the lover sees some need to be fulfilled for the beloved's well being. Care issues in desire for what meets that need. After the beloved's well being, the first object of this desire, the first goal of the dynamism of personal love, is a return of such love by the loved one and, therefore, a union of mutual personal love. This union of mutual love does not by itself constitute personal communion; it is a necessary step toward it and, when the latter is attained, is its very core.

Let me make clear exactly what I am asserting. I am not asserting that reciprocity is necessary for personal love. Although personal love without a return is an incomplete experience, it is neither less truly personal nor less truly love than it is when it is returned in kind. Further, I am not talking of just any desire to be loved personally which a lover might experience. The immature (but developmentally important) self-centered desire to be loved in and for oneself prior to loving others in and for themselves is not under consideration here. I am asserting a desire for a return by the loved one of the lover's personal love for the other.

No complex reasoning or clinical evidence is needed to establish the fact that we have this dynamism. When such evidence can be had, it is welcome help but not necessary. The desire I am asserting is generally recognized by those who experience personal love with any intensity and reflect on their experience. It is less obviously but truly present in less intense experiences. It is evident also if we attend to and reflect on what goes on in the lives of others.

Apart from each person's own experience of the dynamism I am talking about, perhaps the first and most easily noticed sign of it is one that is not peculiar to personal love but certainly applies to it also. This sign is the tendency in lovers, almost irresistible when love is intense, to make their love known to the loved one. The lover tends to declare this love in words, gestures, deeds, and gifts. "This is characteristic of those who love that they cannot be silent about it," writes Aquinas. Gregory the Great makes the point in a sentence that defies satisfactory translation, *qui minus amat, minus clamat*. In some circumstances, care for the loved one requires silence; or the lover may be inhibited or shy; or the love may be so overwhelming as to leave the lover speechless. What is always present is *desire* to make the love known to the loved one; and, when the lover for one reason or another is hindered from doing so, there is the experience of frustration. There may be more than one reason why lovers want to reveal their love to the beloved, but it certainly seems that a principal reason is that given by John Chrysostum: "Nothing so much wins love [in return] as the knowledge that one's lover desires most of all to be himself loved" (*Liturgy of the Hours* 1975, III, 543).

The Surprising and Puzzling Character of This Fact

Although the dynamism of personal love toward a return of love is an evident fact, what has already been shown about personal love and the stages by which human dynamism to such love unfolds in conscious life makes this fact a puzzling one. Recall that in human development the dynamism to be loved personally that appears in conscious life prior to the dynamism to love personally is immature, entirely self-centered, springing from insecurity and need for confirmation of one's own worth. Only after this immature need is fulfilled can the mature dynamism to love with personal love function or at least function freely. Consequently we might expect that the more mature a person becomes and the more truly and fully her love is for the beloved in and for himself, the less she would experience a need and a desire to be loved in return.

It is surprising and puzzling that what happens is quite the contrary. After the good of the one loved and cared for, what, before all else, the one who loves with personal love feels a need and desire for is a return of personal love. Further, the intensity of this need and desire seems to be proportionate to the intensity and purity of the personal love. The more intense and purely unselfish the love, the stronger the dynamism to being loved in return. When love is not returned, the lover experiences frustration of his affective dynamism; when his love is returned, he loves more readily and with a sense of fulfilment—but with a love no less for the loved one in herself for herself.

How can this surprising fact be explained? Answering this question will call for synthesizing much of what we have found in our study of human dynamism to fuller life and in our study of love. It will also bring us to a deeper understanding of personal love.

Explanation of the Fact

The first and most obvious explanation which might occur to anyone is that those who have attained personal love do not (and should not) cease to also love themselves with truthful radical love. Truthful radical self-love does not conflict with truthful radical love for others: in fact, as will be shown later on, the two loves can and should imply each other and in the concrete include each other. Now, radical love for myself modulates into radical care for myself in need of fulfilment. Radical care gives rise to desire for what can fulfil my need; in this context my need is to have my personal love reciprocated.

This explanation is true as far as it goes, but it fails to show how the dynamism to reciprocal love is a dynamism of personal love for the other in herself for herself. It does, however, suggest a possible way of showing how this is so. For it reminds us that personal love necessarily modulates into radical care for the loved other when the lover becomes aware of the other's need and that care issues in desire for what fulfils her need. Since loving in return with personal love will fulfil her dynamism as a person and will open the way toward greater fulfilments (as will be shown), the lover who understands this will desire for the loved one's own sake that she return his love.

Again, this line of thought helps in some ways, but fails to be fully satisfactory. It does show how the desire for a return of love can derive from personal love for the other. Further, it explains why those who are most fully developed as persons, who love most unselfishly and intensely, and who have the least need of being loved in order to love, are the very ones who most need and desire a return of personal love. But it fails to explain why desire for a return of love follows on personal love in every instance. In some instances, the lover will not understand or may not remember that returning his love will fulfil the other and lead to further fulfilments for her; nevertheless, just because of his love, he still experiences a desire for a return of love. Why?

A more satisfactory explanation of the surprising fact we are trying to understand is one based on the features of human dynamism and of radical love as these were described earlier. First, recall several features of human dynamism: It is toward fulness of life by union; it is transcendent, tending to ever greater union with other realities, to ever greater fulness of life by such union; it is above all toward union of all persons by love; it is not exclusively self-centered or exclusively altruistic but is directed toward the fulness of all human life the lover's own and the loved one's and everyone else's. These characteristics of human dynamism need to be kept in mind now and all through the following chapters in which, step by step, the ever greater modes of union and fulness of life that are its goals will be described and established. Second, recall some features of any radical love for others and of personal radical love in particular. Any radical love, we saw, and most of all personal love has these two facets (among others): it is an act by which the lover makes himself a gift to the loved one; it is an act by which he is both in the loved one and actively receives the loved one into himself.

These features of human dynamism and radical love enable us to explain the fact we are concerned with. If you give a gift in the true meaning of gift you intend that it be accepted and be accepted as a gift, that is, as an expression of personal love. If it is not so accepted, the intention of the giver and the meaning of what is offered as a gift is frustrated: what is offered as gift does not fully become a gift until it is received in this way. If this is true of all those gifts that are only signs and expressions of love, much more so is it true of the gift given in the very act of radical love itself, the gift of the lover's own act of being to the loved one as a coaffirmation of the loved one's being. Now, the only way in which the lover's gift of self in personal love can be fully accepted is by the loved one loving the lover in return with personal love.

Likewise, the lover's being in the loved one and receiving her into himself is limited and partially frustrated if the loved one does not, by returning the love, double the mutual indwelling. As explained above, even by any as yet unrequited radical love the lover is in the beloved and the beloved in the lover; but, when radical love is requited by the beloved, she is in the lover not only as his beloved but also as his lover, and he is in her not only as her lover but also as her beloved.

Perhaps all that I have been saying about the lover's need and desire for a return of love can be helped by analogy with the artist's need and desire for receptive persons to contemplate his artistic work and be enriched by it. The artist needs such reception not only because he desires assurance, fame, or fortune (he may well desire these things also), but more deeply because by its very nature his artistic act intends communication of some truth, some beauty, from within him. "All music calls to an ear not the musicians own, all sculpture to an eye not the sculptor's own" (Buber 1955, 25). If the communication is not received, the dynamism of the artist as an artist and of his artistic act is frustrated.

Dynamism of Personal Love to Personal Communion and Personal Friendship

Reciprocal personal love, as shown in chapter 3, is a completion of personal love and is the essential core of personal communion. Personal communion, constituted by mutual love and the other essentials of that experience, is clearly a fuller experience of personal life

than personal love or even mutual personal love without communion. One who loves another with personal love (in the fullest sense)
experiences desire not only for a return of such love but for the yet
fuller experience of communion and experiences the latter as a fulfilment.

Similarly, the earlier description of personal friendship shows it to
be a fulfilling experience which includes and goes far beyond that of
personal communion, opening out to the ultimate mode of fulfilment in personal life. The human dynamism to ever fuller life cannot but reach toward personal friendship, toward an ever more mature
form of it, and bring a sense of fulness in the measure it is attained.

DYNAMISM TO UNIVERSAL PERSONAL FRIENDSHIP

Until now our consideration has, for the sake of simplicity, been confined to personal communion and sharing of lives in personal friendship between two persons. Now it is time to ask whether the transcendent character of human dynamism makes it reach out toward friendships with ever more persons, and if so, whether its reach can stop short of universal personal friendship.

Meaning of Universal Personal Friendship and of Dynamism toward It

To understand the question, the meaning of universal personal friendship or a community constituted by universal personal friendship must be freed from ambiguity. Usually the term universal friendship means no more than a general attitude of kindliness or benevolence among all people in the world, without suggesting that any person knows and loves all persons intimately. Sometimes terms similar to universal personal friendship with a more limited meaning than I will give it are used, especially in ethical and religious writings. Thus, Royce (1968, ch. 2, "The Idea of Universal Community" [75-98]; see also Oppenheim 1987,30), conceives of the "Great Community," an ideal union of all human selves in a universal community. It is to this community that Royce thinks all persons owe "loyalty." In like manner, Calkins (1921, 49) conceives of "the great universe of selves, the totality of conscious beings, the truly universal community" and of "the adequately good man as one loyal to the universe of selves of which he himself is a member" (1921, 51). Macmurray and Johann see in human persons an inherent tendency toward a "universal personal community" and a "universal communion of persons" (Macmurray 1961, 159-65; Johann, 1966, 46-47).

All these concepts move in the direction of what I call universal personal friendship or a community of universal personal friendship but do not arrive at what I mean by those terms. The difference between their meaning and mine can be clearly seen in what Calkins says when defending against her critics the possibility of the universal community as an object of the good man's devotion or loyalty (1921, 57; my italics):

> The plain truth open to observation that men, simple and gentle, ignorant and informed, actually are loyal to great communities, great organisms of interrelated persons—actually are devoting themselves, soul and body, to 'International,' to country or to church—clearly indicates the possibility of an object of loyalty widening to a horizon beyond which there is no conscious creature. For if a man can individualize his class, his country or his church *without knowing, one by one*, all his comrades, all his countrymen or all his fellow churchmen, if he can even individuate and be loyal to a League of Nations, then certainly there is no inherent difficulty in his individualizing the totality of conscious beings *without knowing each of its members as a separate being*.

No more than Mary Calkins do the other authors referred to above seem to be saying that in a universal community or in a universal communion each person knows and loves every other, one by one.

What I shall refer to as universal personal friendship or as a community of universal personal friendship is constituted by actual personal friendship in the most proper and fullest sense of every person with every other one. If the goal of universal friendship in this meaning should ever be achieved, each person would actually know every other person in her unique personality and affectively affirm each one in herself for herself, would even experience personal communion of love and sharing of lives with every one of them, along with all the other essentials of personal friendship noted above. Further, as the goal of personal dynamism, the friendship with each person would be what has been described above as mature, even ideally mature, personal friendship.

Dynamism toward fulness of life in universal personal friendship is implicitly a dynamism toward being the kind of persons in the kind of world necessary for the possibility of that goal. I can do no more here than call attention to these implications which need development in theory of moral virtue, in special ethics, and the areas of study which bear on special ethics such as psychology, sociology, political science, and economics.

First, then, dynamism to universal personal friendship is not dynamism to friendship with every person as he actually is now but as he would be when capable of mature personal friendship with every other one. The goal of fuller life by personal communion and sharing lives in universal friendship is implicitly a dynamism toward a world in which all persons are mature, religiously, morally, emotionally, intellectually, aesthetically, and so on. Unless all persons were so, if any were wicked or painfully defective, they could, in the universal sharing of lives, bring on others and on themselves anguish instead of fulness of life. (For literary illustrations of how this would be, see Herbert's Dune trilogy and Anderson's "Journey's End.") No one could be a participant in this universal personal friendship unless capable of very perfect communion of love and of sharing life with every other person. Think of the unimaginable expansion of conscious awareness and power of attention, the unimaginable greatness of mind and heart, the unimaginable psychic and physical strength and energy such persons would have in order to live such lives without being overwhelmed and shattered by too much life and joy. Think of what an interesting and utterly good and lovable person each one would be. Think of all the interesting and beautiful things that would be going on in the mind and heart of each such person and how open and understanding and appreciative each would be of everything in every other. (There is help in an analogy with what John of the Cross says about the infused divine light received in mystical experience [in the proper sense of that term as he uses it]. This light is at first experienced by the recipient as darkness, even painful darkness, because human weakness as well as sinfulness renders the person unable to bear it. When, however, the person has become purified and strengthened, the very same infused divine light is now experienced as light and delightful. See his famous analogy with a log put in a fire: *The Dark Night* II, 10).

Secondly, universal personal friendship among persons maturely developed in all these ways would involve a transformed world: a world in which the life of universal friendship as understood here is encouraged and supported in all ways, socially, politically, economically, artistically, and so on; a world in which all are freed from the kind of burdens and demands or the kind of suffering which would hinder the growth of persons and their union in friendship. Not every kind of suffering or every kind of obstacle to be overcome necessarily obstructs friendship; some are even helpful. Still, it seems clear that human transcendent dynamism will always tend toward overcoming even these and reach toward a world which is free of all anxiety and anguish over the pain and sorrow of friends or their failures as persons.

When ambiguity about the meaning of universal friendship in this context is cleared away, we still need to point out that asserting human dynamism toward universal personal friendship with all which that implies is not asserting that all persons have an explicit reflective awareness of a dynamism toward this goal. It is only asserting that, whether the persons are so aware of it or not, they do have such an innate dynamism which is at least implicit in what they are aware of. It can, I think, be added, however, that anyone to whom this goal is proposed, who is psychologically and morally healthy and understands the personal wholeness required for every member of a universal personal friendship and the fulness of life to be experienced in it, will in fact spontaneously and consciously desire it unless blocked by fear from doing so.

For fear can hinder us from acknowledging or rejoicing in our dynamism toward universal mature personal friendship as that kind of friendship has been described. To those who have never experienced being loved by another so purely and accepted so totally as to remove all dread of being known through and through by that other, nothing hidden—to them the thought of universal personal friendship, with the mutual sharing of lives involved in it, could be terrifying. To those intimately bound together in romantic love (each the other's "one and only one"), or in exclusive individual friendship, universal communion of love and sharing of lives in personal friendship could be a distressing and fearful prospect.

> For the error bred in the bone
> of each woman and each man
> Craves what it cannot have,
> Not universal love
> But to be loved alone (W. H. Auden 1945, 57).

(Anne Morrow Lindbergh [1956,72-73] accepts the idea that there can be no mutuality between more than two persons and that it is only the desire for permanence of being loved alone that is "The error bred in the bone." Passing "one-and-only moments" are, she thinks, all right. There are two problems with this way of thinking. First, as I hope to show in chapter 13, there can be more than two in mutuality, namely, in an inclusive friendship. Second, even one-and-only moments do not escape the "error bred in the bone" anymore than do desire for permanence of this desire.)

In one way or another the prospect of universal communion of love and universal sharing of lives can be a source of apprehension even for those who intellectually acknowledge the splendor of universal personal friendship, who understand that such friendship by its very nature excludes embarrassment and will only enrich and intensify any union of truthful love already experienced in their lives. Perhaps it is so for anyone other than the person whose love has become so fully purified of self-centered concern and is so all-embracing as to find joy in the prospect of sharing even his or her very dearest one with all others.

The Question of Possibility

Assuming for the sake of discussion (without yet asserting as an established conclusion) that our human transcendent dynamism does reach out toward universal personal friendship, are we talking about a dynamism to an impossible goal? In the face of all the hatred, wickedness, injustice, oppression, and deliberate demonic cruelty in human life, can we take seriously even the possibility of universal personal love?

Even should universal love be thought a possible goal, there is an obvious fact that argues against the possibility of universal personal friendship, a fact noted in writing on friendship from the ancient Greeks until now. That fact is that having many personal friends is, in the concrete, psychologically impossible for us and that trying to multiply such friendships can prevent having any of them. The reason for this is clear: If any union of personal friendship is to grow and bring increased fulness of personal life, the persons must devote time, attention, and energy to being together, to doing things together, to communicating with one another and overcoming obstacles to union from without and from within themselves. Given our limitations, trying to have more than a very few such unions will render all our relationships something less than what has been described as personal friendship. Universal friendship, then, seems to be an obviously impossible goal. All of us, practical wisdom would counsel, need to accept the fact that concretely we are limited to having at most only a few deep and intimate personal friends and are specially blessed if we have even one.

This conclusion is incontrovertible so long as we are thinking about friendship in the present concrete circumstances of human life. Its validity can be questioned, however, if we are concerned, as we are now, with whether, leaving aside our concrete circumstantial limitations, universal friendship is intrinsically possible or whether it is a self-contradictory concept and therefore intrinsically impossible.

Before attempting to answer this last question, we should, perhaps, first ask whether there is any good reason for bothering with it at all. Does it make any difference whether universal friendship is intrinsically possible if it is, without doubt, concretely impossible in human life as we actually experience it?

The answer is very important. For even if the goal of universal personal friendship should be concretely impossible not only now but ever, it would, nevertheless, be a matter of greatest importance to understand whether it is an intrinsically possible ideal toward which human dynamism reaches. For if it is, innate dynamism toward it would reveal something of supreme importance about the constitution of human persons, would give an overall direction to human striving by indicating what kind of persons we are to grow toward becoming, how we are to relate to each other, and what kind of a world we are to bring about if we are to increase the fulness of life that is concretely possible to us as persons. Even if the dynamism to universal personal friendship is thought to be a reaching toward a concretely unreachable goal, uncovering it uncovers something of the glory hidden in every human heart, the splendor of every growth in the direction of that goal or even of just working and striving toward it while failing (Johann 1966, 47-49). With one or two significant reservations what Peter Hawkins says (1985, 27) about the salutary value of utopias applies to the goal of universal friendship:

> Like the kingdom for which we have been taught to pray, utopia may be an unknown entity we are called to press toward if never to find. It may be a 'nowhere" forever standing beyond our reach, whose very unattainability keeps us constantly reaching for more. Perhaps better understood as a dynamic rather than a design, utopia's best gift to us is to keep us actively hoping.

(The main alterations needed in applying Hawkins' statement to the goal of personal dynamism, universal personal friendship, is that Christians believe they are called to actually find the goal, that it will not be forever beyond their reach.)

Given that it is important to consider the intrinsic possibility or impossibility of this goal, let us consider the arguments against and offer an argument to establish its intrinsic possibility. Never have I read any treatment of the possibility or impossibility of many friendships which makes the issue precise by applying the distinction between extrinsic and intrinsic possibility. I have, however, come across two ways of thinking which bear on the question of intrinsic impossibility in this regard, whether or not those who use them are aware of answering that question.

Negative Argument Based on a Quantitative Understanding of Personal Self and Love

One such way of thinking appears in Montaigne's discussion of his friendship with Estienne de la Boetie. This, he thought, was a friendship so "extraordinary," that its like occurs in human history only once every few centuries. While he acknowledged that a person can have more than one ordinary friendship, the extraordinary friendship he was talking about left no room, he thought, for even one other such friendship. The reason he gave seems to go beyond his explicit point and to imply also the intrinsic impossibility of more than a few friendships even of the ordinary kind. (Whether these ordinary friendships of which Montaigne speaks are personal in the sense I use that term is questionable and not answerable from his essay.) He writes (1946, 256-57):

> ... this perfect friendship of which I speak is indivisible, each gives himself so entirely to his friend that he has nothing to dispose of elsewhere; on the contrary, he is grieved that he is not double, triple, or quadruple, and that he has not several souls and several wills to bestow them all on that object. Ordinary friendships can be divided: when we love the beauty of this person, the courtesy of another, the liberality of another; the paternal affection of one man, the brotherly love of another, and so forth; but the friendship that possesses the soul and rules over it in full sovereignty—it is impossible that it should be doubled.

If Montaigne means only that the extraordinary friends so fully devote their available time, attention, and energy to each other that they have none available for sustaining any other friendship, then what he is describing is only the extreme case of the practical impossibility which we have just noted. If, on the other hand, as seems to be the case, what he means is that in the union of such friends, their very personal selves are so completely given to each other that nothing is left to give to any other—if that is what he means, then he is asserting the intrinsic impossibility of having more than one such friendship. Involved in such a way of thinking is the altogether unacceptable assumption that, in the measure a person gives self to another by personal love, the less not only of time and attention but of self and of love there is to give anyone else—in the extreme case, nothing at all. This assumption implies that the personal self and personal love are, like time and energy, quantified and have to be divided up among friends. If this were true, then, in the very nature of things, self and love could be used up by one "extraordinary" friend or by a limited number of ordinary ones, very few if the friends are much loved, more if the friends are little loved. Universal personal friendship in my meaning would clearly be intrinsically impossible.

Negative Argument Based on the Preferential Nature of Friendship

Another and more common way of thinking which implies the intrinsic impossibility of universal personal friendship is that of seeing every friendship as by its nature a preferential relationship. A preferential relationship with every other person at the same time is surely a contradiction in terms. (The question here is closely related with but not the same as the theological question debated for centuries by Christian theologians regarding the relationship between friendship and neighbor-love. Some theologians argue that friendship is not just in present fact but by its very nature preferential and that the universal love to which the New Testament calls us is altogether equal for every person. From these premises they conclude that friendship and Christian charity are incompatible. Others will not grant the premise or, therefore, the conclusion. Recent treatments of the debate can be found in Meilaender 1981, ch. 1 and in Wadell 1989, ch. 4).

Whatever force the argument against the intrinsic possibility of universal personal friendship which is based on the preferential nature of friendship may at first glance seem to have, it can, I think, be shown to be mistaken. It rests on a failure to discern what goes on in a preferential act. That human friendship as we usually experience it does, in fact, have a preferential character cannot be doubted, but this fact gives no ground for concluding that every personal friendship must necessarily be preferential and, consequently, that universal personal friendship is intrinsically impossible.

First of all, even if we should assume that preferential love excludes love for other persons, this assumption could not imply that universal personal friendship is intrinsically impossible. For personal love in friendship is not by its very nature preferential. It is true that, in the actual limits of our human condition, love in friendship becomes preferential when, by reason of limited time and power of attention, we have to choose one or a few friendships and let go of others; but that fact in no way justifies thinking that the love between friends is by its very nature preferential. If the actual limits of our present human condition could be removed, love of friends would not need to be preferential; it is not intrinsic, essential, to such love to be preferential.

Further, even when personal love is in fact preferential, it does not necessarily by that fact exclude personal love for the person or persons over whom another is preferred. Just the contrary, as is clear when we look closely at what goes on in an act of preference. For analysis of preferential acts reveals that preference is in every case an act of giving priority to one component over the other component or components in its complex object when all these components are loved or liked or desired. Unless the components other than the one given priority are also and in the same act loved or desired, the act is not preferential. When I love or desire only one and hate the others or am totally indifferent to them, my love or desire is not preferential—no more so than if I were totally unaware of the others or if they did not exist. I can prefer chamber music to symphonic or ragtime music only if I also like the latter two kinds of music but less than I like the former. Similarly, I have a preferential personal love for one person only if at least one other person is in the same act also loved personally. Unless all the persons or things involved in the complex object of a preferential act, both the one given affective priority and those over which that one is given priority—unless all of these are loved or liked or desired there is no point in speaking of preference.

To conclude, then, there is no sound reason to think that love in personal friendship is by its nature preferential or that, when it is so in fact, this fact excludes any intrinsic possibility of many friendships or even of universal personal friendship. Because the circumstances of concrete human life limit the possible number of friendships among all the desirable ones which could be actualized, those one chooses to actualize are preferential and, concretely, in the present circumstances of human life, exclude actualizing others that appear to be less desirable. If, therefore, human dynamism does reach out toward many possible friendships and even toward universal friendship, it is reaching toward a presently impossible concrete goal but not toward an intrinsically impossible goal, not toward a self-contradiction.

It remains to show that human dynamism not only could be but actually is toward universal personal friendship. This will be done in two steps: first, showing the ground or basis in personal friendship on which the argument will be built and then building the argument on that basis.

The Basis for an Affirmative Argument

The basis on which an argument can be built to establish that transcendent human dynamism does tend toward the full and properly personal friendship of every person with every other is something to be found within every personal friendship. This basis is the unique quality of each friendship. This unique quality is obvious in the sharing of lives that is essential for personal friendship; for each life is without doubt different from every other. But the most fundamentally or radically distinctive quality of every personal friendship lies in the uniqueness of each friend's love and ultimately of each friend as a person.

Recall what was noted earlier, that the affective act of personal love is the expression of the lover's unique personal self and that it is a giving of self to the loved one. The love is the lover in act and is as unique as the person loving. Recall also that personal love is an affective affirmation of the loved one in herself for herself and that this affirmation is intrinsically formed by the unique, unrepeatable, personality of the one so affirmed. In this sense, personal love is the beloved in the lover and is as unique as the person loved. The mutual love at the core of each personal communion, unique and unrepeatable as it is, cannot be replaced by or replace any other mutual love at the core of communion with any other person. Therefore, since communion of love is the core of every personal friendship, every personal friendship is unique and irreplaceable by any other. Now let us see how this insight founds an argument for affirming a personal dynamism toward universal friendship.

Argument to Establish Personal Dynamism toward Universal Friendship

What has been said thus far in this chapter clarifies the question that I am trying to answer and the basis on which I think it can be answered. Given these clarifications, it can now be shown that the transcendent dynamism of personal love does tend (with or without reflective awareness in the person) toward the intrinsically possible (even if concretely impossible) goal of universal mature personal friendship.

Let us begin by asking whether, leaving aside the present concrete limitations already considered, any a priori limit can be set to the number of persons toward whom a human being has an innate dynamism to be joined in a union of mature personal friendship. Is there any point at which it could be said that such a union with one more person would exceed the limits of human transcendent dynamism toward ever fuller life and be of no value for fuller life in the one loving or the one loved or in all others on whom their lives touch? The answer to this question will be clearer and more convincing if it is given in two steps, showing first the dynamism toward universal personal love and then the dynamism toward universal personal communion and friendship.

Dynamism to Universal Personal Love

If, as shown above, each personal love is distinctive, even unique, by reason of the one loving and the one loved, then each such love adds something to the fulness of life that no love for another finite person can. Consequently, given the transcendent character of innate human dynamism, it clearly reaches out explicitly or implicitly, toward ever greater fulness of life by union of personal love with every person.

At some rare moments, for example, when you fall in love and are surprised by the wonder of the beloved falling in love with you, or when experiencing the marvel of loving and being loved by an extraordinary friend—like the one Montaigne described—at such moments there might be no felt need to love more persons and to be loved by them; you feel full to overflowing. But this highly subjective and passing feeling does not correspond with or do away with the objective innate dynamism to ever fuller life in personal union. Loving and being loved by one person or by any definite limited number of human persons, however many, can bring to total rest the transcendent dynamism to ever fuller life.

This conclusion should not be confused with what some writers have asserted, Fromm for instance, when he says (1956, 46) "If I truly love one person, I love all persons." If this statement means that one who does not in some way actually love all persons, who is indifferent to some or hates even one person, cannot truly love anyone, then the statement seems to be clearly at odds with experience. If it means that such a one is inconsistent, that, in all logic, one who personally loves any person should love all persons in that way, then the intended meaning is true but the expression of it could lead to misunderstandings. That a person is inconsistent does not negate her genuinely radical love. However, even if it were true to say that excluding one person from my love made it impossible to truly love anyone with personal love, this "truth" would in no way argue against my having a dynamism toward the fulness of personal life, which, whether I am reflectively aware of it or not, tends toward union with every person in universal personal love. On the contrary, it would strengthen the argument in support of such a dynamism.

Dynamism to Universal Mature Friendship

Even universal personal love without personal communion of love would still be incomplete personal union; personal love necessarily tends toward mutual love, and mutual personal love finds completion in personal communion of love. If each love is unique, then each communion of personal love is also unique, qualitatively different from every other such communion an able to add something to the fulness of personal life that no other communion can.

Similarly, then, with personal friendship toward which personal communion of love tends as its completion and of which it is the essential core. No personal friendship with one person can be qualitatively the same as friendship with another or contribute to the fulness of personal life what another friendship can. Every friendship is uniquely and irreplaceably enriching of personal life. The absence of any one union between any two persons in friendship leaves forever something unrealized and consequently something unrealized in each of them that each could have been for every other person with whom he or she entered into personal relationship. Personal friendship with every other person is necessary if any friendship between two persons is to realize the fulness of life which is intrinsically possible for it. (In all this, I am not taking account of God and communion of love in friendship with God [see ch. 12]. Since every created good is from God and is in God eminently and analogically, personal relationship with God can take the place of relationship with any created person.)

If one union in friendship is more precious, more fulfilling than another, that does not in any way conflict with what I have said. The less precious and less fulfilling is still different and irreplaceable. A more fulfilling and desirable friendship cannot replace the less fulfilling and less desirable—no more than Hamlet or Macbeth can replace a Laurel and Hardy comedy or Beethoven's Ninth Symphony replace "Alexander's Ragtime Band" or a rose replace a daisy.

The inescapable conclusion of all this is that whether the subject of the dynamism is aware of it or not, the transcendent human dynamism in every person toward ever fuller life reaches out toward personal friendship with every other person and toward friendship of all other persons with each other, in short, toward universal personal friendship. If by the word "friend" in a splendid passage by Meilaender means what I mean by personal friend in the fullest and most proper sense (I do not know whether he does), then he could be thinking of universal personal friendship in the meaning this term has for me when he speaks of a glorious

> hope for more than political communities can ever offer... for a day when no one would call another person "citizen" or "comrade" but each would call the other "friend" (Meilaender 1981, 85).

Further, dynamism toward ever fuller life in universal personal friendship cannot but reach toward universal mature, even ideally mature, personal friendship as described above. To begin a personal friendship with one person is to take a step on the road toward ever greater communion and sharing lives in a community of universal personal friendship, in which each friend lives all personal life as it grows ever richer by reason of each friend's growth.

12
DYNAMISM TO PERSONAL FRIENDSHIP WITH GOD

Does personal dynamism to ever fuller personal life extend beyond universally inclusive communion and sharing of lives in personal friendship with human persons? If there are in the universe created personal beings other than human persons, then the argument that supports thinking that our personal dynamism extends to universal friendship with human beings supports also thinking that our dynamism extends to personal friendship with these other beings, whether bodily beings in some other part of the material universe or immaterial persons ("angelic" beings) believed in by most Christians and by many non-Christians.

Does personal dynamism extend even further, to greater fulness of life in some kind of conscious union with God and, if so, in what kind of union? By "God" I mean the uncreated source of all finite beings, infinitely more good beautiful, powerful than created persons and yet more truthfully than in any other way for us thought of as personal, as intelligent, loving and free.

Johann (1966) addresses a question that could be taken to be the very one I am concerned with. His question and his line of argument to answer it are, however, not the same as mine. Nevertheless, I need to acknowledge the light and encouragement received from him for working out an answer to my own question—from him and from those on whom he drew, Macmurray (1961 ch. 7) and Teilhard de Chardin (1959, 254-85). Johann finds an inherent tendency toward a universal, personal community (without yet conceiving of it as universal personal friendship such as described above in chapter 11). This community, he argues, is "inconceivable" without a head who is the source of unity, to whom each member of the community is related and by that relationship is related to every other member; such a head can only be God (Johann 1966, 46-55). Therefore, the inherent tendency in persons toward a universal community is implicitly a tendency toward union with God (but not, by force of his argument, toward personal friendship with God as that is understood in this study).

Evidence in Human Experience

Interpretations of our transcendent dynamism as a drive toward union
with God can be found in religious thought, in theology and philosophy, in literature. The cry that came from Augustine's heart strikes
a responsive chord in the deepest self of most persons: "Our hearts
were made for You, O God, and can never rest until they rest in You"
(*Confessions* bk. 1, ch. 1). Among those who understand human dynamism as a drive toward rest in and union with God, there are different ways of thinking about God and about the kind of union toward which we tend. It would be far beyond my purpose and ability
to show these many ways. I shall only note some hints of the obscure
inmost yearning in human hearts, which on occasion surges into explicit awareness and in some persons becomes an almost continual
experience—the yearning for we know not what, beyond all we know,
beyond all boundaries, a yearning for unimaginable, absolute beauty
and goodness, for God.

C.S. Lewis describes experiences of his atheistic and amoral youth
which he names "Joy," giving the word a technical meaning that has
little likeness to what people ordinarily mean by pleasure or thrills or
feelings of happiness. When trying to describe one such experience,
he wrote (1956, 16; see also 16-18 for similar experiences and Lewis'
comments on them):

> It is difficult to find words for the sensation which came over me;
> Milton's "enormous bliss" of Eden (giving the full, ancient mean-
> ing to "enormous") comes somewhere near it. It was a sensation, of
> course, of desire; but of desire for what?... and before I knew what
> I desired, the desire itself was gone, the whole glimpse withdrawn,
> the world turned commonplace again, or only stirred by a longing
> for the longing that had just ceased. It had taken only a moment of
> time; and in a certain sense everything else that had ever happened
> to me was insignificant in comparison.

The overwhelming momentary experiences came and went without
any possibility of his bringing them to be or extending their duration, without his being able to define the desire in terms of some
specific object of desire.

There is reason to think that many, perhaps most if not all of us,
on occasion, at least a few times during our lives, have like experiences even if in a much lower intensity and without the reflective
awareness that Lewis had. For a passing moment there is a sweet and
exquisitely painful yearning not altogether unlike a touch of home-

sickness in a child left alone away from home, a yearning toward
what is limitlessly desirable, a mere hint of the overpowering "urgent
longings" experienced by a John of the Cross and other religious mystics whose whole conscious lives came to be colored by lastingly influential, intense experiences of this kind:

> One dark night
> Fired with love's urgent longings
> —Ah, the sheer grace!—
> I went out unseen,
> My house being now all stilled
> (John of the Cross 1973, 73, 295)

Does the love in Chesterton's Wild Knight, "among the golden loves
of all the knights...the most hopeless... the love of God," burn at
the core of every person? Does the hope that sings in him sing at the
core of every human spirit?

> For in my soul one hope forever sings,
> That at the next white corner of a road
> My eyes will look on him... (Chesterton 1950, 268-69).

Can we not justly think that in the very groundwork of personal
consciousness, too deep, too tenuous, too continually and pervasively
present to be attended to without a reflective effort that is usually
beyond the present capacity of most persons—can we not think that
there is a sense of loneliness, of being exiled from and homesick for a
home where we have never lived, for a face we have never seen, that
there is a banked up fire of urgent longing smothered beneath the
manifold fascinating trifles that cloud our awareness of the inacces-
sible light for which we are made? Is it not the hardly conscious desire for the undefinable glory of union with unlimited life that explains why our dynamism is always to what is more and better, why
we are the only creatures in the world who can never come to rest in
the world, who seem to be by their very nature rendered restless?

Union with God by Mutual Knowledge and Love
Sometimes this deep yearning is fitted into a system of thought and
interpreted in terms of that system, for example, Plato's eros toward
union with Absolute Beauty by an intellectual vision (*Symposium*,
201D–207A, 210E–211C), or Aquinas' "natural desire" for union
with God by a direct intellectual vision of the divine essence (*Summa
contra Gentiles*, III, 26; ST 1-2, q. 3, a. 4 and q. 4, a. 2). But what has

been shown in the earlier chapters of this book on personal dynamism to union by mutual personal love, communion of love and
sharing of lives in personal friendship with other created persons leads
to thinking that the union with God to which personal dynamism
tends is constituted more by personal love than by intellectual vision. Not that personal love of God is possible without personal knowledge of God or that personal knowledge of God in its fullest sense is
possible without direct vision of God. But even the highest form of
knowledge cannot constitute the ultimate fulness of life in union
toward which personal dynamism tends. It is true that love depends
on knowledge and receives the form of the beloved through knowledge, but it constitutes a union of lover and beloved that is greater
than the union of knower and known.

> Hence it is that even though a soul may have the highest knowledge
> and contemplation of God and know all mysteries, yet if it does not
> love, this knowledge will be of no avail to her union with God as
> St. Paul teaches (I Cor. 13) (John of the Cross, "Spiritual Canticle,"
> [1973] 13:11 [461].

But even such knowledge and love as John of the Cross is talking
about in this passage is not enough unless the lover knows that the
personal knowledge and love is mutual. Seeing and personally loving
the infinitely beautiful God while despairing of being known and
loved by that God could be a taste of hell; even being uncertain of
being known and loved by God would be a taste of bitterness within
the joy, a taste of misery within the glory, a threat of hell.

Personal Dynamism to Personal Friendship with God

Mutual personal knowledge and love do not yet constitute the fullest
kind of personal union or the greatest kind of fulness of life unless
the union becomes friendship in its highest form. There are many
ways of speaking about God as a friend to a human person or about
a human person as a friend to God. In the widest sense, it means
hardly more than that God is benevolent toward the creature and the
creatures are not at enmity with God, that they avoid serious viola-
tions of ethical precepts seen as divine precepts. In a fuller but not
yet the fullest meaning, a friend of God is one who lives a prayerful
life and tries to serve God by caring for other persons or for the
world. In the present context the words "friend" and "friendship" are
given their fullest meaning. (On caring for the world as a basis of
friendship with God, see McFague 1988, ch. 6, "God as Friend";

even those Christians who might be put off by McFague's theology of the Trinity, her Christology, her understanding of the relationship of creation to God, as also by her understanding of the history of thought on friendship can still find much in this chapter that is both enlightening and inspiring.)

It is difficult or impossible, apart from the New Testament, to describe such friendship between God and a human person that is at all, in any measure, satisfactory. Even in a Christian theology based on the New Testament all that can be said will always fall immeasurably short of the mysterious reality. Nevertheless, to omit any philosophical discussion, however inadequate, of human dynamism toward such friendship would be to leave aside what to many is the peak of human thought on friendship and the acme of all human desire.

Certainly, personal dynamism tends toward the lesser forms of friendship with God but also, beyond these, toward friendship with God analogous to the mature personal friendship between two human persons as described above in chapters 5 through 8. That this is so can be shown and clarified by an argument based on the same twofold basis that served for the argument by which universal personal friendship with human persons was shown to be a goal of our personal dynamism. The two factors in that basis are, on the one hand, the unique and limited character of every human person and so of every human personal friendship and, on the other hand, the transcendent character of human dynamism toward ever fuller life.

With some necessary modifications, the parallel of the present argument with the earlier one is so obvious as to eliminate the need for any detailed account of the steps parallel to those by which the latter was carried out. In truth, the dynamism of personal love towards the goal of personal friendship with God follows from the twofold basis at least as readily and clearly as the dynamism toward universal human friendship. For in God's love and lovableness all power of every actual or possible unique but limited created person to call other created persons into fuller life is present preeminently. If the transcendent dynamism to ever fuller life could conceivably ever come to rest, it would do so only in a life of friendship with God that is personal and mature in the fullest sense.

The validity of this conclusion and its full meaning will surely be missed unless some things are kept clearly and firmly in mind. One is that the argument is not intended to establish that this amazing goal can be actually attained by us, but only that we have a dynamism toward it; for the moment, the question of its concrete possibility is not under discussion (no more than it was when showing our transcendent dynamism to complete sharing of lives in ideally mature personal friendship of two or our transcendent dynamism to universal mature personal friendship). The second thing to keep in mind is that without going into the metaphysics of the analogy of being, we must remember that friendship with God is analogous to human friendship and that without a deep understanding of the prime analogate (human friendship) in mind, friendship with God will remain a shallow concept with no great significance for understanding and realizing the awesome mystery of the human spirit. Therefore, in thinking about friendship with God we need to have a lively remembrance of what is involved in human personal friendship as described in chapters 5 to 7. The various possible modes of personal friendship between parent and child, siblings, lovers, spouses, and so on should also be remembered; for, in divine-human friendship, God's love and the created person's love transcend and include these modes.

The Question of Possibility

When discussing the ideal of mature personal friendship between two persons and when discussing universal personal friendship, the question was raised about the possibility of these as goals of transcendent dynamism. Intrinsic and concrete or circumstantial possibility were distinguished, and those goals were said to be intrinsically possible but concretely impossible. What about the goal of personal friendship with God?

There seems to be evidence that it is at least in some sense and to some degree both intrinsically and concretely possible. Many ordinary well balanced religious people (clearly distinguishable from religious neurotics) believe they experience personal friendship with God. They hold God by love at the center of their lives. Their central concern in life is held in common with God, the salvation of the world. They are sure that God knows them through and through, loves them personally, has revealed divine love and desires that they love God, and has given promises of fidelity. In this relationship with God, they come to see all creation as God's gift and word; they contemplate God, and find divine beauty and wisdom and love in all things. They strive to remove from their lives anything that is an obstacle to union with God, to ever more fully radiate God's love and kindness to others, and so to mature in friendship with God. There are also the smaller number of those who come to very mature friendship with God in an extraordinarily complete and intense mystical union, called by some the "transforming union," sometimes experienced as a spousal friendship and called the "mystical marriage" (see Poulain 1978, ch. 19). All these persons live with lively hope for an immortal, ideally mature, personal friendship with God.

13
DYNAMISM TO ONE UNIVERSALLY INCLUSIVE FRIENDSHIP

When describing personal friendship in chapters 5 to 7, attention was limited to the friendship between two persons only. When describing universal personal friendship in chapter 11, I had in mind the friendship of each person with every other, as many friendships as there are other persons. What is to be described now is a richer goal of human dynamism to ever fuller life, union of persons in a single universally inclusive personal friendship.

Meaning of "Inclusive Friendship"

The terms "inclusive" and "exclusive" as applied to love and friendship are used by different writers in different ways, and it will be necessary to make clear the meaning in which they are used here. In some scholarly writing as well as in popular discourse, "exclusive friendship" means one in which the friends not only do not have other friends but are not open to having them. It is a closed as opposed to an open friendship. A friendship is open in one way when each of the friends has or is receptive toward having other friends, whether they do or do not actually have them. It can be open also in a second way when the friends are open to including another or others in their friendship, all to be involved in one friendship. A friendship which is not only open in this second way but actually includes three or more persons is what I mean by an inclusive friendship.

Understood in this sense, inclusive friendship is not merely a combination of friendships, each one between two persons with the persons overlapping, as when A is in friendship with B and B with C and C with A. Even though each of these combined friendships will somehow affect and be affected by the other two, there will still be three separate friendships. By contrast, in an inclusive friendship the relationships between A and B, A and C, B and C "co-inhere" (to borrow a term from Charles Williams) and enhance each other in ways that three distinct friendships do not. The interrelationships in this single friendship are more complex and, other things being equal, constitute, as we shall see, a fulness of life far greater than three fully distinct friendships.

As my efforts will make evident, I find it difficult if not impossible to give a satisfactory descriptive analysis of inclusive personal friendship; and I have been unable to find anyone else from whom I could borrow such a description. C. S. Lewis is one of those who does at least take account of it. Without attempting a sustained descriptive analysis, he does, nevertheless, in a few lines throw a bright light on this experience.

> But two, far from being the necessary number for friendship, is not even the best. And the reason for this is important.
> Lamb says somewhere that if, of three friends (A, B, C), A should die, then B loses not only A but "A's part in C," while C loses not only A but "A's part in B". In each of my friends there is something that only some other friend can fully bring out. By myself I am not large enough to call the whole man into activity; I want other lights than my own to show all his facets. Now that Charles is dead I shall never again see Ronald's reaction to a specifically Caroline joke. Far from having more of Ronald, having him "to myself" now that Charles is away, I have less of Ronald. Hence, true friendship is the least jealous. True friends delight to be joined by a third, and three by a fourth, if only the newcomer is qualified to become a real friend. They can then say, as the blessed souls say in Dante, "here comes one who will augment our love." (Lewis 1960, 73-74).

(Although Lewis is thinking of what I would call an inclusive friendship of three persons, all he says about it could, I think, still apply to three distinct friendships between A and B, B and C, C and A. He does not yet bring out the peculiar richness of inclusive friendship.)

What Lewis says offers a valuable clue to be followed. Using the descriptive analysis of friendship between two persons already made and developing Lewis' remarks, let us try to uncover more of the marvelously rich and complex dynamic structure of an inclusive friendship. Two of the essentials noted in personal friendship between two persons provide a promising starting point. These two are communion of love and sharing lives. Not only are they essential for the constitution of personal friendship, but their ever fuller actualization is the most characteristic goal toward which the dynamism of friendship tends. In the following discussion, the terms "inclusive communion" and "inclusive sharing of lives" will be used in a way parallel to "inclusive friendship," that is, to refer to experiences in which more than two persons are engaged in one act of communion or one sharing of lives.

Inclusive Communion of Love

In chapter 5, it was shown that in communion of love with one other person, I apprehend and love the other as actuated by and revealed in his or her love for me, and also the other way around. (For the sake of simplicity and clarity, let the other essential factors in communion of love be understood even though left unmentioned.) In an inclusive communion of love, involving three or more persons, I apprehend and love each of the others not only as each of them is presently actualized by and revealed in love for me but also as each of them is actualized by and revealed in his or her love for every other person involved in the communion. What holds for me holds for each of the others. Communion between any two in an inclusive communion somehow and in some measure includes and is included in communion between the others involved in the whole. All form one communion, no communion between two persons separate from or even entirely distinct from the others. This is what I mean by saying that all the relationships in an inclusive communion are co-inherent.

Let us try then to make this experience at least less obscure by looking in a more detailed way at the simplest form in which it can occur, an inclusive communion which involves only three persons. So complex are the mutually inclusive relationships that, as more persons are included in the communion, its dynamic structure exceeds imagination and defies coherent analysis. Nevertheless, I hope that what I say will serve the purpose here. For my realistic aim is not to make a complete and accurate description of what will go on in an inclusive communion even of only three if it is ever actualized. All I want to do is to give some indication, however incomplete, of how inclusive communion of three or more persons differs from several distinct communions among these same three or more persons and in so doing to give some hint of the amazing fulness of life in universally inclusive communion at the core of a universally inclusive friendship.

If communion between A and B, B and C, and A and C were three fully distinct communions of persons who have three distinct friendships, it would be enough to say that A knows and loves B as B is actualized in knowing and loving A and the other way around and similarly with B and C and with C and A. Each person would, of course, bring to communion with each of the friends what he or she has become by reason of friendships with each of the others; but this communion of two would not include communion with any other friend in one act of communion—as happens in an inclusive communion. In the latter, all that is involved in the mutual responses of A and B, of B and C, of C and A are so interwoven and interpenetrated as to render each of these presently actual mutual responses in its full concreteness unintelligible and impossible apart from the other two presently actual responses. Thus, if we begin with A's relationship with B, we have to say that A knows loves B as B is presently actualized and revealed in his love for A as A is actualized in love for C as the latter is actualized and revealed in love for A and for B. Parallel statements can be made about B's love for A and for C, as also for C's love for A and for B.

Every person beyond three added to an inclusive communion brings into it for all the others not only the added richness of that one's personality and love but also the new richness in every one of the other friends as they now actually respond to that new one in each one's own distinctive way. It brings also the added richness of their responses to each other as they are each actualized by their unique responses to this new friend. "Here comes one who will augment our loves." To imagine and clearly describe the amazing interweaving and interacting, the relations within relations, of knowledge and love in such communion even between a few friends seems to be an impossible task. The very experience of trying and failing, however, can give an impression of the fulness of life to be experienced in inclusive communion.

Is experience of inclusive personal communion really possible? Without explicitly employing the terms concrete and intrinsic possibility or impossibility, as I have done, Nédoncelle seems to be making such a distinction when discussing what he calls a we that is a triad or quadrad. By this term he means "a community in which three or four individuals are simultaneously translucent to each other in such a way that each turns lovingly to the others as if they were but one and receives from them simultaneous and equal attention" (Nédoncelle 1966, 35). In the human condition, he says, the we seems to be limited to a dyad: "subjective awareness does not achieve real reciprocity except between two personal beings. Such is our situation" (1966, 34). On the other hand, he allows that "the subjective we may be indifferent, in principle, to the number of its associates and capable of indefinite extension" (1966, 34). Even the dyad he points out, is in our human condition "weak, intermittent, and maintained in a fragmentary fashion" (1966, 34). Much more so if any we beyond the dyad should occur at all. Nédoncelle makes no mention of a universal we, but it is not hard to surmise what he would say if he did consider it.

While I cannot agree with his unqualified denial of the possibility of reciprocity in our human condition except between two persons, the rest of what he says seems to me largely true and leads me to think that inclusive personal communion even between three is something that, if it happens in our world, does so very rarely and only momentarily. What is commonly found in actuality is a group (three or more) of persons, among whom each one experiences a dyadic communion with each other one in the group, these communions in some way affected by, colored by, relationship with the whole group. Each person goes back and forth from one dyadic communion to another without the whole group experiencing one inclusive personal communion.

This concession to the limits of inclusive communion of love in the concrete human condition in no way diminishes the value of asserting the intrinsically possible ideal of universal communion or hinders establishing it as a goal of human dynamism, no more than the difficulty raised before about the concrete possibility of severally universal friendship diminishes the value of describing that goal or hinders establishing the human dynamism to it. Whether inclusive communion of love (as also sharing of lives) is possible in our present human condition, and, if it is, whether it actually happens even rarely, these questions are peripheral, even irrelevant, to my present main concern.

Inclusive Sharing of Lives

The limits and value of describing as best we can inclusive communion will hold also for inclusive sharing of lives. Recall that by "lives" in this context is meant whatever the persons consciously do, whatever happens to them of which they are aware; how they think and feel about these acts and happenings. Recall also that sharing lives in friendship presupposes mutual affective identification by personal love along with mutual communication, that it involves the experience by each friend of the other as an other self, knowledge by each of the other from within, experience by each of the other's life as one's own in the other and of one's own life as the other's life in oneself—all this believed (at least implicitly and non-reflectively) by each to be mutual.

Without attempting to describe the bewilderingly complex dynamic structure of inclusive sharing of lives, it seems enough for our purpose to say that when personal friendship is inclusive, by reason of each added friend beyond two, the sharing of lives becomes more complex and richer in a way that parallels inclusive communion of personal love.

A wonderfully interesting fictional account of what happened in mature friendship among many persons might give some hint of what could go on in an extensive inclusive friendship, the inclusive communion of love and the sharing of lives. Howard Fast's short story entitled "The First Men" (1974, 317-43) is a story of how a group of extraordinarily gifted, good, learned, and experienced educators created for forty children a secret and guarded environment of total love and security in which the children had no need to develop any mental blocks. In this environment, the children flourished in every way, physically, emotionally, intellectually. At an early age they surpassed their educators and finally went beyond the latter's ability even to follow and learn from them. In the story not much is said explicitly about friendship, but interpreting it in terms of this study, what happened was that the forty children all became joined in a union such as I have been speaking of as an inclusive mature personal friendship. In their growth to this loving union, the children reached a point at which they were totally telepathic to each other. As a consequence, not only was there no need or desire to lie, to deceive, or even to have secrets from one another; there was no possibility of these things. They entered into each other's thoughts freely. Their memories became one common memory. They had, as it were, one mind—and one heart also. All understanding, all joy and sorrow, all pleasure and pain were common to all. There was never any anger or annoyance among them; for every one of them experienced the life of every other one in the group as each one's own life in the other and each one's own life as the life of every other in him or her.

Yet each had to remain his or her own unique self or else personal communion and sharing lives in personal friendship would have ceased, to be replaced by some loveless collective consciousness that would destroy personal life. In fact, it must be said that each of the persons in such an inclusive personal relationship would actualize more and more each one's own unique self; for in personal friendship, each unique friend brings to life in a way that only she or he can some dimension of the other's unique self that would otherwise remain latent, an unrealized potentiality. Each friend actualizes and comes to know his or her self precisely as enlivened by every one of the other friends. It is this personal self so actualized by relationship with every other person in the inclusive friendship that each one gives in love to every other, is received in love by every other, who in turn gives his or her self in the same way.

Life in Universally Inclusive Friendship

In the light of what has been said about inclusive communion and sharing of lives in an inclusive friendship of three or more, what can now be said about universally inclusive personal communion and sharing of lives in universally inclusive personal friendship? When answering this question, it is imperative to keep in mind what was said about the kind of persons who alone would be able to enter into severally universal friendship and the kind of world that would be necessary for its possibility. All that holds equally for universally inclusive friendship.

As remarked above, with every added friend beyond three, the interrelationships would become more complex and bewildering—that is to say bewildering to anyone who tried to analyze these interrelationships descriptively. The friends, of course, would simply experience them without reflective analysis. Nevertheless, it is possible to extrapolate reflectively from the simplest form of three to an inclusive friendship of many persons and finally to a universally inclusive friendship and still retain some intelligibility. One can understand in some very limited and very vague way the meaning of a billion to the millionth power, without any image or clear concept of that many units. In like manner, some altogether inadequate statement of what is involved in universally inclusive personal communion and sharing of lives in personal friendship can serve to suggest, even though it does not clearly explicitate, the inexpressible fulness of life that will be in a universally inclusive friendship if it should ever come to be.

In it, every friend would be united by conscious acts and preconscious dispositions (the virtue of friendship) in personal communion of love and sharing of lives with every other friend as that friend is presently uniquely actualized by every other in the universal union. That is to say, each one would experience the whole of personal life among all persons as they are all actualized by their universally inclusive union. Each one would experience this whole life from within every other who is living it. Since every other person would be to him as an other self, he would experience that whole life in each one as his own life in every one of them. She would also experience her own life, including her living all personal life, as the life of every other person who by love identifies with her as an other self and experiences her life from within.

When descriptively analyzing personal communion of love between two persons we found that it is in some sense and in some measure one composite act of two agents. In like manner, it seems that we are justified in thinking of personal life in an inclusive friendship as one composite life of many friends and of personal life in a universally inclusive friendship as one composite life of all persons, a life which each person experiences as totally his own and totally every other's, each finding even greater fulfilment and joy because it is totally every other's than because it is his own.

Dynamism toward a Universally Inclusive Friendship

All the preceding description and clarification have been preparatory to understanding and answering the question whether human dynamism as it is channeled through personal love tends not only toward the goal of severally universal personal friendship but beyond that toward one universally inclusive personal friendship.

From what has been said, an affirmative answer to the question follows. For human dynamism, as we saw, is of its nature transcendent, tending toward ever greater fulness of life in union with other persons. Therefore, even an experience of inclusive personal friendship such as that of the children in Fast's story could not be in any sense the final goal. If such a union as is described in that story were ever achieved, transcendent human dynamism would still drive not only toward an intrinsically possible deeper and fuller personal union among the friends in that group but also toward a friendship that included ever more persons. Ultimately it would drive toward a universally inclusive personal communion and sharing of lives in an ideally mature universally inclusive personal friendship. Even should it be true that dynamism toward such a goal does not become explicitly conscious, unless very rarely in very rare human persons, there is in every person an actual innate preconscious dynamism to that goal implicit in our conscious personal dynamism to ever fuller life. It would be so even if no human person were ever explicitly conscious of it.

Another way of arriving at this conclusion is by drawing out the implications of severally universal friendship. For, if personal friends in the full sense that is understood here have a dynamism to share their lives with each other ever more fully and to bring each other to the greatest possible fulness of life and joy, then surely they have a dynamism to share with each other what is so precious in their lives, their friendships with other persons. If, then, in severally universal friendship each one of us as persons is joined in personal friendship with every other, we will have a dynamism to share with each and every one of these friends as fully as possible all our other friendships. The only complete way of doing so would be by bringing every friend into inclusive communion of love and sharing of lives in one universally inclusive personal friendship. The tendency of transcendent dynamism of personal love cannot stop short of that presently impossible but intrinsically possible glorious goal.

Can it stop short of a universally inclusive personal friendship which includes God? If personal dynamism (human dynamism formed and directed by personal love and care) tends toward ever greater fulness of personal life for the loved one, how could each human person in severally universal personal friendship not experience a dynamism toward the supreme fulfilment of every "other self" by union of personal friendship with God, the actually infinite fulness of life, by participation in which alone every other life is possible. In other words, how could the members in a human universal friendship not desire a severally universal friendship of each member with God—and, beyond that, the ultimate and most glorious mode of personal union, an inclusively universal divine-human personal friendships, in which each one experiences not only all human life but all life, uncreated as well as created.

Epilogue
A Tragic Conclusion and the Hope of Overcoming It

Whether our conviction of experiencing genuine personal communion of friendship with God now is true and whether our hoped-for perfect eternal union hereafter is concretely possible these are questions that only religious faith can answer, either affirmatively or negatively. Without appeal to faith we are left at best with uncertainty about the possibility of ever attaining the goal of our deepest desire and at worst with certainty that our transcendent dynamism is tragically doomed to frustration.

Likewise, whether the intrinsically possible lesser goal of universally inclusive ideally mature personal friendship among human persons (or even ideally mature friendship of two) will ever be concretely possible escapes any certain and satisfactory answer outside the realm of religious belief. We might hope that, as billions and billions of years of human evolution go by, the human race might develop greater and greater freedom from the bonds of egoism, greater and greater powers of awareness, of attention, of personal love, and so grow toward this goal. But who knows whether our race will not destroy itself or become the victim of a cosmic accident before any great progress toward that goal? And even apart from these possible catastrophes, is there any reason to think that time and human effort alone could ever entirely heal human egoism? Even if the human race should after billions of years reach such a goal, will we who live now and all those before us or those who will live and die during those billions of years, will we and they have any part in it? And those who would attain the goal would they die also? Without religious faith in salvation, resurrection, and immortality, there can be no way of escaping the conclusion that personal dynamism is doomed to tragic frustration. For a destiny to fail of living all of personal life in the union of universally inclusive divine-human personal friendship and of living it forever would surely be a tragic one, even though it is not experienced as such by those who have no understanding of their personal dynamism and little or no realization of the grandeur of beings who have such a dynamism.

For those, however, who have Christian faith and hope, this tragic conclusion is overcome. Their faith gives believers assurance that the goals of personal transcendent dynamism are not only intrinsically possible but that they are included in our God-given destiny, made concretely possible in Jesus Christ, a destiny to which we are all urgently called by God, even lovingly commanded to seek, but are free to reject and to take the horrifying consequences of doing so.

Beyond that assurance, Christian faith in the triune God, in the incarnation of the Divine Word, and in the mystical body of Christ, also marvelously clarifies how this destiny is to be achieved, in a way that human intelligence and imagination at their furthest reach could never conceive of. "What no eye has seen nor ear heard, nor the human heart conceived, what God has prepared for those who love God, has been revealed to us through the Spirit" (I Cor. 2:9-10).

All that is divinely revealed to us about our destiny can be understood (as far as we can understand what is ultimately mystery) only "in Christ Jesus." Of him it is written: "All the promises of God find their Yes in Him" (II Cor. 1:20)—all God's promises and all the intimations from our personal dynamism which God created in us.

What has been shown in this volume is, then, all preliminary to an interpretation of the goals of personal dynamism in the light of Christian revelation, an interpretation of human personal dynamism as it is transformed in Christ. Only in this interpretation, founded on faith in Jesus Christ and the gospel, can we reach the fullest understanding of human persons as they actually are in a world created to receive, beyond our wildest hope or imagining, the gracious gift of God in Christ Jesus, for whom all is created.

BIBLIOGRAPHY

Aelred of Rievaulx. 1977. *Spiritual Friendship*, trans. Mary Eugenia Laker. Kalamazoo MI: Cistercian Publications.

Alighieri, Dante. 1962. *La Vita Nuova*, trans. Mark Musa. Bloomington: Indiana University Press.

Anderson, Poul. 1969. "Journey's End," in Robert Silverberg, ed., *Dark Stars*. New York: Ballantine Books.

Aquinas, Thomas. 1941. *Summa theologiae*, trans. from the edition of the Institute of Medieval Studies, Ottawa.

Aristotle. *Nicomachean Ethics*.

Augustine, Aurelius. *The Confessions*.

———. 1900. *De Civitate Dei*. Ed. Emmanuel Hoffmann. Vienna: Corpus Scriptorum Ecclesiasticorum Latinorum.

Auden, W. H. 1945. "September 1, 1939," in *The Collected Poetry of W. H. Auden*. New York: Random House.

Badhwar, Neera K., ed. 1993. *Friendship: A Philosophical Reader*. Ithaca NY: Cornell University Press.

Benoît, Hubert. 1955. *The Many Faces of Love*, trans. Philip Mairet. New York: Pantheon.

Bentham, Jeremy. 1948. *An Introduction to the Principles of Morals and Legislation*. New York: Columbia University Press.

Bergson, Henri. 1946. *The Creative Mind*, trans. Mabelle L. Andison. New York: Philosophical Library.

Bernard of Clairvaux. 1951. *On the Love of God*, trans. Terence L. Connolly. Westminster: M.D.: Newman Press.

Bernards, Neal and Terry O'Neill, eds. 1989. *Male\Female Roles: Opposing Viewpoints*. San Diego: Green Haven Press. Essays by Michael E. McGill, "Men Do Not Have Strong Friendships," Drury Sherrod, "Men Have Strong Friendships," and Letty Cottin Progrebin, "Men and Women Cannot Be Friends."

Brain, Robert. 1976. *Friends and Lovers*. New York: Basic Books.

Broad, C. D. (Charlie Dunbar). 1952. "Egoism as a Theory of Human Motives," in *Ethics and the History of Philosophy*. New York: Humanities Press, pp. 218-231.

———. 1930. *Five Types of Ethical Theory*. New York: Harcourt, Brace.

Brodrick, James. 1952. *St. Francis Xavier: 1506-1552*. New York: Wicklow Press.

Brontë, Emily. 1963. *Wuthering Heights*. New York: W.W. Norton.

Buber, Martin, *I and Thou*, 2d., trans. Ronald Gregor Smith. New York: Macmillan.

———. 1955. *Between Man and Man*, trans. Ronald Gregor Smith. New York: Scribner.

Burnaby, John. 1938. *Amor Dei*. London: Hodder & Stoughton.

Calkins, Mary Whiton. 1921. *The Good Man and the Good*. New York: Macmillan.

Chesterton, Gilbert Keith. 1950. "The Wild Knight," *The Collected Poems of G.K. Chesterton*. London: Methuen.

Cooper, John M. 1977. "Aristotle on the Forms of Friendship" in *Review of Metaphysics*, 30.

Crowe, Frederick E. 1959. "Complacency and Concern in the Thought of St. Thomas," *Theological Studies*, 20: no. 1 (March), no. 2 (June), no. 3 (September).

Dante. *Paradiso.*

D'Arcy, Martin C. 1956. 2d ed., rev. *The Mind and Heart of Love.* New York: Meridian Books.

Davies, Robertson. 1983. *The Rebel Angels.* New York: Penguin.

Donnelly, Dody H. 1984. *Radical Love: Toward a Sexual Spirituality.* Minneapolis MN: Winston Press.

Emerson, Ralph Waldo. 1904. "On Friendship," in *The Collected Works of Ralph Waldo Emerson.* Boston: Houghton-Mifflin.

Farley, Margaret A. 1988. *Personal Commitments: Beginning, Keeping, Changing.* San Francisco: Harper & Row.

Fast, Howard. 1974. "The First Men," in *Introductory Psychology through Science Fiction,* ed. by Harvey Katz, Patricia Warwick, and Martin Harry Greenberg. Chicago: Rand McNally.

Fiske, Adele M. 1970. *Friends and Friendship in Monastic Tradition.* Cuernavaca, Mexico: Centro Intercultural de Documentacion.

Fletcher, Joseph. 1966. *Situation Ethics.* Philadelphia: Westminster Press.

Freud, Sigmund. 1961. *Standard Edition of the Complete Psychological Works* (=SE), trans. James Strachey. New York: W.W. Norton. SE 18 "Group Psychology and the Analysis of the Ego" in SE 18. "Civilization and its Discontents" in SE 21.

Friedman, Maurice S. 1955. *Martin Buber: The Life of Dialogue.* Chicago: University of Chicago Press.

Fromm, Erich. 1955. *The Sane Society.* New York: Rinehart .

———. 1956. *The Art of Loving.* New York: Harper .

Gilleman, Gerald. 1959. *The Primacy of Charity in Moral Theology,* trans. William F. Ryan and André Vachon. Westminster: Newman.

Gilson, Etienne. 1936. *The Spirit of Medieval Philosophy,* trans. A.H.C. Downes. New York: Scribner.

Guitton, Jean. 1951. *Essay on Human Love,* trans. Melville Channing-Pearce. London: Rockliff .

Hallett, Harold Foster. 1957. *Benedict De Spinoza: The Elements of His Philosophy.* Fair Lawn NJ: Essential Books.

Hassel, David J. 1982. "Indwelling Prayer: in God, Self, Others," in *Review for Religious,* 41.

Hazo, Robert G. 1967. *The Idea of Love.* New York: Praeger.

Haule, John R. 1990. *Divine Madness.* Boston: Shambala.

Hawkins, Peter. 1985. *Getting Nowhere: Christian Hope and Utopian Dreams.* Cambridge MA: Cowley.

Hildebrand, Dietrich von. 1966. *Man and Woman.* Chicago: Franciscan Herald Press.

Hobbes, Thomas. 1950. *Leviathan.* New York: Everyman's Library.

Hunt, Mary. 1991. *Fierce Tenderness: A Feminine Theology of Friendship.* New York: Crossroad.

International Encyclopedia of Social Sciences. 1968. New York: Macmillan.

Johann, Robert O. 1955. *The Meaning of Love.* Westminster: Newman.

———. 1966. *The Pragmatic Meaning of God.* Milwaukee: Marquette University Press.

John of the Cross. 1973. *The Collected Works of Saint John of the Cross*, trans. Kieran Kavanaugh and Otilio Rodriquez. Washington DC: ICS Publications.

Johnson, Robert A. 1983. *We: Understanding the Psychology of Romantic Love*. San Francisco: Harper & Row.

Kierkegaard, Søren. 1946. *Works of Love*, trans. David Swenson and Lillian Marvin Swenson. Princeton: Princeton University Press.

Lepp, Ignace. 1963. *The Psychology of Loving*, trans. Bernard B. Gilligan. Baltimore.

Leonard, Elmore. 1988. *Bandits*. New York: Arbor House.

———. 1964. *The Ways of Friendship*, trans. Bernard Murchland. New York: Macmillan.

Lewis, C. S. (Clive Staples). 1956. *Surprised by Joy*. New York: Harcourt, Brace.

———. 1960. *The Four Loves*. London: Geoffrey Bless.

Lindbergh, Anne Morrow. 1956. *Gift From the Sea*. New York: Pantheon.

Liturgy of the Hours. 1975. New York: Catholic Book Publishing Company.

Macmurray, John. 1961. *Persons in Relation*. New York: Harper.

Madinier, Gabriel. 1938. *Conscience et Amour: Essai sur le "nous."* Paris: Presses universitaires de France.

Marcel, Gabriel. 1960. *The Mystery of Being*, trans. G.S. Fraser. Chicago: H. Regnery.

Maslow, Abraham. 1962. *Toward a Psychology of Being*. New York: Van Nostrand.

———. ed. 1959. *New Knowledge in Human Values*. New York: Harper.

May, William. 1957. "The Sin vs. the Friend: Betrayal," in *Cross Currents*, 17: 159-170.

May, Rollo. 1953. *Man's Search for Himself*. New York: Norton.

McFague, Sally. 1988. *Theology for an Ecological, Nuclear Age*. Philadelphia: Fortress Press.

McGuire, Brian P. 1988. *Friendship and Community: The Monastic Experience*. Kalamazoo MI: Cistercian Publications.

McGlynn, James V. and Jules Toner. 1961. *Modern Ethical Theories*. Milwaukee: Bruce.

Meilaender, Gilbert. 1993. "Men and Women—Can We Be Friends?" in *First Things*, No. 34.

Millor, Michael V. 1987. *New York Times*, December 27. Book review section, p. 23.

Montaigne, Michel de. 1946. "Of Friendship," in *The Essays of Michel de Montaigne*, trans. George B. Ives. New York: Heritage Press.

Morgan, Douglas N. 1964. *Love: Plato, the Bible and Freud*. Englewood Cliffs NJ: Prentice-Hall.

Nédoncelle, Maurice. 1966. *Love and the Person*, trans. Ruth Adelaide. New York: Sheed & Ward.

Norton, David. 1976. *Personal Destinies: A Philosophy of Ethical Individualism*. Princeton: Princeton University Press.

Nygren, Anders. 1953. *Agape and Eros*, trans. Philip S. Watson. Philadelphia: Westminster.

O'Neill, Terry, and Neal Bernards, eds. *Male\Female Roles: Opposing Viewpoints*. San Diego: Green Haven Press. Essays by Michael E. McGill, "Men Do Not Have Strong Friendships," Drury Sherrod, "Men Have Strong Friendships," and Letty Cottin Progrebin, "Men and Women Cannot Be Friends."

Oppenheim, Frank M. 1987. *Royce's Mature Philosophy of Religion*. Notre Dame IN: University of Notre Dame Press.

Ortega y Gasset, José. 1957. *On Love: Aspects of a Single Theme*, trans. Toby Talbot. New York: World Publishing Co.

Outka, Gene. 1972. *Agape: An Ethical Analysis*. New Haven: Yale University Press.

Peck, M. Scott. 1985. *The Road Less Traveled*. New York: Simon & Schuster.

Pieper, Josef. 1974. *About Love*, trans. Richard and Clara Winston. Chicago: Franciscan Herald Press.

Pitt-Rivers, Julian A. 1954. *Transactions of the New York Academy of Science.*

Plattel, Martin C. 1965. *Social Philosophy*. Pittsburgh: Duquesne University Press.

Poulain, Auguste. 1978. *Graces of Interior Prayer*, trans. Leonora L. Yorke Smith. Westminster VT: Celtic Cross.

Radar, Rosemary. 1983. *Breaking Boundaries: Male and Female Friendships in Early Christian Communities*. New York: Paulist.

Ramsey, Paul. 1962. *Nine Modern Moralists*. Englewood Cliffs, NJ: Prentice Hall.

Raymond, Janice. 1986. *A Passion for Friends: Toward a Philosophy of Female Affection*. Boston: Beacon Press.

Reik, Theodor. 1957. *Of Love and Lust*. New York: Grove Press.

Reisman, John M. 1979. *Anatomy of Friendship*. New York: Irvington Publishers.

Royce, Josiah. 1968. *The Problem of Christianity*. Chicago: University of Chicago Press.

Rougemont, Denis de. 1945. *Love in the Western World*. Garden City NY: Doubleday.

Russell, Letty. 1979. *The Future of Partnership*. Philadelphia: Westminster Press.

Shanley, Mary Lyndon. 1993. "Marital Slavery and Friendship," in N. K. Badhwar 1993 (q.v., above): 267-284.

Scheler, Max. 1954. *The Nature of Sympathy*, trans. Peter Heath. New Haven: Yale University Press.

Shideler, Mary McDermott. 1962. *The Theology of Romantic Love*. New York: Harper.

Singer, Irving. 1966. *The Nature of Love: Plato to Luther*. New York: Random House.

Schneider, Isidor, ed. 1964. *The World of Love*. New York: George Braziller.

Spinoza, Baruch. 1914. *Ethica Ordine Geometrico Demonstrata*, 3d edition of J. Van Vloten and J. P. N. Land, Benedicti De Spinoza Opera. The Hague.

Tallon, Andrew. 1997. *Head and Heart: Affection, Cognition, Volition as Triune Consciousness*. New York: Fordham University Press.

Teilhard de Chardin, Pierre. 1959. *The Phenomenon of Man*. New York: Harper and Row.

Telfer, Elizabeth. 1970. "Friendship," *Proceedings of the Aristotelian Society*, Vol. 71.

Tillich, Paul. 1954. *Love, Power and Justice*. New York: Oxford University Press.

———. 1957. *The Dynamics of Faith*. New York: Harper.

———. 1963. *Systematic Theology*. Chicago: University of Chicago Press.

Toner, Jules. 1964. "Focus for Contemporary Ethics," *Thought*, 39: 5-19.

———. 1968. *The Experience of Love*. Washington DC: Corpus Books.

Unamuno, Miguel de. 1954. *Tragic Sense of Life*, trans. J. E. Crawford Flitch. New York: Dover.

Vacek, Edward Collins. 1994. *Love, Human and Divine: The Heart of Christian Ethics*. Washington DC: Georgetown University Press.

Vella, Arthur G. 1964. *Love Is Acceptance: A psychological and theological investigation of the mind of St. Thomas Aquinas*. Rome: Gregorian University Press.

Wadell, Paul J. 1989. *Friendship and the Moral Life*. Notre Dame IN: University of Notre Dame Press.

Williams, Charles. 1941. *Religion and Love in Dante*. London: Dacre Press.

Wolfson, Harry. 1934. *The Philosophy of Spinoza*. Cambridge: Cambridge University Press.

Wylie, William P. 1958. *The Pattern of Love*. New York: Longmans.

Yeats, William Butler. 1962. *Selected Poems and Two Plays of William Butler Yeats*, ed. M.L. Rosenthal. New York: Collier.

INDEX